Small Developing Countries and Global Markets

Small Developing Countries and Global Markets

Competing in the Big League

Walter Kennes

Published by PALGRAVE
Houndmills, Basingstoke, Hampshire RG21 6XS and
175 Fifth Avenue, New York, N. Y. 10010
Companies and representatives throughout the world

PALGRAVE is the new global academic imprint of
St. Martin's Press LLC Scholarly and Reference Division and
Palgrave Publishers Ltd (formerly Macmillan Press Ltd).

Outside North America
ISBN 0–333–80088–5

In North America
ISBN 0–312–23358–2

This book is printed on paper suitable for recycling and
made from fully managed and sustained forest sources.

A catalogue record for this book is available from the British Library.

Library of Congress Catalog Card Number: 00–022309

10   9   8   7   6   5   4   3   2
09   08   07   06   05   04   03   02   01

Printed and bound in Great Britain by
Antony Rowe Ltd, Chippenham, Wiltshire

Contents

Preface and Acknowledgements

The current globalization process offers opportunities for developing countries, but it also poses important risks and challenges. Opening the economy is generally considered as the key to take advantage of globalization and become better integrated into the world economy. The economic success of a growing number of developing countries has demonstrated that integration into the world economy is indeed possible and beneficial. However, there are also countries that fear increased marginalization. There is no single best road towards openness. Developing countries can open up on their own while taking advantage of the framework provided by the multilateral trading system. They can also look for various kinds of partnership and open their economies to these partners. Partnerships can be established within a region and with similar countries, but they can also be with more distant and more diverse partners. Small developing countries face particular problems for their integration into the world economy, mainly because of their lack of diversification. Depending on the measure that is used, there are nearly one hundred countries that can be considered small in economic size. This is more than half the sovereign states in the world.

Integration into the world economy is not desirable for its own sake, but as a means towards achieving sustainable improvements in the welfare of the most vulnerable groups in a society. This book does not attempt to outline or recommend a unique best strategy. Rather, it attempts to describe and assess the ingredients of a number of strategies. The main purpose is to facilitate decision-makers and advisers exploring the strategy mix that seems most promising in the given circumstances.

The work on this text started in 1996 during a six-month fellowship at the Brookings Institution in Washington, DC, financed by the European Commission. I am very grateful to Bernard Petit for his generous support. Robert Litan of the Brookings Institution stimulated me to write about the integration of small developing countries into the world economy. The period necessary to finish this text was longer than anticipated. This was at least to some extent because so many things relevant to this subject were happening. I would like to mention only one: the start of the negotiations between the European Union and the group of ACP countries in 1998 and specifically the debates about a new trade regime between the EU and the ACP group.

I owe a great debt to the many writers and observers on the international trading system and regional integration. I would like to acknowledge the useful suggestions and help of Daniel Bach, Alice Landau,

Terrence Lyons, Claude Maerten, Gillian Nkhata, Guy Platton, Wolfgang Reinicke, John Roberts, Maurice Schiff, Graham Sims, Remco Vahl and Maryse Vanderstraeten. I am particularly grateful to Simon Horner for providing extensive editorial comments on the whole text. The drafting and redrafting took a large amount of free time and I would like to thank my family for their encouragement and patience. It goes without saying that none of the persons mentioned is responsible for the views expressed or for any inaccuracies. The views expressed in this book should not be ascribed to these persons or to the European Commission.

WALTER KENNES

List of Tables and Figures

List of Abbreviations

ACP	African, Caribbean and Pacific countries
ADB	African Development Bank
AEC	African Economic Community
AERC	African Economic Research Consortium
APEC	Asia Pacific Economic Cooperation
ASEAN	Association of South East Asian Nations
BLNS	Botswana, Lesotho, Namibia, Swaziland
CACM	Central American Common Market
CAEMU	Central African Economic and Monetary Union (see CEMAC)
CARICOM	Caribbean Common Market
CBI	Caribbean Basin Initiative
CEAO	Communanté Economique de l'Afrique de l'Quest
CEMAC	Communauté Economique et Monétaire de l'Afrique Centrale
CEPR	Centre for Economic Policy Research
CET	Common External Tariff
CMA	Common Monetary Area
COI	Commission de l'Océan Indien
COMESA	Common Market for Eastern and Southern Africa
CU	Customs Union
EAC	East African Cooperation
EC	European Community
ECA	Economic Commission for Africa
ECCAS	Economic Community of Central African States
ECO	Economic Cooperation Organization
ECOWAS	Economic Community of West African States
ECLAC	Economic Commission for Latin America and the Caribbean
ECU	European Currency Unit
EFTA	European Free Trade Association
EPZ	Export Processing Zone
EU	European Union
EURO or €	European Single Currency as of 2000
FDI	Foreign Direct Investment
FTA	Free Trade Area
FTAA	Free Trade Area of the Americas
GATS	General Agreement on Trade in Services
GATT	General Agreement on Tariffs and Trade
GCA	Global Coalition for Africa

GCC	Gulf Cooperation Council
GSP	Generalized System of Preferences
HET	Harmonized External Tariff
IMF	International Monetary Fund
IOC	Indian Ocean Commission
ISO	International Organization for Standardization
LAFTA	Latin American Free Trade Association
LAIA	Latin American Integration Association
LDC	Least Developed Country
MERCOSUR	Mercado Común del Sur
MFA	Multifibre Arrangement
MFN	Most-Favoured-Nation
MIGA	Multilateral Investment Guarantee Agency
MSG	Melanesian Spearhead Group
NAFTA	North American Free Trade Agreement
NTB	Non-Tariff Barrier
OAS	Organization for American States
OAU	Organization of African Unity
OECD	Organization for Economic Cooperation and Development
OECS	Organization of Eastern Caribbean States
OR	Origin Rule
PTA	Preferential Trade Area for Eastern and Southern Africa
REPA	Regional Economic Partnership Agreement
RIA	Regional Integration Agreement
RTA	Regional Trading Agreement
ROW	Rest of the World
SAARC	South Asian Association for Regional Cooperation
SACU	Southern African Customs Union
SADC	Southern African Development Community
SAP	Structural Adjustment Programme
SDE	Small Developing Economy
SIDS	Small Island Developing States
SPF	South Pacific Forum
SMP	Single Market Programme
SPARTECA	South Pacific Regional Trade and Economic Cooperation Agreement
SSA	Sub-Saharan Africa
STE	Small Transition Economy
TPRM	Trade Policy Review Mechanism
TRIMs	Trade-Related Investment Measures
TRIPs	Trade-Related Intellectual Property Rights
UDEAC	Union Douanière et Economique de l'Afrique Centrale
UEMAO	Union Economique et Monétaire de l'Afrique de l'Ouest
UNDP	United Nations Development Programme

UNECA	United Nations Economic Commission for Africa
UNCTAD	United Nations Conference on Trade and Development
VER	Voluntary Export Restraint
WAEMU	West African Economic and Monetary Union (see UEMOA)
WTO	World Trade Organization

1
Introduction

Over the past decade, policy-makers have been confronted with the trends of globalization and regionalization. Economic activity across national borders has been increasing rapidly, creating new opportunities, but also leading to fears of exclusion or marginalization. At the same time there has been a new wave of regionalism, involving industrial as well as developing countries. Developing economies are strongly encouraged to embrace 'openness' – in other words, to dismantle their barriers to trade and investment. Openness is presented as the key to participation and integration in the world economy, which will stimulate economic growth.

However, integration into the world economy implies various kinds of adjustment, to new ideas, new goods and new methods of production. Adjustment can be costly and risky, because some industries may be forced to close down before new opportunities have materialized. There are not only economic adjustment costs. There is also a wider educational and cultural adaptation process when a country becomes more integrated into the world economy. While there are costs and risks for all countries, small developing economies face special problems because they are more vulnerable than other countries. Small developing nations are often not able to participate effectively in the multilateral trading system. Many have tried some form of regional integration, but, so far, these efforts have been largely unsuccessful. Many also continue to rely on special arrangements or privileges granted by the industrial countries, but the advantages of these arrangements are dwindling. Moreover, some of these arrangements are increasingly being challenged. For all these reasons, small developing economies need to reflect carefully on their strategy to reposition themselves in the new world economic context.

This book is addressed firstly to economic policy-makers in smaller developing countries who are confronted with the issues of globalization and regionalization and who must develop a coherent policy response.

At the same time, the subject is relevant more generally for those interested in how the trade and development cooperation policies of the industrial countries can facilitate the integration of smaller developing countries into the world economy.

Globalization and regionalization go together

Since the beginning of the 1990s, globalization has been at the top of the world economic policy agenda. This consists in the widening of the scope of economic activities across national boundaries, taking the form of trade in goods, provision of services, direct and portfolio investment and migration. Globalization is driven by a combination of technological progress and economic policies. It is not a new phenomenon. Trade and investment at a global level have been widespread at least since the sixteenth century and arguably much earlier.[1] There have been several waves of globalization, generally following technological breakthroughs in sectors that have many linkages to the rest of the economy (for example, transport and energy). The current wave is due, in the first instance, to technological advances in the areas of information processing and telecommunication, but also in some other fields such as biotechnology. The second driving force is the increased openness of economic policies. Since the Second World War, trade and investment barriers have been removed at an accelerated pace. Even though globalization is usually not regarded as a political phenomenon, the demise of the communist systems in Central and Eastern Europe was an important enabling political factor.

Globalization influences all economic sectors, but financial services are particularly affected. As a consequence, financial markets have become highly interdependent across countries. Enterprises worldwide cannot avoid taking into account these developments. The investment decisions of large multinationals, but increasingly of small and medium-sized enterprises as well, reflect a global analysis of opportunities and constraints. Sub-contracting networks involve companies in many countries. Inputs are procured from many places and shifts can occur as a result of small price movements.[2]

Another characteristic of globalization is that more and more countries have become members of international regulatory institutions. Membership of the International Monetary Fund (IMF), whose main task is to promote monetary stability and orderly currency convertibility, is nearly universal. A large majority of countries in the world have become members of the World Trade Organization (WTO) that was established in 1995, taking over and extending the responsibilities of the General Agreement on Tariffs and Trade (GATT). Once the countries with applications in the pipeline become members, this organization will also become nearly universal.[3] The IMF and the WTO carry out key functions supporting the global economic system. Both are public sector institutions, which provide public goods in the form of international monetary and trade rules. However, there are also private-sector-driven bodies providing public goods on a worldwide scale. An example is the International Organization for Standardization (ISO) – whose members are national standardization bodies involving private companies. The spread of international technical norms is an important aspect of globalization.[4]

It is striking that, during the 1990s, alongside the globalization trend, there has also been a new wave of regional integration. The European Union (EU) completed its single-market programme at the beginning of 1993. Two years later, three new member states joined: Austria, Finland and Sweden. Discussions are ongoing on how the EU institutional structures can be adjusted to accommodate possibly ten new member states, mainly from Eastern Europe, over the next decade. The United States, notwithstanding its traditional emphasis on multilateralism, has become much more involved with regionalism, in the first place through the North American Free Trade Agreement (NAFTA), which became operational in 1994. Although there were earlier US trade agreements with Canada and Israel, NAFTA has a broader scope and its possible expansion was envisaged from the outset. The United States was also behind the launching of the idea to establish a Free Trade Area of the Americas (FTAA) and takes an active part in the Asia Pacific Economic Cooperation (APEC) process.

The new wave of regionalism has certainly not been restricted to the industrialized countries. In the developing world, regional initiatives have been revitalized or strengthened and new groupings have been formed. For example, in 1992, the Association of South East Asian Nations (ASEAN) agreed on a trade liberalization agenda and more recently accepted Vietnam, Laos and Myanmar as new members. In the Latin American and Caribbean region, the Central American Common Market (CACM), the Caribbean Common Market (CARICOM) and the Andean Community have all recently been strengthened. The most striking development in Latin America was the establishment in 1991 of MERCOSUR, grouping countries in the Southern Cone, comprising Argentina, Brazil, Paraguay and Uruguay. Trade liberalization within MERCOSUR has led to a rapid rise in the level of intra-regional trade. In sub-Saharan Africa a new Economic and Monetary Union was formed in 1994 among the West African members of the CFA Franc zone. In addition, there was the creation of the Common Market of Eastern and Southern Africa (COMESA), while the Southern African Development Community (SADC) adopted a new strategy of market integration.

Initially, it was thought that the increased attention being given to regionalism stemmed from the delay and frustration in reaching a satisfactory outcome in the Uruguay Round negotiations. However, the successful conclusion of the Uruguay Round with the creation of the WTO in 1994 has not diminished the trend towards regionalism. It is fair to say that globalization and regionalization will move together for some time to come.

Developing countries need to reposition, but how?

It is often stated that developing countries should react constructively rather than defensively to the new globalization and regionalization trends. Discussing the outlook for Jamaica and other Caribbean nations, Bernal (1996) calls for a 'strategic global repositioning'. Some developing countries have clearly repositioned successfully, but many more appear to be by-passed or even excluded. There is now a broad consensus that a certain degree of openness of the economy is a vital ingredient for economic growth. Indeed, there are no examples of countries that have been able to increase the welfare of their citizens in a sustainable way through a strategy of isolation and autarky. Several developing nations have successfully opened their economies and reaped impressive benefits in terms of growth and welfare (e.g. South Korea, Malaysia, Taiwan, Thailand, Singapore, Chile and Mauritius).[5] However, there are other developing countries, that have been opening their economies, which have not yet reaped the rewards of significant or sustained growth. There are also many developing states that have still to open their economies.

Even though openness is widely believed to stimulate economic growth, there is controversy about the kind of openness that should be pursued and about the best timing and sequencing of policy reforms.[6] Some analysts recommend openness across the board for all economic sectors and towards all trading partners. This can be done by the unilateral dismantling of trade barriers. Such unilateral reforms have been among the key ingredients of the structural adjustment and stabilization programmes promoted by the World Bank and IMF. Others suggest that *regional* openness should precede and complement *global* openness. This is often the view of politicians and trade officials. An important argument for politicians to be in favour of regionalism is that concessions can be obtained from partner countries that can be politically exploited. With unilateral liberalization, there are no such concessions.

Regionalism can be compared to the multilateral liberalization that took place under the successive GATT rounds. Regional openness usually allows one to go faster in certain areas, with a group of like-minded countries, than is possible in the multilateral context. Lawrence (1996) emphasizes that regional openness makes it possible to deal with matters that are not (yet) covered by the multilateral trading system such as, for example, competition policy, social policy, industrial standards and environmental regulations. These issues are often referred to as '*deep integration*' in contrast to '*shallow integration*' that essentially concerns the removal of barriers at the border. Regional arrangements can thus constitute a laboratory for multilateral liberalization.

A large part of the recent debate on the desirability of regional integration has addressed the question of whether or not regional groupings are 'stumbling blocks' or 'building blocks' towards worldwide free trade.[7] The background to this controversy is the perception of some analysts that the world is moving towards three inward-looking continental trading blocs: a European, a North American and an East Asian bloc. If such hegemonic trading blocs exploit their monopoly power, there will be damage to the world economy, especially for developing countries. Hallet and Braga (1994) consider that large trading blocs will display a natural tendency to become inward-looking and therefore express concern about the growth of regionalism. However, economic history over the past half-century does not confirm the view that large trading blocs have exploited their monopoly power to the detriment of world welfare. The United States enjoyed an overwhelming dominance on the world economic and trading scene during the two decades following the Second World War, but its weight was used to promote and secure the multilateral liberalization initiated through the GATT.[8] The European Community brought together economies with very different traditions as regards openness. Yet, on the whole, European integration has coincided with sustained trade liberalization.[9] By the mid-1960s, when the European customs union was achieved, the average tariff on manufactured imports from developing countries was around 14 per cent, slightly lower than the tariffs of the USA and Japan (see World Bank, 1996). The possible negative effects of a three-bloc world have obscured the very different debate on the desirability of smaller regional groupings that do not possess significant monopoly powers. The analysis of hegemonic trading blocs is of no use in assessing the relevance of regionalism for small developing countries.

Regardless of the theoretical debate, many developing countries have recently created new regional groupings and revitalized existing ones. In other words, some kind of regionalism appears attractive. For policy-makers, the issue is not so much whether regionalism contributes to multilateral trade liberalization, but rather how to open their economies successfully.

Small developing countries face specific constraints

The main purpose of this book is to outline and assess the options of *small developing economies* (SDEs) in relation to their beneficial integration into the world economy. Integration into the global economy is a different story for large developing countries like China, Brazil or Indonesia, that control vast human and natural resources and already constitute a sizeable potential market, when compared with states such as Burkina Faso, Malawi, Laos, Bolivia, St Lucia or Guyana – to mention just a few examples of SDEs. The economic opportunities available and the scope for autonomous policies are much broader for the former category of countries.[10]

The most important characteristic of small developing economies is *lack of economic diversification*. Very often, exports are dominated by a single sector or even a single product or company. Without diversification, it is difficult to absorb economic shocks. This applies, for example, to fluctuations in the prices or yields of food or export crops. In large, ecologically diverse countries, overall agricultural production will tend to be relatively stable. Lack of diversification strongly affects public finance. Taxes on only a few commodities or companies may dominate government revenue. Hence revenue can be very unstable.

Small economies tend to suffer more from inward-looking policies than large ones. Economies with little diversification have no choice but to import a wide range of products. Small economies, therefore, naturally have a high ratio of imports and exports to GNP. Inward-looking policies lead to distortions between imported, exported and non-traded goods in the form of high tariff barriers or overvalued exchange rates. Such distortions are more costly when exports and imports represent a large share of GDP, as in small economies. Large diversified economies can more easily afford to be closed.

Small economies clearly face disadvantages in relation to the provision of public goods such as transport infrastructure or specialized education. A typical problem of SDEs that often tends to be overlooked is the high *cost of governance*. This makes it difficult for such countries to participate effectively in multilateral negotiations that can be lengthy and technically complex. An important argument in favour of regional groupings is that they can help to reduce the cost of bargaining and increase its effectiveness for SDEs.

Another common characteristic of SDEs is their *vulnerability to natural disasters*, both slow-onset events such as drought and random catastrophes such as floods, earthquakes and volcanic eruptions. Vulnerability is also related to geographical characteristics such as *insularity and landlockedness*. Among developing countries, virtually all island and landlocked states are small economies. Being landlocked always implies dependency on a transit system that can be costly and may be easily disrupted because of conditions in coastal states. The effects of both insularity and lack of access to the sea are sometimes exacerbated by remoteness resulting in very high transport and communication costs (for example in the

South Pacific and Central Asia). Moreover, many island states are archipelagos, with large distances between different islands.[11]

It is useful to introduce a criterion of 'smallness'. There are many
ways to characterize smallness. Trade theory defines a small economy
as one whose international trade does not affect world prices. However,
this is not a practical way of identifying small countries, because of
measurement problems. There are three more straightforward criteria:
population size, size of the economy and physical area of the country.
Size of territory has some obvious disadvantages, because part of the
land may not be suitable for habitation. Moreover, there are often large
differences in the quality of land as an economic resource.

Population size is a commonly used criterion of smallness.[12] An advantage is that it is easy to measure. Population size is also related to
economic indicators such as the (potential) size of the market and the
labour force. For the purpose of this text, the size of the economy,
rather than population size is preferred as an indicator of smallness.
The economic size or GNP of a country reflects reasonably well the
trade-theory notion of lack of weight on international markets. A possible and admittedly arbitrary cut-off point could be a GNP value of
US$ 10 billion.[13] Using this criterion, small developing countries turn
out to be concentrated in three geographical areas: sub-Saharan Africa
(where all countries are small, with only two exceptions, Nigeria and
South Africa), the Caribbean Basin and the South Pacific. Countries
such as Ethiopia, Tanzania or the Democratic Republic of Congo, despite their large populations, are still small economies. Some key
characteristics of small developing economies are set out in Appendix
B (Tables B1–B3).[14] In addition to SDEs, there is also a relatively large
group of *small transition economies* (STEs), most of which emerged from
the break-up of the Soviet Union. The focus in this text is on developing countries, but most of the themes covered are also relevant for
STEs. Table B4 contains key characteristics for these countries. All in
all, around 95 countries, or more than half the sovereign states in the
world, fall into the category of small developing or transition economies as defined above. However, in population terms, they make up
only around 10 per cent of the global total. It should be stressed that
the specific criterion of smallness is only introduced for illustration
purposes. The reasoning in the subsequent chapters does not hinge
upon any criterion or cut-off point.

The countries listed in tables B1–B3 are certainly not a homogeneous
group. They can be divided in two main subgroups: countries with a
very low per capita income and possibly a large population – such as
Ethiopia with more than 50 million people, and middle-income countries with a very small population such as Barbados with only 0.3 million.
The first group almost totally coincides with the category of *Least Developed*

Countries (LDCs) as officially defined by the United Nations.[15] Of the 48 LDCs, only Bangladesh, with annual per capita income of US$ 220, has a GNP above US$ 10 billion, because of its very large population of 120 million.

It might be argued that the differences between the group of very poor countries with a relatively large population and the group of middle-income countries with a small population are so important that they cannot be dealt with together. However, while these differences should not be disregarded, there are also striking similarities in relation to some of the characteristics mentioned above, such as lack of economic diversification and vulnerability.[16] Moreover, countries in the two groups are often neighbours and frequently participate in the same regional groupings. For example, Haiti, the poorest nation in the Western Hemisphere, is a member of CARICOM, together with much wealthier countries such as Jamaica and Trinidad & Tobago. Mozambique, one of the poorest countries in Africa, borders South Africa, a large middle-income country. Both belong to SADC.

The prospects of small developing economies matter for affluent countries

The affluent part of the world is increasingly concerned about the situation of many smaller developing countries. Lack of prospects in these economies will make them more susceptible to the problems of 'new interdependence' that feed back to the affluent states. These include money-laundering, drugs and arms trafficking, illegal migration, spread of contagious diseases and environmental degradation.

For a long time the industrial nations have recognized the special situation of small developing economies and responded by setting up special arrangements. This led the United States, for example, to adopt the Caribbean Basin Initiative (CBI), while the European Union entered into a broad partnership with a large group of developing economies through the Lomé Convention. Presently, there are 71 Lomé members, virtually all of them small and very small economies, covering sub-Saharan Africa, the Caribbean and the South Pacific. The EU also has a special arrangement with the small Central American states. All these arrangements provide privileged trade-access together with other advantages for small developing economies.

The Multifibre Arrangement (MFA) was designed in the 1970s to protect textiles and clothing in the industrial economies. Many small developing economies received a better deal in textiles and clothing than the larger ones. But the Uruguay Round agreement includes a general reduction of protection, leading to erosion of the preference margins for small developing countries as well as the phasing-out of the MFA over ten years, starting in 1995. Small developing economies will lose on both accounts and will need to adjust.

In addition to the Uruguay Round there are other developments that negatively affect the prospects of SDEs. The creation of NAFTA undermined the privileges of the Caribbean countries. A new trade arrangement, involving NAFTA parity, has been promised, but nothing significant has been done so far. The planned enlargement of the European Union towards Central and Eastern Europe is also perceived as a threat by many small developing countries that enjoy privileged access to the European market.

Without timely corrective action, the phasing-out or diminished importance of several special arrangements that disproportionately favour small developing countries will tend to undermine their security and stability. Hence the need for the affluent countries to assist with a coherent strategy for the integration of these countries into the world economy.

What are the options for integrating into the world economy?

It should be stressed that integration into the world economy is not worthwhile merely for its own sake, but is rather an element of a wider strategy to contribute to the fundamental objective of sustainable and equitable growth. Autarkic approaches such as emphasizing import-substitution behind high tariff walls have not led to sustainable growth. Therefore, some degree of outward orientation is a common characteristic of all the options or strategies considered below.

Membership of the World Trade Organization (WTO) can be considered as a base-line strategy. It requires a minimum degree of openness. Most important, it provides countries with orderly, rule-based and fairly liberal access to world markets. The use of new forms of protection such as anti-dumping measures, which spread rapidly during the 1980s, has been made more difficult and transparent under the WTO than was the case previously. The procedure for complaints against unfair practices has been strengthened and made more accessible to developing countries.[17]

Notwithstanding its positive aspects, WTO membership provides only a general framework and some minimum requirements in terms of openness. A wide range of policy decisions still need to be taken on opening the economy. Countries can pursue liberalization of trade and deregulation of investment on their own. This strategy is called *unilateral economic liberalization*. Structural adjustment programmes have strongly emphasized this approach.

But small developing economies can also constitute regional groupings among themselves or with larger developing countries. This strategy can be called: *South–South regionalism or regionalism among developing countries*. Despite the limited success of many past initiatives, regionalism continues to figure prominently on the agenda of many developing countries. It is important that such regionalism does not pursue regional autarky, but is outward-oriented.

During the 1960s and 1970s developing countries were barely involved in the GATT negotiations on tariff reductions. Instead, they emphasized 'special and differential treatment' which formed the basis of the notion of non-reciprocity. Developing countries could be granted special preferences by the industrial countries without having to return the same favour. Small developing countries disproportionately benefited from these non-reciprocal preferential arrangements with industrialized economies. One might wonder whether such arrangements can be considered a strategy because of their asymmetric nature, i.e. the industrialized economies determine which concessions to make and for how long. However, the lobbying of small developing countries during the Uruguay Round to minimize the erosion of preferential arrangements shows that they certainly regard it as a strategy. This strategy can be called *non-reciprocal arrangements with industrial countries*.

The adherence of Mexico to NAFTA has stimulated attention for a quite different approach where developing countries become part of a *reciprocal* arrangement with industrialized nations. In other words, developing countries no longer enjoy special treatment, but accept the same obligations as industrialized members in the grouping. The transition period can, however, be asymmetric, giving more time to developing countries for adjustment. Such a strategy of *North–South regionalism* is viewed positively by several analysts, mainly because of its effect on the credibility of trade liberalization and macroeconomic policy reform in the South and because there is a natural trade complementarity between the North and the South.

The five strategies distinguished above will be presented and assessed in the following chapters. They are not mutually exclusive. The challenge is to find the right strategy-mix, taking into account specific circumstances.

Guide to the text

The main purpose of this book is to review and assess the strategies for beneficial integration of small developing countries into the world economy, in other words, integration that makes them better off. Integration into the world economy is not an objective as such, but it is an element of a strategy to improve prospects for sustainable growth. Given the broad coverage of the text, there is no analysis of any particular countries or regional groupings. The references to countries or groupings only serve to illustrate the reasoning. Appendix A contains a brief narrative on the objectives and achievements of the main regional integration organizations.

While the emphasis is on the options of small developing economies, the reasoning is based on theoretical analysis that is valid more generally. In fact, there is no specific body of theory that is valid only for small developing countries as defined above. It should also be recalled that the category of small developing economies is quite heterogeneous.

The book is organized as follows. Chapter 2 outlines the evolution of the role of developing countries in the multilateral trading system. It summarizes the benefits of membership of the World Trade Organization for (small) developing countries. Chapter 3 contains an overview of the shift from inward-looking policies towards more outward orientation and discusses advantages and disadvantages of unilateral liberalization. Chapter 4 deals with regional economic integration among (small) developing countries, in other words South–South regionalism. The assessment pays attention to a few themes that do not figure prominently in the literature, such as the preconditions for success and institutional design. The implications of industrialized countries' non-reciprocal arrangements in favour of small developing economies are the subject of Chapter 5. It is demonstrated that SDEs disproportionately benefit from these arrangements. Chapter 6 examines the advantages and disadvantages of North–South regional integration arrangements from the point of view of (small) developing countries. The final chapter contains a number of conclusions and recommendations.

Each chapter summarizes the main views on the subject and puts these in the context of the strategies for small developing economies towards integration into the world economy. A few sections use graphs to illustrate some of the reasoning. These sections are starred(*) and can be skipped without losing the general line of reasoning. The chapters are generally self-contained and can be consulted in any order.

2
WTO Membership: What's in It for Small Developing Countries?

The lengthy negotiations needed to reach a satisfactory outcome in the Uruguay Round prompted pessimism about the future of the multilateral trading system. The coincidence of the completion of the European single market and the signing of the NAFTA agreement around the end of 1992, while the GATT discussions were in their seventh year, with little prospect of a conclusion, reinforced these views. Several analysts felt that further progress on international trade liberalization would be obtained within and between regional blocs such as the EU and NAFTA. Some went as far as stating that 'the GATT is dead' (Thurow, 1992) or that 'the GATT system is clearly crumbling' (Krugman, 1992). However, the successful conclusion of the Uruguay Round with the Marrakesh agreement in April 1994, and the creation of the World Trade Organization enjoying significant new areas of competence, has restored confidence in the important role of the multilateral trading system.[1]

This chapter highlights the evolution of the relationship between developing countries and the world trading system, from the GATT as agreed in 1947 to the WTO. It assesses the relevance for developing countries of several new provisions agreed under the Uruguay Round (sector coverage, safeguard measures, dispute settlement, intellectual property, investment, trade policy surveillance).[2] It then addresses the advantages and limitations of WTO membership for small developing economies. We conclude that WTO membership provides a beneficial general framework for small developing economies, but that it still leaves wide scope for specific trade policy. In other words, countries should complement the provisions of WTO membership by additional unilateral and/or regional policy measures. Small developing countries may not have the resources to take full advantage of WTO provisions, hence the importance of providing assistance. As a reference, some of the frequently mentioned GATT articles are listed in Table 2.1.

Table 2.1 Frequently mentioned GATT Articles

I	Requires general Most-Favoured-Nation (MFN) treatment; excludes any discrimination among products based on the country of origin.
III	Requires national treatment, once border measures are satisfied (*).
V	Requires freedom of transit.
VI	Allows anti-dumping and countervailing duties (*).
X	Requires the publication of trade laws and regulations; complemented by the Trade Policy Review Mechanism and various notification requirements.
XI	Requires general elimination of quantitative restrictions (*).
XII	Allows restrictions to safeguard the balance of payments or achieve a reasonable increase in the level of reserves (*).
XIII	Requires non-discriminatory administration of quantitative restrictions (*).
XVI	Sets out provisions on subsidies, including notifications (*).
XVIII	Allows developing countries to restrict trade to promote infant industries, protect the balance of payments or ensure a reasonable level of reserves (*).
XIX	Allows safeguard action to restrict imports of particular products (*).
XXII	Provides for consultation between parties that have a trade dispute – a necessary condition for invoking Article XXIII.
XXIII	Dispute settlement provision (*).
XXIV	Sets out the conditions under which the formation of Free Trade Areas and Customs Unions is permitted (*).
XXVI	Provides for entry into force of GATT-1947, allowing simple entry for former colonies.
XXXIII	Provision for accession.
Part IV	Articles XXXVI–XXXVIII, calls for differential and more favourable treatment of developing countries (*).

(*) amended by GATT 1994. Based on Hoekman and Kostecki (1995).

Developing countries and the multilateral trading system

Over the past few decades, there has been a marked evolution in the attitudes and expectations of developing countries towards the multilateral trading system, especially since the beginning of the Uruguay Round in 1986.[3] Several developing economies, including Brazil, Chile, Cuba, India and Pakistan, were among the original 23 contracting parties of the General Agreement on Tariffs and Trade (GATT) in 1947. Nevertheless, they did not play a significant role in the early tariff reduction rounds. This situation was to continue into the 1960s when many newly independent developing countries, especially in Africa, joined the GATT. As observed by Haggard (1995), accession for these countries was quasi-automatic and did not demand policy reform on their side. Under Article XXVI, former colonies could accept the obligations initially negotiated by the metropolitan government. They did not need approval for a tariff schedule. On the other hand, countries that were not ex-colonies had to negotiate their accession under Article XXXIII. This implied more commitments, including acceptance of a tariff schedule and reasonable tariff 'bindings'.[4] In addition, accession needed a two-thirds majority vote of the contracting parties.

Special and differential treatment

From the 1950s to the 1970s, developing countries played a minor role in the GATT. The provisions for developing countries to apply protection for establishing infant industries or to cope with balance of payments problems (Art. XVIII) did not alter their suspicion of the multilateral trading system. The general development thinking made their expectations about trade with industrialized economies very pessimistic. Under the intellectual leadership of economists such as Raoul Prebish and Samir Amin, the view was advanced that international trade and investment would be to the disadvantage of the 'periphery'. On the other hand, it was believed that autonomous planned economic strategies, along the lines of those adopted in the communist countries, would lead to rapid industrialization, which was perceived as the cornerstone of economic modernization. These views were at the origin of the widely applied import substitution approach. They also led to the creation of the United Nations Conference on Trade and Development (UNCTAD) in 1964 as a separate body. Unlike the GATT, it put trade issues into a wider development context and responded more to the perceived needs of the developing countries. While the developing countries considered the multilateral system to be biased against them, the industrial countries felt that the developing countries were often acting as 'free riders', whose main aim was to avoid the disciplines of the global system.

The reaction of the GATT contracting parties to the creation of UNCTAD was to adopt a new part IV on trade and development, endorsing provisions for '*special and differential treatment*' for developing countries. Special and differential treatment formed the basis of the principle of *non-reciprocity* that would dominate trade relations between industrial and developing countries for two decades until the beginning of the Uruguay Round. Reciprocity implies mutual obligations and concessions and is one of the cornerstones of the GATT edifice.[5] It was agreed that developing countries could be granted special preferences by the industrial countries without having to reciprocate. Special and differential treatment implied that developing countries did not have the same obligations as the other contracting parties. The Tokyo Round (1973–79) consolidated the approach of special and differential treatment of developing countries by approving the so-called '*Enabling Clause*', whose full title is 'Differential and more favourable treatment, reciprocity and fuller participation of developing countries'. This clause provided a legal basis for non-reciprocal preferential arrangements such as the Generalized

System of Preferences (GSP). These arrangements are particularly important for small developing economies. An assessment is made in Chapter 5. The enabling clause also contains a provision for regional arrangements among developing countries that do not have to follow the rules of Article XXIV (see Chapter 4). Despite these changes – or some would say, because of them – developing countries continued to be marginalized in the multilateral trade discussions.

Towards real participation

The Uruguay Round (1986–93) marked a fundamental reorientation in the attitude and role of developing countries in the world trading system. Right from the start, there was much more active participation by developing countries in the debates than had occurred in any of the previous rounds. Several important developing countries became new members of the GATT, most prominently: Mexico, Colombia, Venezuela and Thailand. One of the main explanations of the change in attitude was probably the success of the East Asian economies based on a strategy of export orientation. In addition, all over the developing world, structural adjustment programmes were promoting openness and export orientation. Around the beginning of the 1990s the rapid breakdown of the planned economies further strengthened the case for openness and against inward-looking policies.

The overall assessment of the Uruguay Round for the developing countries is that through their bargaining they obtained significant concessions from the industrialized nations. More importantly, these concessions were obtained on the basis of reciprocity, even though special and differential treatment continues to apply in many areas. The main benefits for developing countries will flow from reduced protection in the textiles and clothing sectors with the phasing out of the restrictive Multifibre Arrangement (MFA),[6] and in agriculture. Other positive points for developing countries, especially the newly industrialized ones, are: the prohibition of Voluntary Export Restraints (VERs), the more tightly regulated and transparent anti-dumping provision, the new arrangement for dispute settlement and the increased provisions for technical assistance by the WTO Secretariat.

However, developing countries do not only gain from the Uruguay Round. Some of the new aspects are expected to have mixed or negative effects on them: the agreements on services, trade-related investment measures (TRIMs) and trade-related aspects of intellectual property rights (TRIPs). In reaching the final agreement in Marrakesh in 1994, the industrialized countries tabled the subjects of environmental and labour standards for future discussions, against the wishes of the developing countries. There is increasing concern among developing states that such standards will be abused as new protectionist tools.

Still, the completion of the Uruguay Round made it clear that the developing countries as a group can gain from participation in the multilateral trading system on a reciprocal basis. At the same time various quantitative studies demonstrate that the gains from multilateral trade liberalization are not spread equally among developing states. For example, while some countries with a large export capacity, such as Argentina, Brazil, Chile, Mexico, Malaysia, Thailand and Singapore, are expected to benefit strongly from the reduction of protection by industrialized countries, the anticipation is that several other countries, especially in sub-Saharan Africa, will suffer, at least in the short run.[7]

The Uruguay Round recognized the special problems of the least-developed countries. It was decided that the latter are only required to undertake commitments and concessions to the extent consistent with their development, financial and trade needs and administrative and institutional capabilities (WTO, 1995). For the least-developed countries, as well as for food deficit countries, it was also recognized that trade liberalization in agriculture could have negative effects, including difficulties in financing normal levels of imports of basic foodstuffs, because prices are expected to increase. For this group of developing countries, it was agreed that improvements would be made in the provision of additional food aid as well as technical and financial assistance to improve their agricultural productivity and infrastructure.

Four years on from its creation, a large majority of developing countries had joined the WTO or had applied for membership. By early 1999 there were 134 WTO members, including 99 developing countries. As regards small developing economies, Tables B2 and B3 in Appendix B show that WTO membership is almost universal in Latin America, the Caribbean, Asia and the Pacific. However, as Table B1 reveals, a number of countries in Africa, including Ethiopia and Sudan, remain outside the WTO. The main benefit of WTO membership for all countries, including large and small developing economies, is orderly and rule-based access to world markets.

The post-Uruguay Round relationship between developing countries and the multilateral trading system is characterized by two tendencies. First, for many developing countries, the system of differential and more favourable treatment is changing. There is a gradual move away from a permanent lower level of obligation to a system which simply offers a longer time-horizon for implementation, combined with provisions for technical assistance. There is also increasing pressure on the newly industrialized countries to assume full obligations. Second, there is more explicit recognition and special assistance for the problems of the least-developed countries in relation to the multilateral trading system.[8]

Relevance of new WTO provisions for developing countries

The new WTO provisions that are probably most relevant for the developing countries are the broadening of goods coverage, the agreement on services, the implementation of anti-dumping measures, the agreement on subsidies and countervailing measures and the agreement on safeguards. Other important new provisions include the mechanism for dispute settlement, the provisions on investment and intellectual property and the trade policy surveillance mechanism. In addition, the Marrakesh agreement committed the contracting parties to start discussions on labour and environmental standards, two issues of great concern to the developing countries. We will briefly review these provisions.

Goods coverage

The most important changes as regards product coverage are in textiles and clothing, and agriculture. As regards *textiles and clothing* the Multifibre Arrangement (MFA) that restricted exports from developing countries through a complex system of quotas is to be phased out over a period of ten years, starting in 1995. As a result, consumers in industrial countries will benefit from lower prices. The agreement is less favourable than it looks, because the phasing out will be 'back-loaded' towards the end of the transition period. Furthermore, it is likely that the benefits in terms of increased exports will go mostly to large exporting countries such as China, India, Pakistan and South Korea, whereas small countries such as Mauritius and Jamaica that obtained relatively large MFA quotas will suffer.[9]

One of the reasons why the Uruguay Round was a breakthrough was that it was the first time a multilateral trade negotiation had covered *agriculture*.[10] The agreement requires the conversion of all kinds of import restrictions (such as quotas and the EU's variable levies) into tariffs and a reduction of tariffs by 36 per cent over ten years. Again, the agreement on agriculture is less dramatic than it seems because the tariff reductions start from an inflated base-year level. But the Uruguay Round made a beginning with the dismantling of agricultural protection. One of the expected effects of the agreement is a rise in world market prices for those agricultural products due to lose a significant amount of protection (for example cereals, sugar and meat). The likely overall effect of agricultural liberalization on developing countries is positive. Several of these states, with a large agricultural export capacity, are expected to obtain sizeable benefits (for example Argentina, Brazil and Thailand). However, food-deficit countries, among which there are many small developing and least-developed economies, will pay more.

Services

Including *services* in the multilateral trading system through the new *General Agreement on Trade in Services (GATS)* was another major achievement of the Uruguay Round. Trade in services has been rising more rapidly than trade in goods and its share in total trade reached 22 per cent in 1993. At the beginning of the discussions on services, developing countries were not very keen to take part. Gradually, however, developing countries came to realize their strong position in the provision of various services such as tourism, business services (for example, accounting), construction and transport. In the case of services, it is not just the large developing countries that expect to benefit, but very much the small ones as well. Caribbean nations, for example, have genuine potential to boost their export income in certain service sectors.

The GATS covers *four basic modes of supply of services*:

* *cross-border supply*: services provided from the territory of one member country to the territory of another (for example, accounting);
* *consumption abroad*: services supplied in the territory of a member country to consumers of another (for example, tourism);
* *commercial presence*: services supplied through a business or professional establishment of one member country in the territory of another (for example when a company with headquarters in one member state establishes a branch in another); and
* *temporary presence of natural persons*: services provided by nationals of one member country in the territory of another (for example, construction and consultancy).

The main general provisions of GATS are the Most-Favoured-Nation principle and transparency. The latter requirement obliges WTO members to publish all measures of general application to services such as laws, procedures and administrative arrangements. In addition, member governments are invited to draw up schedules containing liberalization commitments for specific services. Commitments can entail, for example, improved market access, the extension of national treatment and steps to remove restrictions on payments. Once a commitment has been made, it is 'locked-in', meaning that it cannot be rolled back without negotiation and compensation for those affected. The GATS contains provisions to facilitate increasing participation by developing states, especially the least-developed countries. However, the GATS contains no specific provision designed to lighten the obligations on developing countries, thereby illustrating the new trend mentioned above.

The extent of liberalization of trade in services depends on the actual content of the schedules and commitments. The positive list approach constitutes a serious limitation as well as a complication. Altinger and Enders (1996) conclude that developed and transition economies have made significant commitments, while developing countries have made only limited ones. Services liberalization is closely linked to Foreign Direct Investment (FDI). As of the early 1990s, roughly 60 per cent of FDI flows were related to service activities (Hoekman and Kostecki 1995). The GATS commitments made by individual countries give a signal to investors. However, because developing countries have made such limited commitments, this is likely to have a small impact on the FDI flows they receive.

Anti-dumping

Anti-dumping measures are permitted under Article VI of the GATT. They can be imposed on goods exported at prices lower than those charged in the home market where the effect is to cause injury to an industry in the importing country. Anti-dumping has become the most widely applied trade defence measure. Its use, mainly by industrial countries, increased so much during the 1980s that many trade analysts considered it to be a major threat to the multilateral trading system (Abbott, 1996). Recently, anti-dumping measures are being used increasingly by developing countries – especially the more advanced ones such as Brazil and Mexico.[11]

The Uruguay Round has clarified and restricted the use of anti-dumping. There are now stricter rules to determine whether or not dumping takes place and to measure the size of the dumping margin. Temporary protection is normally restricted to five years (the 'sunset ' provision) and may not be applied if the dumping margin is less than 2 per cent or if the level of injury is negligible (*de minimis* provision). Despite these improvements, there is a continuing risk of the spread of anti-dumping measures as more countries start applying them. If this happens, disputes are likely to become more frequent. The extent of unwarranted use of anti-dumping measures will depend very much on the success of the provisions for dispute settlement (see below).

Subsidies and countervailing measures

The objective of countervailing duties is to offset the injurious effects of specific subsidies. Like anti-dumping duties, they are allowed under GATT Article VI. Both address 'unfair' trade practices. Together, they are sometimes referred to as contingent protection – in other words, protection that depends on specific circumstances. Subsidies can take the form of direct financial support or indirect support through tax exemptions or government purchase practices. In order to impose countervailing duties, the importing country must prove that the subsidy caused injury to domestic industry. The possibility of countervailing duties came into the GATT because the United States had prior legislation on this subject. The US has also been the heaviest user of countervailing duties.

With the Agreement on Subsidies and Countervailing Measures, the

Uruguay Round has tightly circumscribed the use of countervailing duties and has created multilateral disciplines on subsidies. The agreement is quite complex and only a few general points are described below. Three categories of subsidy are distinguished: prohibited ('red box'), actionable ('amber box') and non-actionable ('green box'). Prohibited or red-box subsidies are export subsidies and subsidies contingent upon the use of domestic over imported goods. The non-actionable or green category includes subsidies with an economy-wide impact (for example, general infrastructure, education and basic research) and those with a non-economic purpose (for example, reducing regional income disparities or promoting new environmental requirements). Actionable subsidies are an intermediate category. They may have an impact on domestic as well as export sales.

With regard to subsidies, the Agreement provides for two types of remedy for complaining countries: dispute settlement and countervailing measures. Dispute settlement is a multilateral remedy: a WTO panel may recommend that subsidies should be withdrawn or their adverse effects eliminated. If the recommendation is not followed, the complaining country may be authorized to take appropriate measures. Countervailing measures are unilateral actions to protect domestic industry from the effect of subsidies in other countries. Strict conditions apply before any countervailing duties can be imposed: the existence of a countervailable subsidy must be demonstrated and domestic industry must be damaged. A causal link between the subsidy and the injury should be established. Countervailing duties have to be eliminated within five years.

For red-box subsidies, fast-track dispute-settlement is possible without evidence of adverse effects. The subsidies in the amber box can only lead to dispute settlement when there are adverse effects. The green-box subsidies can lead to dispute settlement if they cause serious adverse effects, which in practice is extremely unlikely. Both prohibited and actionable subsidies are countervailable, provided they cause or threaten to cause injury to domestic industry. For subsidies in the non-actionable category, countervailing duties are not permitted.

There are several special provisions for developing countries. Least-developed countries and developing countries with less than US$ 1000 per capita GNP need not eliminate export subsidies and have a time-limited exemption for subsidies contingent upon the use of domestic over imported goods. Other developing countries must phase out all export subsidies within eight years (by the end of 2002). In special circumstances an extension of this period can be agreed. Stricter conditions apply in the event that developing countries have reached 'export competitiveness'. This is when their share in world exports for a particular product exceeds 3.25 per cent in two consecutive years. In that case, developing countries must phase out export subsidies over two years. Least-developed countries and developing countries with less than US$ 1000 per capita GNP still receive eight years. In practice, developing countries can maintain a modest level of specific subsidies. If during an investigation it is established that the level of subsidy for a certain product is less than 2 per cent or 3 per cent respectively for developing or least-developed countries, the investigation will be terminated because the level of subsidy is *de minimis*. It is considered that such a low level of subsidy cannot cause injury.

Safeguards

Safeguard measures have always been possible under GATT Article XIX to counteract situations where imports cause serious problems to domestic producers even though there is no 'unfair' trade practice as such. However, the rather strict conditions of Article XIX discouraged its use. Governments instead preferred to use 'grey-area' measures such as Voluntary Export Restraints (VERs) and other market-sharing devices.

The WTO Agreement prohibits grey-area measures. All VERs must be eliminated by the year 2000. The Agreement sets out criteria for the assessment of 'serious injury' to a company or industry. The duration of safeguard measures should not exceed four years, though under certain conditions this can be extended to eight years. Measures must be progressively relaxed after one year. Safeguards shall not be applied against products of a developing-country member as long as its share of imports does not exceed 3 per cent and provided that developing-country members with less than 3 per cent import share collectively do not account for more than 9 per cent of total imports of the product concerned.

Balance of payments provisions

Article XVIII always permitted trade restrictions by developing countries to protect their foreign exchange reserves or balance of payments or to help the establishment of infant industries. Many developing countries routinely justified protection in the form of quantitative restrictions on balance-of-payments grounds. However, it became clear that quantitative restrictions were often not an appropriate policy response to external payments problems that resulted from bad macroeconomic policies (for example maintaining an overvalued exchange rate). According to Hoekman and Kostecki (1995), the challenge for the Uruguay Round negotiators was to close this important balance of payments loophole. In the context of structural adjustment programmes, developing countries were often required to refrain from quantitative trade restrictions and encouraged to use other policies to combat balance-of-payments problems.

The Uruguay Round understanding on balance-of-payments provisions involves a shift from quantitative restrictions to price-based measures. Furthermore, price-based measures, such as import surcharges, must normally be applied across the board. Exemptions can only be allowed for goods to meet basic consumption needs or imports of vital capital goods or inputs. In collaboration with the IMF, the surveillance of measures adopted on balance-of-payments grounds has been strengthened. Each year, countries applying balance-of-payments restrictions must notify the WTO and provide complete information.

Dispute settlement

Dispute settlement is a key aspect of the functioning of the multilateral trading system. The dispute-settlement provisions offer protection against non-application or abuse of GATT rules. Before the WTO came into existence, dispute settlement almost exclusively concerned industrial countries. It was not very effective because any country could delay the setting-up of a GATT panel to discuss a dispute or even block a panel ruling. The new dispute settlement mechanism is more open, timely, automatic and binding. It covers not only goods, but also services and intellectual property rights. It reflects better the interests of developing countries. Specific time limits are imposed on all aspects of the procedure. The creation of a panel to deal with a complaint is almost automatic, its terms of reference are standardized and blocking a panel ruling requires a unanimous vote. In cases brought by developing countries, there must be at least one panelist from a developing country. The dispute-settlement understanding of the Uruguay Round further adds a new element to the mechanism by creating a standing '*Appellate Body*', which hears appeals of the parties involved about panel decisions and can confirm, reverse or modify these decisions. Nonetheless, not everything is positive for developing countries. Dispute settlement involves the use of expensive legal expertise, which represents a serious constraint for developing countries. However, the new understanding requires the WTO Secretariat to provide legal technical assistance to developing countries.

Despite the above improvements, there remain important constraints, especially for small developing countries involved in a dispute. Even with technical assistance, developing countries may find it difficult to pursue a dispute successfully. According to Abbott (1996, p. 31): 'The ultimate sanction – although virtually never invoked – has been trade retaliation in an amount offsetting the effect of the violation; yet this sanction is virtually meaningless for a developing country acting against an economically powerful state.'

Intellectual property

The agreement on Trade Related Intellectual Property Rights (TRIPs) is an important addition to the multilateral trading disciplines. The agreement covers intellectual property rights such as patents, copyrights, designs of integrated circuits, geographical indications and industrial designs. The inclusion of TRIPs in the Uruguay Round was done at the insistence of the industrial countries. It was pushed by a number of industrial interests, including pharmaceutical, film and software producers, against the wishes of developing countries. The attitude of the latter moderated over time, with some countries such as Brazil and India becoming new exporters of software. It is probably reasonable to say, however, that developing countries only accepted the TRIPs agreement as part of a bargaining process that helped to secure the reforms in agriculture and textiles. From the point of view of the industrial countries, the agreement will curtail the 'free-riding' of some developing countries in relation to intellectual property.

The TRIPs agreement is innovative because it implies measures that are 'beyond the border', such as the harmonization of policies of the participating countries. This is novel when compared with the agreements on goods and services that mainly require governments to refrain from creating impediments at their frontiers. WTO members must put procedures in place under their own law to protect intellectual property rights. For example, action should be taken against firms that do not respect the patent rights or copyrights of foreign companies. The overall assessment of the TRIPs agreement is that it will be a new burden for the developing countries. Rodrik (1995, p. 107) states: 'Since developing country policies are unlikely to have much impact on global innovative activity, tighter patent or copyright protection entail, in the first instance, a redistribution of income from poor to rich countries.' Martin and Winters (1995), however, expect the agreement to have a positive impact on developing countries, resulting from the expected stimulus for new investment in knowledge-based industries.

Investment

Another innovation of the Uruguay Round is the Agreement on Trade Related Investment Measures (TRIMs). Trade and investment have become ever-more intertwined. Investment is also increasingly linked to trade in services and often precedes trade in goods. A large part of international trade consists of transactions taking place within multinational companies.[12] The rapid rise in foreign direct investment (FDI) over the past decade underlines the need to achieve adequate multilateral rules. This applies both to industrial countries as the main source of FDI and developing countries as the main destination, even though South–South FDI is also becoming more important.

Developing countries have been concerned in the first place about minimizing the negative effects and maximizing positive effects of FDI. In developing countries with a large protected market, FDI was sometimes a form of *'tariff-wall jumping'*. In such cases, the host government had an incentive to introduce measures to recapture some of the rents created by its protection. Small developing countries could not offer much in terms of tariff-wall jumping and therefore were less concerned by such rent-seeking.

TRIMs typically include local content requirements, export performance targets, restrictions on the remittance of profits and limitations on ownership. TRIMs may be mandatory or there may be an arrangement under which compliance is necessary to obtain an advantage (for example a tax break). Such measures are usually considered to be inefficient in much the same way as goods market distortions. Sometimes, measures are taken to combat over-invoicing of imports and under-invoicing of exports (transfer pricing). The latter practices can be used by firms to avoid taxation.

As in the case of intellectual property rights, the developing countries were reluctant to have TRIMs included in the Uruguay Round negotiation. The industrial countries, on the other hand, were keen to make a first step towards international harmonization of investment requirements. Under the TRIMs agreement, various practices are to be phased out. Developing countries received five years to do so, the least developed countries got seven years, while industrial countries had to do it in two years.

The measures to be eliminated include investment policies requiring firms to purchase domestic products or limiting purchasing of imported inputs to an amount related to the value of exports. The TRIMs agreement addresses market imperfections resulting from government interference. It does not, however address market imperfections resulting from monopoly situations. The agreement also does not cover export performance requirements.

A distinction must be made between the trade-related investment measures and more general measures to attract or regulate foreign investment. The latter are not within the scope of the WTO even though there is certainly a need to achieve more harmonization. Presently, there are large numbers of bilateral investment deals and it would be beneficial to agree on multilateral rules.[13] Certain investment rules have already been agreed in the field of services (on the right of establishment and the right to conduct business). The TRIMs agreement contains an important provision, which foresees a start to discussions on a multilateral competition policy. Investment provisions and rules of competition are already dealt with in several regional arrangements, for example in the EU and NAFTA. It may be possible gradually to extend the rules and principles of such regional arrangements to the multilateral framework. Morrissey and Rai (1995) criticize the TRIMs agreement for being weak and deficient. They argue that the system prevents developing countries from responding adequately to the various restrictive business practices of transnational corporations engaging in FDI. They recommend dealing with investment measures, not only those related to trade, in a wider framework such as the United Nations. They also favour technical assistance – provided by UNCTAD – to help developing countries cope with the restrictive business practices of foreign investors. Others such as Krueger (1995) and Srinivasan (1996) maintain that the TRIMs agreement is positive for developing countries, because it will diminish their use of regulations that are inherently inefficient. In their view, the agreement is likely to increase the attractiveness of developing countries for FDI.

Trade policy surveillance

The Trade Policy Review Mechanism (TPRM) was introduced during the Uruguay Round negotiations in 1989 and has become a permanent feature of the WTO. Each WTO member is requested to submit periodic reviews of its trade policies. These reviews are the basis of discussions between the WTO and the government. The reports prepared by the trade policy review body of the WTO are made available to all members. The periodicity of report preparation (every two, four or six years) is related to the country's share in international trade. Only the four largest traders: the EU, the US, Japan and Canada (the 'quad'), are reviewed every two years. The WTO's trade policy surveillance complements the ongoing IMF's surveillance of monetary and balance-of-payments policies.

The surveillance mechanism increases the transparency of trade policy. Developing countries will have a better basis to challenge harmful practices. Surveillance should also lead to a greater role for the WTO in collecting comparable data on trade policies and practices. This is important for the quality of technical assistance that the WTO can provide to developing countries in various areas including dispute settlement.

Environmental and labour standards

Although environmental and labour standards are not part of the new WTO provisions, they should be mentioned because they have become a major concern in relation to the international trading system. Industrial countries are concerned because they perceive a risk that their own politically negotiated standards will be undermined by so-called 'ecodumping and social dumping'. With free movement of capital, many observers fear a 'race to the bottom' with investors travelling around the world seeking the least restrictive environmental or labour standards. Developing countries are concerned because they view restrictive environmental or labour norms as a disguised form of new protection and an unacceptable interference in their domestic affairs. The issues related to environmental and labour standards are extremely divisive, both within industrial and developing countries and between them.

The WTO established a Committee on Trade and Environment, with a mandate to promote greater transparency and more objective analysis of the relationship between the environment and trade. While environmentally sound development is undoubtedly desirable, it is debatable whether trade policy is a suitable instrument to achieve 'green' objectives.

As regards the harmonization of labour standards, there has already been a long-term, but not much publicized, effort in the context of the International Labour Organization (ILO). Several conventions have been prepared, calling for core standards such as freedom of association, the right to collective bargaining, protection against discrimination and prohibition of forced labour. However, those conventions have not yet been ratified by all WTO members. For the moment, the WTO only permits restrictions on products made with prison labour. It does not recognize other uses of trade policy in response to labour conditions. Several trade policy analysts, for example Srinivasan (1996), Bhagwati (1997) and Krueger (1995), advise extreme caution on multilateral labour standards. A ban on child labour, for example, may be unenforceable in poor developing countries. It would be more appropriate to address poverty alleviation directly rather than through trade policy measures. The latter may simply shift the problems so that they become less visible or, worse, they may actually increase poverty and child mortality.

Small developing economies and the WTO

What do the new aspects of the Uruguay Round mean for Small Developing Economies (SDEs)? For them, the results of the Uruguay Round are certainly not unequivocally positive. Because most SDEs benefit in an important way from non-reciprocal preferences made available by industrial countries, their access to those markets cannot be improved very much. Hence, they will not gain from the general lowering of tariffs by the industrial countries as agreed under the Uruguay Round. The lowering of MFN tariffs will, on the contrary, erode the effect of special preferences (see Chapter 5). Small developing countries, including the least developed, will therefore face more stringent competition in the industrialized markets. During the Uruguay Round negotiations, several small developing countries lobbied against tariff reductions and the phasing-out of preferential arrangements.

Benefits of membership

Despite preference erosion in the industrial country markets, there will be significant gains in market access because of tariff reductions in the more advanced (large) developing countries and the transition economies. It is likely that import demand in both groups of countries will grow more rapidly than in the industrial nations.[14] There are several new aspects of WTO membership that are likely to be beneficial for small developing countries. These include the limitations put on anti-dumping measures and the new dispute settlement procedures. Kuruvila (1997) observes a remarkable increase in the participation of developing countries in the WTO dispute settlement compared to the situation under the GATT. For the first time complainants include small economies such as Costa Rica and Honduras. However, small countries still face many difficulties in effectively handling disputes. The cost of legal expertise can be insurmountable and they cannot implement meaningful retaliation.[15] The WTO Secretariat has the obligation to provide technical assistance, but it lacks capacity to handle all the specialized assistance that may be required. With around 500 staff members, the Secretariat is in fact rather small. It should be strengthened in order to be able to provide adequate assistance to small developing economies. Michalopoulos (1999) considers that the WTO Secretariat can provide general technical assistance and training on procedures, but cannot really help developing countries in specific dispute settlement, because this would violate neutrality. He favours establishing an independent advisory centre on WTO law to be funded by donors and by developing-country users. For such a centre to be successful, it should indeed be independent of lobbies in developing and industrial countries. Regional organizations could also help with defending the specific interests of their (small) members in the multilateral discussions. This point is raised in Chapter 4.

The new provisions on services are generally believed to be positive for small developing countries. But, the benefits of new trade in services will not at all be automatic and will require a repositioning of the private sector. Again, this is an area where increased assistance should be provided.

Membership of the WTO will have some indirect benefits, especially in combination with IMF membership and with the elimination of restrictions on current account transactions (what is called 'fulfilment of the obligations of Article VIII of the IMF's articles of agreement'). Investors and traders will clearly be more confident about doing business with small developing economies that participate in the multilateral system and 'play by the rules' than with those remaining outside this system. The Trade Policy Review Mechanism can also play a signalling role towards investors.

A related benefit of WTO membership is its contribution to the stability and credibility of trade policies through tariff bindings and the elimination of quantitative restrictions. Tariff bindings can be a way to 'lock in' trade policy reform. However, the scope for the WTO to enforce the lock-in of policies of small developing economies is limited. One of the explanations is the tiny weight of these countries in international trade. The WTO approach is to reduce tariffs by offering mutual concessions. Small developing countries cannot make concessions that are significant in the world trading system and therefore do not have much incentive to lower tariff bindings. Furthermore, developing countries can still invoke differential and more favourable treatment as a reason for not making concessions. The situation for sub-Saharan Africa (SSA) has been analysed by Sorsa (1996), who concludes that most SSA countries did not make meaningful liberalization commitments on protection in agriculture, industry or services. Exceptions are South Africa and Zimbabwe. Sorsa therefore considers the Uruguay Round a missed opportunity for the African countries. We will argue below that regionalism offers better possibilities to increase the credibility of trade policy reforms.

Membership of the WTO carries only limited non-economic benefits. It will not help in any direct way to consolidate peace and security or to achieve good governance and strengthen the rule of law. It will also not help to reduce the inherent vulnerability of small developing countries. Furthermore, it does not prevent threats from large countries or trading blocs. Small developing economies may expect more from regionalism in relation to these aspects.

Costs of membership

What can be said in general about the costs of being a member of the WTO? One aspect of these costs is the contribution to the budget for the functioning of the WTO Secretariat. However, there are other types of costs. As mentioned by Blackhurst (1997b) one should also take into account the cost of keeping delegates in Geneva and the cost of support staff in the capitals. An important characteristic of the WTO is that its activities are driven by its member states. Hence, the importance of being able to take part effectively in meetings, negotiations and dispute settlements. Other cost aspects derive from constraints on sovereign policies that countries may wish to pursue and the need to demonstrate compliance through various notifications.

The WTO budget is rather small – about US$ 80 million in 1995. The member countries contribute in proportion to their share in international trade. This implies a relatively small financial contribution from developing economies.[16] The cost aspect in terms of constraints on sovereign policies is also likely to be small for developing economies. The Uruguay Round did not abolish special and differential treatment for them. Developing countries generally receive more time for compliance and sometimes have more limited obligations. Furthermore, the WTO does not require developing countries to achieve low tariff levels. This is mainly because the level at which their tariffs are bound remains in many cases quite high. Hence, membership of the WTO, while necessary for successful trade liberalization, is certainly not sufficient on its own.

The costs of representation in Geneva often pose insurmountable problems for small developing countries. Two-thirds of the least-developed countries that are members of the WTO have no representation in Geneva. Even a small representation would not be of great help because there are hundreds of specialized meetings taking place each year. Small developing countries could achieve significant savings by setting up representations on a regional basis involving regional organizations.

The need to demonstrate compliance through various notifications (for example, in relation to subsidies, TRIMs and TRIPs) may not a big issue for large countries, but it poses real problems for small ones. Small developing countries will need assistance to deal with these notifications.

Conclusion

Summing up, membership of the WTO is an important and worthwhile, even necessary step towards integration into the world economy. Not being a member of the WTO sends a negative signal to traders and investors. It is thus recommended that small developing economies that have not yet done so join the WTO. However, being a member does not bring many automatic benefits. There is certainly a need to go beyond purely formal and minimal membership and to accept meaningful obligations such as reasonable tariff bindings on goods and real offers for liberalization in services. Furthermore, small developing countries require assistance for a wide range of complex issues in order to participate effectively in the multilateral system. The WTO Secretariat is not adequately equipped to provide such assistance. It should be strengthened in order to help small developing countries with their participation. The issue to be examined further is how best to complement the requirements of WTO membership. In the following chapters we will examine ways of doing this.

3
Unilateral Economic Liberalization

In assessing the membership of the WTO from the perspective of small developing countries, it was concluded earlier that this membership does not settle many policy matters that must be dealt with regarding beneficial integration into the world economy. The framework offered by the WTO is only a starting-point and needs to be complemented by further economic policy decisions. WTO members can still maintain relatively closed economies. It has been noted that many developing countries entered the WTO with high tariff bindings. They can also continue to impose trade restrictions, for example on balance-of-payments grounds, relying on special and differential treatment. All in all, developing countries that have become WTO members must still make a variety of policy choices in order to achieve openness. Some choices relate to the sequencing and the speed of economic liberalization measures. Countries must also choose whether to move towards openness in a unilateral way or in a regional integration grouping. Whether openness is pursued unilaterally or regionally, it will increase interdependence and lead to constraints on economic policy. The size of the economy will affect the advantages and costs of these choices.

For many small developing countries, macroeconomic policy reform takes place in the context of structural adjustment programmes (SAPs) formulated and implemented in collaboration with the World Bank and the International Monetary Fund. Trade liberalization has invariably been a key component of SAPs. Small developing countries are more affected by interdependence resulting from increased openness than large ones.

This chapter examines the strategy of unilateral economic liberalization from the point of view of small developing economies. The main areas of liberalization are trade policy, investment regulations and payments mechanisms. Before examining the unilateral liberalization strategy, the historical origin of inward-looking policies and the relationship between growth and openness will be described. We find that the inward-looking strategies pursued by many developing countries put a serious brake on their economic growth. The empirical evidence that openness improves economic growth performance is convincing. There are theoretical arguments that under certain assumptions unilateral trade liberalization increases welfare. However, unilateral trade liberalization is not a panacea. It has several limitations. For example, it does not improve market access, adjustment costs may be large and income distribution effects may be quite strong. Moreover, many small developing countries find it difficult to raise government revenue except through trade taxes. Where it is not coordinated with neighbouring countries, unilateral liberalization can easily lead to cross-border problems. These arise because of differences in the macroeconomic situation of neighbouring countries. For example, policy-induced price differences will stimulate smuggling or unrecorded trade. For economies vulnerable to such macroeconomic spill-over effects, the SAPs should take account of the regional dimension, rather than be purely national. Especially for small countries, another limitation of unilateral trade liberalization is that it may lack credibility. Policy reversals are frequent. These themes will be elaborated below.

From import substitution to export orientation

During the 1950s and 1960s, many newly independent developing countries followed inward-looking strategies to promote economic growth. These strategies reflected the dominant economic opinions of the period. During the depression of the 1930s most industrial economies had become closed, with high tariff barriers and inconvertible currencies, not only in Europe, but also in the wider western hemisphere. The colonial system extended this strategy to a large part of the developing world. During the 1950s, central planning and government intervention seemed to be the quickest way towards industrialization, which was seen as the key to economic development and modernization. This view was strengthened by the apparently continuous decline of raw-material prices and the persistent protectionism of industrial countries for labour-intensive agricultural and manufactured products. Import substitution behind high tariff walls became the dominant policy advice to achieve industrialization. The 'infant industry' argument provided a theoretical justification for high tariffs. The theory was that the newly established industries would gradually become more efficient so that tariff protection could be reduced.

This period also coincided for many developing countries with the build-up of their state structures and an understandable political preoccupation with fully exploiting the privileges of sovereignty. One aspect of this was the granting of export and import monopolies to marketing boards. The build-up of the state apparatus logically called for increased taxation. Tariff revenue was almost always the most convenient way to raise new revenue for the state. State-owned companies and marketing boards, sometimes remaining from colonial times, were used to raise money for the state. Because the state system was predominantly urban, these mechanisms typically channelled resources from rural producers to urban consumers, leading to the phenomenon of urban bias.

In the spirit of consolidating sovereignty, Foreign Direct Investment (FDI) was not viewed positively. Governments certainly have a legitimate concern about the contribution of foreign-owned companies to national welfare. Promoting development in the host country is clearly not the first objective of foreign investors, even though the profitability of investments may be enhanced by economic development. In order to avoid foreign investors transferring excessive profits, governments would impose various restrictions, as well as taxation to get maximum benefit for the treasury. In doing this, they disregarded the positive externalities of FDI on the rest of the economy.[1] In some cases investments were nationalized without adequate compensation, further exacerbated by foreign exchange restrictions. In many instances a heavy regulatory framework was established, discouraging new FDI.

Another crucial aspect of exercising sovereignty concerns monetary policy. In many newly-independent countries, monetary institutions enjoyed little freedom from government interference. Instead, the central bank was put at the service of the treasury. Inflationary financing of an increasing government budget deficit was usually politically easier than collecting new taxes. The resulting inflation was often not reflected in a depreciation of the official exchange rate. Keeping nominal exchange rates fixed in the presence of inflation led to overvalued currencies and consequent loss of competitiveness. Imports were excessively stimulated for those with access to foreign exchange and exports were discouraged, leading to chronic shortages of foreign exchange. Overvalued exchange rates resulting from budget deficits often had another important consequence: governments borrowed money abroad, resulting in rising foreign debt that gradually became unsustainable. In order to cope with the shortage of foreign exchange, many governments introduced elaborate systems of exchange controls. These led to the development of parallel exchange markets. In several cases, the difference between the official fixed (nominal exchange) rate and the black market or parallel rate became very large, leading to disruption of normal international trade and encouraging smuggling.

It should be underlined that the prevalence of inward-looking policies and the negative consequences did not only occur in developing countries. As mentioned already, most industrialized countries resorted to similar policies in their attempt to cope with the great depression of the 1930s. It is paradoxical that during the post-Second World War period, industrialized countries successfully reversed their earlier economic policies while, at the same time, many newly independent states gradually introduced them. The spread of inward-looking policies in developing countries probably had more to do with political ideology and nation-building than economic policy insight or an objective assessment of the facts.

The above description is admittedly stylized and incomplete. The situation was far from uniform across developing countries and over time. During the 1970s, some developing countries started revising their inward-looking policies because of a lack of tangible results. The economic turbulence of the 1970s, following the fall of the Bretton Woods system of fixed exchange rates and the oil price shock in 1973, probably confused policy-makers and delayed the move away from inward-looking and urban-biased policies. During this period, there were unprecedented fluctuations in the prices of food and other basic commodities, as well as in interest and exchange rates. Developing countries became sharply divided into exporters of oil and a few other commodities that saw export revenues rise rapidly and others that faced unprecedented import bills. Several developing countries that benefited from transitory gains increased government spending in a way that could not easily be reversed later and the response to this was to extend restrictive, inward-looking policies. Furthermore, the windfall gains in export earnings of a particular sector could lead to an appreciation of the real exchange rate, thereby undermining competitiveness and penalizing exports outside the booming sector. This phenomenon has been called 'Dutch disease', in reference to the effects of rapidly increasing natural-gas revenue in the Netherlands in the 1960s. The conditions during the 1970s were not the same for small and large developing economies. Small economies are more vulnerable to shocks and Dutch disease effects than large ones. Inward-looking policies usually impose a greater cost on small economies.

In summary, until the end of the 1970s, inward-looking economic policies dominated the macroeconomic policy environment in developing countries. The three main elements here are protective trade barriers, restrictions on inward investment and extensive foreign exchange controls. Because all three require detailed administrative management, they are also linked to governance problems and created many opportunities for corruption.

Around the beginning of the 1980s, when the industrialized countries had learned to cope with shocks in commodity prices, interest and exchange rates, the negative consequences for economic growth of the inward-looking policies outlined above became fully visible. Import substitution behind high tariff walls had failed to deliver economic growth. Even its contribution to non-economic objectives such as nation-building was looking increasingly questionable. At the same time the spectacular success of a few strongly export-oriented economies such as South Korea and Taiwan attracted attention. The dominant development policy advice started to shift towards outward orientation.

A lot of the policy advice on openness became part of the standard recipe in structural adjustment programmes (SAPs). During the 1980s most of the poor small developing economies embarked on SAPs formulated with the help of the International Monetary Fund and the World Bank.[2] In virtually all cases, the SAPs promoted a reversal of the inward-looking policies. However, for small developing economies, the success rate of SAPs in terms of achieving sustainable economic growth has been below expectation. Even in countries where SAPs were considered reasonably successful (for example in Ghana), it took more time to achieve success than had been anticipated.

In many cases, developing countries were not able to implement effectively the recommended policies. The effects on income distribution of the reforms could be so drastic that they became politically and/or socially impracticable. The inward-looking policies had led to the existence of strong vested interests that resisted reform. In other cases, the reforms were implemented, but there was not much supply response from the private sector. Several reform programmes were actually stopped or even reversed.

Of the main areas of reform of inward-looking policies, exchange-rate devaluation has often been among the first measures undertaken, though it was generally politically controversial. Most countries implementing SAPs have been able to put an end to currency overvaluation. In practice, what often happened was massive devaluation. At the same time restrictions on current account transactions, such as foreign exchange licensing, have been eliminated so that exchange rates are more market-determined. An increasing number of countries have accepted the obligations of Article VIII of the IMF's articles of agreement, i.e. current account convertibility.[3] Also, in the area of investment, the bias against foreign investors has been reduced or eliminated. However, for many small economies, reforms in both policy areas have not resulted in significant new exports or in new foreign direct investment. The third policy area, trade liberalization, has been the one which has been implemented most slowly. The rest of this chapter focuses on trade policy.

Openness and economic growth

The shift in development policy advice from import substitution towards openness has been underpinned by many empirical studies. In his survey on openness, trade liberalization and growth in developing countries Edwards (1993) makes a distinction between in-depth country case-studies and analysis based on a cross-section of countries. Detailed case-studies on countries such as Chile and South Korea have probably been the most influential for policy advisers and politicians. Many of the cross-section studies reviewed by Edwards have been plagued by empirical and conceptual shortcomings. One empirical problem has been the way to measure openness. Some of the early studies used the simple ratio of exports, imports or the sum of both to GDP. The disadvantage is that small countries, even if they are relatively closed, tend to have high ratios, whereas large countries that are open may have low ratios. Small economies generally have a higher trade share because of their lack of diversification.

In its report 'Global Economic Prospects and the Developing Countries', the World Bank (1996) considers openness as identical to integration in the world economy. A distinction is made between fast, moderate, weak and slow integrators, according to the value of a 'speed of integration index'. This index avoids the problem mentioned above because it is based on changes of variables between the early 1980s and the early 1990s, rather than their levels. The variables are the ratio of trade to GDP, the ratio of FDI to GDP and the institutional investors' credit ratings. The World Bank study demonstrated that over the decade 1984–93, the fast integrators among developing countries achieved on average 2 per cent per capita GDP growth per year, whereas the slow integrators experienced an average decline of 1 per cent.

Sachs and Warner (1995) made a detailed and influential analysis of the relationship between openness and growth. This study is particularly interesting for the way in which the problem of measuring openness is dealt with as well as for the detailed documentation of the data. Openness is measured by the *absence* of one or more of five conditions:

- non-tariff barriers covering at least 40 per cent of trade;
- average tariff rates of 40 per cent or more;
- an official exchange rate that is overvalued by at least 20 per cent on average relative to the black-market exchange rate;
- a socialist economic system;
- a state monopoly on major exports.

Many economies that are classified as closed satisfy several of these conditions. For small developing and transition economies, the Sachs and Warner measure of openness is reproduced in Appendix Tables B1 to B4.[4] The authors note a strong association between growth and openness for the period 1970–89. Per capita GDP in open developing economies grew at 4.5 per cent per year, whereas in closed developing countries it grew at only 0.7 per cent. However, it was also demonstrated that open economies were more susceptible to the economic shocks that occurred in the 1970s. Nonetheless, while open economies experienced more fluctuations, there was not a single year where their growth rate was lower than the growth rate of closed economies.

Even though the empirical analysis demonstrating the positive relation between openness and growth over the past few decades is convincing, a number of questions regarding interpretation still arise. If openness pays off so well in terms of economic growth, one wonders why it took such a long time for most countries to open up. Another question concerns the relationship between openness and the role of the state as a promoter of economic development.

Openness has usually been advocated in combination with other reforms, such as a reduced role for the state and democratization. However, some of the countries that are often referred to as examples of export success, such as Japan, South Korea, Singapore and Taiwan, heavily relied on state guidance and support to foster import substitution. Wade (1990) provides a revealing account of how the government in Taiwan encouraged export growth. Why were some countries successful with import substitution while so many others failed? An import substitution strategy in fact requires only selective protection. It does not call for generalized protection, a massively overvalued exchange rate or a restrictive investment regime.

A study by Vamvakidis (1996) extends the analysis by Sachs and Warner over a much longer period and offers some insight into the differences between large and small economies. Vamvakidis uses the same definitions as Sachs and Warner, extending the length of their time series for as many countries as possible. He demonstrates that the positive correlation between openness and growth in the 1970s and 1980s disappears in the 1950s and 1960s and becomes negative in the 1920s and 1930s. His explanation for these startling observations is that for a country, openness pays off mainly when the rest of the world is also open. The policy rationale is that openness, when others are closed, increases vulnerability to external shocks. Vamvakidis also adds a regional perspective. Countries that are near to other open economies tend to grow faster than those having closed neighbours. As a result, there is a tendency for countries to open up in regional groups. This was the case for Western Europe in the 1950s, for a sizeable part of East and South-East Asia in the late 1960s and early 1970s, for Latin America in the second half of the 1980s and for an increasing part of Africa since the beginning of the 1990s. When the rest of the world, and especially neighbours, are increasingly open, protection usually reduces the growth rate.

Vamvakidis (1996) also presents some results related to the size of the economy. He finds that small closed economies grow more slowly than large closed economies, suggesting that market size and scale economies matter for economic growth. While import substitution policies have sometimes been successful in large economies, this has almost never been the case for small ones. The latter do not have a domestic market that is sufficiently large for infant industry protection to work. In large economies, the infant industry approach can succeed, as demonstrated for example by the Japanese car industry. This grew under protection during the 1950s and 1960s and conquered the world market during the 1970s and 1980s.

The case for unilateral trade liberalization (*)

As mentioned in the historical overview, the negative results of inward-looking policies of small developing economies led to the adoption of structural adjustment programmes (SAPs) that included trade liberalization as a key component. As the SAPs were conceived and implemented in a national context, the policy advice on trade always amounted to *unilateral trade liberalization*. This is to be contrasted with *multilateral trade liberalization* undertaken through the successive GATT Rounds and *regional trade liberalization* undertaken in the context of regional integration groupings. This section reviews the arguments in favour of unilateral trade liberalization from the point of view of small economies.

The arguments for unilateral trade liberalization are the mirror image of the reasoning against protection. A simple graph can clarify the main point. Consider the case of a market of a single product in a small country. The item is not produced in the country. Protection, in the form of tariffs, is generally paid for by consumers through higher prices, while the government receives the tariff revenue. Referring to Figure 3.1, based on Corden (1974), the world market price is at level OC. The small country can import whatever quantity it wishes at that price. It is further assumed that the exchange rate is in equilibrium so that the import price can be considered to reflect the true social cost of imports. Without a tariff, demand curve D would lead to an imported quantity of CF. If the price rises by the tariff value AC, the import quantity decreases to AB. The government receives tariff revenue represented by the rectangle a. However, the tariff revenue is not enough to compensate for the loss in consumer welfare represented by the decline of the consumer surplus (equal to the decline of the area below the demand curve and above the price line), this is areas a plus b. The net loss is therefore represented by triangle b which is usually called the 'deadweight loss'. Market distortions resulting from government interventions or other factors lead to welfare losses that can be represented by triangles such as area b.

It is easy to add a supply curve S representing local production as done in Figure 3.2. This leads to an additional triangular area welfare

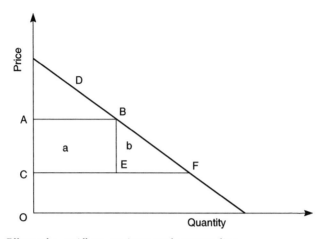

Figure 3.1   Effect of a tariff on an imported commodity

loss resulting from a tariff. This can be explained as follows: introducing again a tariff at level AC reduces the total consumer surplus by the sum area a + b + c + d. Area a represents the increase in producer surplus (the area under the price line and above the supply curve). This is extra income going to the producers because of the protection they receive. Area c is the tariff revenue received by the government. The net welfare loss is therefore equal to b + d. Area b is the loss represented by inefficient production above the world market price.

Figure 3.2 illustrates that protection for a small country leads to welfare losses because consumers would prefer more imports at lower prices and because producers are pushed towards inefficient production. Maximization of welfare in the simplified world represented by Figure 3.2 would imply elimination of all tariffs in all markets so that there is no longer any deadweight loss to the economy resulting from protection.

It is interesting to make a brief digression to examine the case of market distortions that do not result from government interventions. These can arise, for example, because of a monopoly situation or externalities.[5] Tariffs are sometimes justified to correct for such distortions. However, it can be demonstrated that, under certain assumptions, tariffs are a less efficient way of compensating for distortions than policy measures that directly address the root cause of the distortion. For example, a production externality can best be dealt with through a production subsidy rather than a tariff. This is illustrated in Figure 3.3 where the dotted supply curve S' represents the true marginal social cost of production that is situated below S. A frequently mentioned cause of such a situation in developing countries is an institutionally fixed wage rate in manufacturing that is above labour productivity in

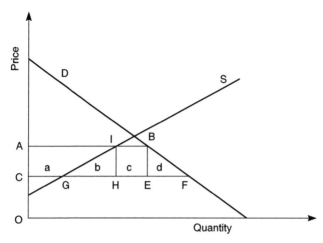

Figure 3.2 Effect of a tariff with demand and supply

the rest of the economy. A production subsidy of AC per unit will lead to a production increase of GH such that the social marginal production cost equals the import price OC. The triangular area e represents an increase in social welfare. Up to a quantity CH it is socially efficient to produce the given commodity, rather than to import it. Consumers are not affected and continue to demand CF. A tariff of the same magnitude as the subsidy AC would lead to the same production level, but would reduce demand by EF, implying a loss in consumer surplus represented by area d. While the subsidy leads to an unambiguous welfare gain, it is not possible to tell whether the tariff will lead to a net gain. This depends on the relative size of the areas d and e.

Even though the above reasoning is appealing, it is useful to recall several important assumptions that are necessary for the result. Lack of fulfilment of one or more of these assumptions may, in some cases, explain the prevalence or persistence of tariffs. In addition to the limitations of the partial equilibrium framework the following assumptions are made:

- taxation needed to pay for the subsidy will not upset any marginal conditions reducing welfare in the rest of the economy;
- there are no collection costs of taxation;
- there are no distribution costs of the subsidy and
- income redistribution from taxpayers to subsidized producers does not imply a welfare loss.

While tariffs may lead to a welfare loss, other policy interventions such as subsidies may also reduce welfare if the above assumptions are not valid. The tariff has the advantage that it is often relatively easy

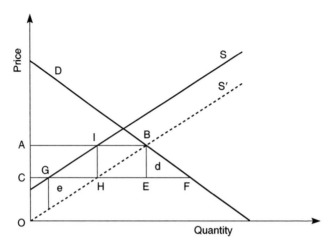

Figure 3.3 Comparison of tariff and a subsidy to deal with a production externality

and cheap to collect. Furthermore, it is also possible that the distortion actually originates with imports. In this case a tariff will be the best policy response. An example is a tariff to compensate for overvaluation of the exchange rate. If the exchange rate is overvalued, imports are cheaper than they should be and a tariff can compensate for this. This situation occurred for many small African economies before the devaluation of the CFA Franc at the beginning of 1994. Several members of the CFA zone such as Côte d'Ivoire used tariffs to compensate for overvaluation.

The limitations of unilateral trade liberalization

It might seem surprising that, given the economic costs of maintaining tariff protection, not all small economies have reduced their tariffs towards zero. The main economic arguments in favour of tariff protection, the terms of trade and the infant industry arguments, are not particularly relevant for small countries. The terms of trade or optimal tariff argument refers to a situation where a country has a certain degree of monopoly power and can lower its import price by restricting demand through tariffs. The optimal tariff is the one that maximizes welfare.[6] This is clearly not applicable in the case of small developing economies. The infant industry argument is a valid argument for *temporary* protection in the event of dynamic economies to scale, i.e. cost savings that can only be realized over time (see Corden, 1974). Dynamic scale economies can be internal or external to the firm or the industry. In developing countries, dynamic economies are typically related to capital market imperfections and to the accumulation of experience and knowledge (learning by doing). However, the infant industry tariff can only promote the establishment of an industry if the internal market is sufficiently large. This is not applicable in small economies.

There is also a frequently used non-economic argument against unilateral tariff reduction. As long as the rest of the world has not liberalized completely, it would be useful to keep a margin for tariff bargaining. This reflects the mercantilist nature of international tariff negotiations. One's own tariff concessions are used to 'buy' concessions from others. This argument does not make sense in the case of small developing economies. Clearly, small economies cannot expect to be able to influence the tariffs of the rest of the world by offering concessions themselves. Only in the case where small economies would be able to create a successful customs union constituting a sizeable market (even if this is only for a few selected commodities), can they expect to play a significant role in the international tariff bargaining under the aegis of the WTO.

So, if the most frequently used arguments are not valid, why do many small countries maintain tariffs? There are at least four other reasons why small economies do not necessarily think it is to their advantage to go very far in the direction of unilateral trade liberalization. First, reducing tariffs unilaterally will increase imports, but will not increase market access and therefore exports in any direct way. Second, tariff reductions will lead to adjustment costs and changes in income distribution. Third, tariffs are often a convenient way to collect revenue. Fourth, unilateral tariff reductions may not be considered credible by investors. These arguments are developed below.

Unilateral tariff reduction by a small country will reduce the price of imported products, which will lead to increased imports. However, apart from drawing down international reserves or obtaining extra balance-of-payments support, increased imports must as a rule be paid for by increased exports. Since the rest of the world has not reduced its tariffs, there will be no rapid increase in exports. What may happen instead is a deterioration in the trade balance leading to a depreciation of the exchange rate. This will again raise the domestic price of imports and decrease their volume. The lowering of tariffs may have a gradual effect on exports by improving the competitiveness of producers relying on imported materials, which are becoming cheaper. Such producers may expand into new markets, but this is likely to take more time than the rise in imports mentioned above. Some African countries, such as Zambia, have unilaterally reduced tariffs at a rapid pace in the context of structural adjustment programmes. In Zambia's case, extra balance of payments support has limited the decline of the exchange rate. The result has been a rapid increase in imports from South Africa. Non-traditional exports are increasing, but only slowly. For tariff reductions to be sustainable, their pace should be in line with the pace of new export growth.

Tariff reduction will lead to the closure of firms that can only compete because of protection. Even if these are not particularly efficient operations, their closure will imply adjustment costs. The issue of adjustment costs is often neglected in the trade policy literature.[7] Thomas, Nash and associates (1991), in their analysis of trade liberalization, tend to minimize their importance. They refer to adjustment costs as merely 'discomfort of firms and sectors harmed' (page 85). In practice, replacing inefficient production will always entail sizeable costs. Capital market imperfections may prevent a smooth transition to other industries. This could lead to a permanent loss of skills (the reverse of the infant industry argument). If opening of the economy is done together with neighbouring countries, the transition may be easier. The historical analysis of Vamvakidis mentioned earlier demonstrated the positive growth effect of opening the economy when the rest of the world and especially neighbouring countries were opening as well.

Unilateral trade liberalization can be risky for a small economy, especially if it has a large neighbour that is not opening its markets at a comparable speed. This situation is applicable, for example, to small economies in Southern Africa that, in the context of structural adjustment programmes, have sometimes unilaterally reduced tariffs at a faster pace than the dominant economy of the region: South Africa. During 1996, firms in adjusting countries in Southern Africa such as Malawi and Zambia lost competitiveness in relation to South African firms because of their pace of liberalization and, in addition, because of the depreciation of the rand. This is an argument for *orderly* liberalization or, in other words, for taking into account the regional dimension in the formulation of national adjustment programmes. A regional integration arrangement is the logical way to achieve orderly liberalization. The benefits of redesigning structural adjustment programmes by taking into account the regional dimension of adjustment are underlined by Mistry (1996).

Trade liberalization has an effect on income distribution. Tariffs will increase the share of revenue going to production factors that are intensively used in protected sectors. Rodrik (1998) considers the effect on income distribution as the main explanation for the difficulties in bringing about trade reform in Africa. Using a simple model and some plausible assumptions, he demonstrates that the distributional implications of trade reform can be overriding. The main distributional effect of tariff reduction in Africa involves a shift of revenue from the protected urban sector (urban workers, employers and government officials) to the farmers and informal sector workers. The shift in income distribution can be much larger than the value of the efficiency gains of tariff reduction. Hence trade liberalization will be politically delicate.

Another reason for not reducing tariff levels to zero is to keep the tariff revenue as a component of government revenue. For small developing economies, tariff revenue is often a sizeable component of total revenue. Even after some rounds of adjustment programmes, the share can be above 20 per cent and there are situations where it is above 50 per cent. Collecting tariffs is usually easy in comparison to other ways of raising revenue, such as a value-added or income tax. In economies with a large subsistence component, both value-added and income taxes are difficult to set up and administer. Furthermore, in the case of small economies, import duties are not very different from other indirect taxes, especially if there are only few tariff rates. Small economies will always need to import a wide range of commodities, hence tariffs are almost equivalent to consumption taxes. If the tariff structure is reasonably uniform, the tariffs are mainly for revenue and will not have much welfare-reducing effect. This assumes that government expenditures are equally welfare-enhancing than private expenditures.

Another limitation of unilateral trade liberalization in small developing countries is that it may lack credibility. Lack of diversification makes it relatively easy for pressure groups representing vested interests to push for policy reversals. Investment in more efficient industries is the key to reaping the benefits from liberalization. But domestic and foreign investors may not be confident that the unilateral measures will not be reversed. Lack of investment response may upset a liberalization programme so that lack of credibility becomes a self-fulfilling prophecy. There are a number of ways to boost the credibility of reforms. Conditionality of support under structural adjustment programmes is one approach. However, Collier *et al.* (1997) find that conditionality as currently practised, on the basis of a promise of policy reform, is not very credible. Once the aid has been received, the vested interests may push for reversal and a new round may start. As observed in Chapter 2, tariff bindings under the WTO are also a relatively weak instrument to enhance credibility. Other approaches to increase credibility involve some form of regionalism, either between developing countries or with industrial countries. With regionalism, policy reversals may be discouraged by the application of sanctions. The effect of regionalism on credibility of economic reforms is examined in Chapters 4 and 6.

Assessment

The points that emerge from the discussion on the limitations of unilateral trade liberalization should not be interpreted as arguments against outward orientation. They are mainly arguments about the pace and sequencing of liberalization and in favour of complementary measures. They are also arguments to explore the contribution of regionalism, as will be done in Chapter 4. The limitations of unilateral approaches that have been identified do nothing to undermine the lessons of historical experience and theoretical insights about openness. A fair amount of unilateral liberalization can be considered necessary, even vital, for integration into the world economy. It is indispensable to reduce or eliminate 'big' distortions that have effects throughout the economy, such as an overvalued exchange rate, negative real interest rates or an institutionally fixed manufacturing wage. Such distortions impose a heavy cost in terms of economic growth. Currency convertibility should be achieved at least for current account transactions. The exchange rate should reflect the real value of the currency and foreign exchange licensing should be abolished. The investment regime should also be made transparent and stable. In most circumstances, foreign investors should have the same rights and obligations as national investors. Procedures for approving investments should be relatively light and short. The possibilities for corruption should be minimized. It is helpful to create a single investment promotion agency that is a focal point for relevant information and is able to organize all the regulatory requirements.

An obvious advantage of unilateral policy measures in comparison to the regional approaches that are discussed in later chapters is precisely that they are unilateral. There is no need to invest resources in a negotiation process. There is also no need to wait until other partners have done their part of the deal. These are significant practical considerations.

In the area of trade liberalization, there is a broad consensus on what should be done and what should be avoided. Non-tariff barriers such as quantitative restrictions and import licensing should be abolished or replaced by tariffs. Peak tariff rates should be reduced quite quickly. Raw materials and capital goods should have low tariff rates in order not to discourage exports. Customs procedures should be clear and fair. Trade monopolies should be avoided and if they do exist, they should be free from government interference and have a clear objective (for example, assisting small producers).

The welfare benefits of eliminating the big distortions are sizeable. Small developing economies have little justification to postpone the elimination of such distortions. The speed of elimination should be determined with a view to minimizing adjustment costs. However, once the big distortions are gone, the benefits of further unilateral action become less obvious. Improvements in market access for new exports will be important for further gains. These cannot be obtained unilaterally. Small developing countries cannot bargain much in exchange for their own market liberalization. They cannot, on their own, play a big role in multilateral negotiations. A possibility is to improve their market access through regional integration. In addition, regional integration will increase their bargaining power.

4
South–South Regionalism

There are virtually no developing countries that are not members of one or more regional groupings. Regional partnership among developing countries with a comparable economic situation is a widely followed strategy to overcome the limitations of small economic size and to acquire more bargaining power. So far, however, the success of most groupings has been limited. In many cases the initial high expectations have not been fulfilled.

There have been two waves of regionalism in developing countries (Bhagwati, 1993). The first wave followed the successful beginning of regional economic integration in Europe in the 1950s. For many developing countries, especially in Africa, this coincided with the immediate post-independence period. A second wave of regionalism started around the end of the 1980s and the beginning of the 1990s. This coincided with the preparation of the European single market programme that was completed at the end of 1992. In the developing world, the single market programme led to fears of a 'fortress Europe' that would become exclusive and inward-looking. The formation of NAFTA led to similar fears of exclusion in the Caribbean and Latin America. By making or strengthening their own groupings, developing countries felt that they could better cope with the groupings of industrial countries and with globalization. Some observers also link the second wave of regionalism to the disappointment with the GATT system that had been unable to counteract the rise of new forms of protectionism (for example 'Voluntary Export Restraints' and anti-dumping measures) and to the difficulties during the prolonged negotiations of the Uruguay Round.

There is a seemingly never-ending controversy on the merits of regional economic integration. Krugman (1991) speaks of a 'fundamentally murky debate', which is due to the inherent ambiguity of the welfare implications of integration arrangements. A complicating factor is that regional integration invariably has important political motives and objectives in addition to the economic ones.

This chapter assesses the merits and difficulties of regional integration as a strategy for small developing countries. Regional integration is not presented as a panacea, but rather as a way to complement what can and should be achieved through participation in the multilateral trading system and through unilateral action. Politicians often tend to overestimate the gains from regional integration and to underestimate the problems to be overcome. On the other hand, many trade economists (generally supported by the Bretton Woods institutions) look at regional integration with considerable suspicion, tending to see it as an obstacle on the road towards the 'first best' situation of worldwide free trade. In this view, unilateralism within the WTO framework is the best strategy and regional trading arrangements are an unnecessary and costly distraction. The section below on the outcomes of regional arrangements summarizes the key aspects of the debate. It maintains that regional integration should build on the multilateral system and should not deal with issues that are more effectively handled in a unilateral way. Even within these boundaries, a sizeable potential remains for regionalism to contribute to economic growth in small developing countries. However, for this contribution to be realized, developing countries should pay much more attention than in the past to the preconditions for successful regional integration, to institutional design and to effective implementation. These aspects are dealt with below. The discussion of these issues refers mainly to European experience, because this is relevant for an appreciation of some neglected aspects of the debate on regionalism among developing countries.[1] If certain preconditions are not fulfilled or if the institutional design is not suitable, regional integration among developing countries is likely to fail. Before addressing these topics, the next section will refresh some basic concepts.

Levels and types of integration

The literature on economic integration usually distinguishes *Free Trade Areas (FTAs)*, *Customs Unions (CUs)*, *Common Markets* and *Economic Unions* (see for example Pelkmans, 1997). In FTAs, trade in goods is liberalized within the grouping, but the partner countries maintain a separate trade policy towards third countries. It is understood that FTAs also eliminate all quantitative constraints such as quotas and other non-tariff barriers, for example import licensing. Sometimes, reference is made to Preferential Trade Areas (PTAs), meaning that the tariffs are not (yet) fully eliminated between member states and only preferential treatment is given.[2] Usually PTAs are considered as interim arrangements towards FTAs. CUs are like FTAs, but with the establishment of a Common External Tariff (CET) towards third countries. In other words, CUs require a *common* trade policy. In a Common Market, free movement of production factors, capital and labour is added. FTAs and CUs may cover not only trade in goods, but also in services.[3] Finally, an Economic Union maintains all the requirements of a Common Market, adding the harmonization of macroeconomic policies. There is no precise definition of an Economic Union in the sense that there can be different policies that are harmonized and the degree of harmonization may also be flexible.

A separate category of economic integration is a monetary union, where the partner countries share a common currency or where different currencies are fully convertible and the exchange rates are irrevocably fixed. There can also be weaker forms of monetary cooperation, such as limiting exchange rate fluctuations or mutual credit facilities among the central banks. Because, in the European experience, the establishment of a monetary union was firmly put on the agenda only after achievement of an Economic Union, it is sometimes thought that this is a necessary sequence. This is not the case. A monetary union can be combined with an FTA, a CU, a Common Market or an Economic Union. A monetary union is even possible without trade integration. Still, it is true that monetary instability and competitive devaluations will tend to undermine all forms of economic integration. Hence the pressure to step up monetary cooperation, as economic integration progresses.

Recent literature on economic integration pays a lot of attention to the concept of 'deep integration' which is contrasted with 'shallow integration' (see for example Haggard, 1995, and Lawrence, 1996). The latter refers mainly to FTAs and CUs that eliminate border restrictions such as tariffs and quotas. Deep integration refers to elimination of constraints that operate within countries such as: industrial and environmental standards, government procurement rules, and health and phyto-sanitary regulations.[4] The European single market programme that was completed in 1993 addressed the elimination of such barriers and is an example of deep integration. With the progressive decline in tariffs through the multilateral trade negotiations, and because of more complex technological processes and the increasing importance of environmental standards, the deep integration aspects are becoming ever more prominent. Removal of fiscal disparities, not related to tariffs, is another aspect of deep integration.

It is useful to characterize economic integration possibilities in a slightly more general way in the form of a matrix. This requires a notion of which sectors, policy areas or themes are covered; in other words, how 'broad' the integration process is. One can refer to *broadening* of integration as increasing the number of themes that are covered. This is to be distinguished from the more frequently used term *widening* of integration, which indicates that more countries adhere to an integration initiative. There is also a need to describe what can be called the 'intensity'

of integration. Increasing the intensity of regional integration is referred to as *deepening* of integration.

Using the above notions, it is possible to construct a table indicating
how 'broad' and how 'deep' a specific integration arrangement is. For
each sector, policy area or theme, at least four levels of integration can
be distinguished. The minimum position is simply the *exchange of information*, whereas the maximum position is the formulation and
implementation of *common policies*. Between those levels, there is a range
of intermediate possibilities going from weak *coordination of policies* towards
more compelling *harmonization of policies*. There is no standard definition of the above concepts. An illustration can be provided referring to
indirect taxation. A coordination approach could mean that all countries install a system of value added tax (VAT). Harmonization of indirect
taxation goes further and could lead to agreement on similar categories
of goods to be taxed and on a range of possible tax rates for each of
these categories. In a harmonized system, each government has some
leeway to choose specific tax rates within the agreed bands in view of
its preferences or budgetary requirements. A common policy would imply
that both classifications and tax rates would be identical across countries.

As an illustration one can refer to the European integration process
which has been characterized by progressive widening (adding new
member states from the original six in 1958 to the 15 in 1995), broadening (adding more themes) and deepening (moving in the direction
of more harmonized and common policies). Table 4.1 illustrates in a
very stylized way the current situation for the EU.

The theoretical analysis of regional economic integration has almost
exclusively been made for trade in goods. Looking at Table 4.1 one
sees that this analysis covers only a small proportion of regional economic integration possibilities. Trade is certainly a key aspect, but when
theoretical analysis, based exclusively on trade liberalization, is used to
offer conclusions on the overall integration process, confusion can be
the result. The increasing attention to deep integration will stimulate
analysis of the non-trade aspects of integration. Regional cooperation
in areas such as transport, environment and education is often referred
to as *functional cooperation* to make a distinction with more specialized
market-based regional integration.

For trade in goods and services, another level of integration should
be mentioned: *mutual recognition of standards*. It is situated more or less
between harmonized and common policies. Sometimes, it is easier for
countries to recognize each other's standards rather than agree on common
ones. The process of developing a common or even a harmonized standard can be frustratingly slow. For companies, the advantage of mutual
recognition is that they have to demonstrate only once that a product
fulfils a standard.[5] Mutual recognition is only realistic when the capac-

Table 4.1 Illustration of broadening and deepening of integration: the current status of EU integration

Themes/sectors	Level of integration			
	Exchange of information	*Coordination of policies*	*Harmonization of policies*	*Common policies*
Trade in goods				x
Trade in services			x	
Agricultural policy				x
Monetary policy			x	
Competition				x
Investment policy			x	
Cohesion				x
Social policy			x	
Transport			x	
Environment			x	
Education			x	
Research			x	
Fiscal policy			x	
Industrial policy		x		
Consumer protection		x		
Public health		x		

ity to develop and control standards is comparable across member states. For smaller developing countries, it is often more cost-effective to adopt the standards of one of the main industrial trading partners rather than to develop their own standards. Mutual recognition of standards is not only applicable in the area of trade, but also, for example, in the area of recognition of diplomas and certificates, which is a requirement for the free movement of professionals.

Regionalism within the multilateral system

Regional integration has always been permitted under the GATT system, if certain conditions are fulfilled. The famous GATT Article XXIV allows Free Trade Areas (FTAs) and Customs Unions (CUs) provided that participating countries liberalize among themselves *substantially all* trade, and external protection is *not on the whole higher or more restrictive* than before. The purpose of these requirements is to ensure that regional trade arrangements facilitate trade between the parties to the agreement and do not raise barriers to the trade of third countries. Their interpretation has been the source of lengthy discussions.[6] In several cases, one or more important sectors of the economy – for example, agriculture – has been left out of regional arrangements. There is no unambiguous answer to the question of how much trade can be left out while still covering 'substantially all' trade. A rule of thumb of 90 per cent of trade has sometimes been advocated, but there is no agreement on a particular share. There is also no obvious way to measure aggregate protection for a group of countries and for substantially all trade. There are different methods to define aggregate protection. In several cases, a simple arithmetical average of tariff rates has been used. This was done, for example, to establish the customs union among the original six European Community member states. The requirement that protection cannot be increased is designed to protect the interests of third countries, while recognising that countries have the right to pursue regional integration. It should also be observed that Article XXIV does not allow PTAs. Tariffs or equivalent measures must be abolished completely between the integration partners except in the context of an *interim arrangement* towards the establishment of an FTA or CU.

All regional arrangements must be notified to the GATT. Upon notification, a working party is established to review whether the arrangement conforms to the obligations. If the working party finds that the arrangement does not fulfil the requirements of Article XXIV, the contracting parties can ask for revision or possibly agree on compensation measures. In practice, partly because of the difficulties of interpretation and measurement, the GATT follow-up of regional arrangements has been very weak. According to Samson (1996) only one agreement has been found to conform fully. This is the CU between the Czech Republic and the Slovak Republic established in 1992. At the same time no agreement has ever been formally rejected. A frequent source of contention has been whether the level of tariffs towards third countries should be based on applied rates or on bound rates. The latter can be substantially higher. Samson (1996) finds that what constitutes full conformity is not clear-cut.

As regards regional arrangements among *developing countries*, the follow-up under the GATT has been even less significant than for industrial countries. Regional arrangements among developing countries can also be justified under the 'Enabling Clause', agreed in 1979 during the Tokyo Round of negotiations. The Enabling Clause provides, in the first place, a legal basis for non-reciprocal trade concessions granted to developing countries, such as the Generalized System of Preferences (GSP), but it also permits preferential trading arrangements among developing countries. Under the Enabling Clause, regional agreements of developing countries are not obliged to eliminate tariffs completely and are not required to cover substantially all trade; hence, almost anything goes. The Enabling Clause does not refer to Article XXIV. It is not clear whether it represents, for developing countries, a complete alternative to Article XXIV or whether it affects the terms of application of that article (see WTO, 1995). So far, virtually all developing-country arrangements have only been notified under the Enabling Clause (for example ASEAN,

MERCOSUR and COMESA). An exception is the notification of CARICOM under Article XXIV in 1973. A clear difference of interpretation surfaced as regards MERCOSUR. Its member states, supported by other developing countries, maintained that its notification could be settled under the Enabling Clause. However, industrial countries felt that MERCOSUR should fulfil the requirements of Article XXIV. In fact, many arrangements among developing countries were simply not notified (WTO, 1995).

Views among analysts differ on whether or not it is in the interest of developing countries to allow flexibility in their regional agreements by using the Enabling Clause. Blackhurst (1997a) argues that it is better for developing countries to accept the obligations of Article XXIV, as this would reduce pressures from interest groups for exclusions of various kinds that would diminish the trade liberalization effect.[7] It should also enhance the credibility of the integration effort in the eyes of investors. Others such as Thomas (1997) argue that the flexibility of the Enabling Clause is necessary to help developing and least-developed countries.

The Uruguay Round resulted in an *Understanding on the interpretation of Article XXIV* that made some of the obligations more explicit. The assessment of the level of tariffs in CUs towards third countries must be based on a (trade)-weighted average of *applied* rates. The assessment shall be based on import statistics for a representative period. The transition period is now limited to ten years, apart from exceptional circumstances, which require a full explanation. It is further understood that no 'major sector' of trade should be excluded. Even though there is no precise definition of what constitutes a major sector, it is clear that, for example, agriculture as a whole should not be excluded. Exclusions of specific products are still permitted. In addition, the supervision of correct implementation of existing arrangements versus third countries has been made more stringent. The Understanding states that the dispute settlement provisions can also be used on any matters arising from the application of Article XXIV. It confirms the reporting requirements for members of regional arrangements. Because of all this, the verification of regional arrangements should become more thorough. A new Committee on Regional Trade Agreements was established for this purpose in 1996. The committee will also examine the systemic implications of regional trade agreements and the relation between regionalism and multilateralism. Still, the Understanding has not solved all the controversies that surround the interpretation of Article XXIV. One of the tasks of the committee is to organize discussions on the interpretation and revision of Article XXIV.[8]

It is doubtful whether the application of the Understanding will lead to important changes in the case of trade agreements among developing countries. As with several other WTO provisions, one could argue that the transition period could be longer for developing countries, because exceptional circumstances can more easily apply. However, the Understanding does not solve the issue of whether the Enabling Clause can fully justify regional trading arrangements among developing countries that deviate significantly from Article XXIV. In December 1996, during the Singapore ministerial meeting, the WTO pledged to devote more resources towards assisting developing countries with their multilateral trade obligations. This also implies assisting them with their regional arrangements.

More and more regional integration agreements cover both goods and services. The relative importance of trade in services is rapidly increasing. It is fortunate that the Uruguay Round introduced a *legal basis for regionalism in the area of services*. Article V of the GATS is the equivalent of Article XXIV of the GATT. The provisions are comparable, but not identical. According to Article V of GATS, there should be substantial sector coverage and elimination of substantially all discrimination. Article V also serves to ensure that regional integration will not penalize third countries. The level of barriers *within each* of the sectors covered shall not be raised towards third parties. Hence, there is no notion that trade barriers in services should be 'on the whole' not higher or more restrictive, as in the case for goods. In the goods case it is possible for an increase in certain tariffs to be offset by a decrease in others. Such 'averaging' is not permitted with services. Developing countries are granted flexibility in the application of the above provisions. In addition, they are not obliged, as other countries are, to extend privileged treatment to service providers within the region that are controlled or owned from outside the grouping, but with substantive activities in the region.

Preconditions and success factors

It is surprising that the vast literature on economic integration pays little attention to what we might call preconditions and factors of success.[9] Similarly, institutional design is bypassed in the economic analysis even though it receives attention in the political and historical literature. This is unfortunate, especially for the debate on regionalism as a strategy for developing countries, because inadequate design and lack of fulfilment of basic preconditions have been the most frequent causes of failure of developing countries' regional arrangements.[10]

It is helpful to distinguish non-economic, mostly political preconditions and economic preconditions. The most important political preconditions are peace, security, respect for human rights, prevalence of the rule of law and good governance. Civil strife within countries

ound macroeconomic management. Currency convertibility and
onably converging inflation rates are necessary for cross-border in-
ment and to sustain trade. Informal trade or barter can circumvent
e of the problems caused by inconvertible currencies, but this al-
s implies a sizeable increase in the cost of transactions. Macroeconomic
ility depends on, among other things, the degree of independence
he central bank, the overall quality of the budgetary process and
rules for deficit financing (see also Chapter 3).

the European context, an interesting view about the Marshall Plan
ms that it served in the first instance to put in place some of the
ic preconditions for future economic integration. De Long and
engreen (1992) have called the Marshall Plan 'history's most suc-
ful structural adjustment programme'. The Plan indeed required a
ole battery of economic policy reform measures including an orderly
getary process and sound monetary management. The Organization
European Economic Cooperation (OEEC), set up to administer the
rshall Plan, organized the elimination of non-tariff barriers across
eficiary countries. Through the European Payments Union (EPU),
Plan also promoted currency convertibility, which was achieved by
7, just before the signing of the Rome Treaty on the European Econ-
ic Community.

n the way that the Marshall Plan facilitated early European integra-
n, structural adjustment programmes in developing countries are
sently doing more or less the same thing. These programmes pro-
te sound macroeconomic policies and trade liberalization. This implies
le facto degree of convergence of economic policies, improving the
is for economic integration.[12] In this way structural adjustment im-
ves the prospects for regional integration. There are indeed some
lications that the recent second wave of integration initiatives among
justed countries' is more successful than the first wave. MERCOSUR
ld be mentioned as an example, as well as the West African Econ-
ic and Monetary Union (UEMOA).

n Europe, the much debated 'Maastricht criteria' are an example of
ict preconditions for entry into the European Monetary Union.[13]
onomic integration reduces mutual barriers and increases economic
teraction, leading to more vulnerability to negative spillover effects
policy measures among integration partners. Macroeconomic stab-
ty requirements are a way to avoid the situation where countries abuse
gional openness and cause damage to the economy of partner coun-
es (for example, through competitive devaluation). In order to assess
e fulfilment of the macroeconomic stability requirements, the EU
troduced a system of *multilateral surveillance* focused on the budget-
y management of the member states. Such surveillance requires a
rmonized information system, close collaboration and mutual trust.

and conflicts between countries are obvious deterrents for any gr
enhancing cross-border economic activity. Still, absence of conf
rarely mentioned as a fundamental requirement for regional integ
to succeed. Many regional arrangements between developing cou
include one or more members that have recently been or still ar
fronted by serious conflicts or civil strife. Examples are easy to
ECOWAS, COMESA and SADC in Africa and, CACM and the A
Community in Latin America. While peace is a precondition for suc
integration, the success of integration itself may tend to contrib
the consolidation of peace and help to avoid renewed conflict. Pro
tion of peace was among the fundamental motivations for Eur
integration.

Respect for human rights and the rule of law are also fundar
preconditions. Countries can only cooperate successfully if thei
and political systems are compatible. Why would businesspeop
gage in cross-border trade and investment with a chance of hara
by customs authorities, a possible need for expensive bribes, l
and costly procedures and a risk of loss of property without any
bility of legal recourse? A democratic system is generally a
guarantee the rule of law, respect for human rights, and transp
and accountability of governance. This does not mean that deve
countries should adopt all aspects of a Western-style democracy
is certainly room for other traditions.

From its inception, the European Community put forward
racy as a strict requirement for the accession of new member
This is the reason why Greece, Portugal and Spain could only join
the 1980s. As observed by Wallace (1994), full EC membership of
(in 1981) and Spain and Portugal (in 1986) was seen by both si
reward for their transition to democracy and as a means for
dating that democracy. It is also the reason why the widening
EU towards Eastern Europe has only been put on the agenda fo
their political transition. In 1993, the Copenhagen European (
adopted explicit political criteria for their accession: 'member:
quires that the candidate country has achieved stability of inst
guaranteeing democracy, the rule of law, human rights, and res
and protection of minorities'. In contrast, integration arrangement:
developing countries do not pay much attention to political pr
tions.[11] Discussions about prospective North–South agreements g
cover political issues. The second summit of the Americas in (
April 1998 reiterated the importance of strengthening democr:
tice and human rights on the way towards the FTAA. The
concluded and prospective free trade agreements between the
developing countries all contain a political and human rights
There are also important economic preconditions that are mostl

It is interesting that the Treaty of the West African Economic and Monetary Union also foresees the installation of a system of multilateral surveillance.

In addition to the political criteria mentioned above in relation to accession to the EU, there are also economic conditions, including a functioning market economy and the capacity to cope with the competitive pressures within the Union. A functioning market economy implies requirements such as: equilibrium between demand and supply established by the free interplay of market forces, absence of barriers to market entry and exit, a legal system respecting property rights and allowing contract enforcement, a sufficiently developed financial sector and macroeconomic stability.[14]

The discussion in Chapter 2 made it clear that membership of the WTO and IMF (especially through acceptance of the requirements of Article VIII on current account convertibility) already represents an important step towards fulfilment of certain minimum macroeconomic preconditions. The standard surveillance of the IMF under its Article IV and the Trade Policy Review Mechanism of the WTO are useful starting points for a closer economic surveillance implemented at the regional level.[15] Civil society in developing countries may have more confidence if 'their own' regional body carries out surveillance rather then distant organizations such as the IMF or the WTO. Surveillance should not necessarily be linked to the application of tough sanctions. The linkage of the results of surveillance to any kind of sanctions is a particularly delicate undertaking that normally calls for a supranational rather than an intergovernmental design (see below).

In some respects, the word 'preconditions' used in this section may sound too strict. One can easily imagine, after all, an authoritarian regime abolishing its trade barriers and maintaining macroeconomic stability. Some of the political preconditions outlined above could be better interpreted as 'factors that enhance the chances of success'. There are many more factors in addition to those mentioned above that boost the prospects for success – such as a common language, culture and history, and a comparable social situation and social security system.

An illustration of the relevance of some of the above factors is the reluctance of CARICOM member states to accept the Dominican Republic as a new member. In addition to the different language and history, the population of the Dominican Republic exceeds the combined population of the original member states.[16]

An important success factor that, in some cases, effectively constitutes a precondition, is the *absence of large disparities* across member states in the level of development, income, industrial structure and (arguably) size. Disparities in the level of income and industrial structure are closely related to the possibilities of benefiting from integration as well as to the fair allocation of contributions to finance common policies. The collapse of the East African Community during the 1970s was attributed largely to the perception that Kenya, with its relatively advanced industrial sector, was getting a disproportionate share of the benefits at the expense of Tanzania and to a lesser extent Uganda. Within a unitary or federal state, there are powerful mechanisms, such as centralized taxation and unrestricted migration, to reduce disparities relatively quickly. Moreover, these mechanisms are more or less invisible and automatic. They are part of the political consensus. In addition, governments frequently use direct interventions to speed up convergence, because rising disparities can easily become a source of political instability. In a regional grouping there will be no centralized taxation that automatically reduces disparities while cultural and other constraints will usually limit migration. The EU has gradually developed a range of regional and social redistribution policies to promote cohesion and reduce disparities.

In several regional groupings of developing countries, initiatives have been mounted with the aim of reducing disparities. However, many of these have not been successful. Examples that did not fulfil expectations are the ECOWAS fund and the mechanism set up under the former West African Economic Community (CEAO).

Shallow integration, essentially trade and payments liberalization, can be mutually beneficial even when disparities are large. It will slowly lead to a reduction of disparities. However, convergence will be more rapid when barriers on factor movements are also diminished. Cohesion policies such as those established in the EU are linked to deep integration and are designed to speed up the convergence process. It would be unwise for groupings of developing countries to try to install cohesion policies when the shallow integration stage is only just beginning. The budgetary outlays would be difficult to collect and to justify. The allocation of funds will be politically very difficult. A more affordable approach to promote convergence would be to facilitate investment flows towards the less developed partner countries. A successful example is the Caribbean Development Bank, which has channeled resources to the less developed member states of CARICOM.

Institutional design

The success of regional economic integration also depends on the institutional design. Deeper and broader integration calls for appropriate institutions to ensure effective policy formulation and implementation. In most discussions about regional economic integration in developing countries, little reference is made to the institutional set-up. This applies especially to Africa and Asia, and less to Latin America. It contrasts with the situation in Europe where there has always been a lot of debate on the role of institutions and especially about the balance of power between and within institutions. From the beginning, European integration has been driven by a strong institutional system. NAFTA on the other hand is very 'light' on institutions.

It is helpful to explain in a nutshell, the main characteristics of the EU institutional system.[17] There are five main institutions: the Council of Ministers, the Parliament, the Commission, the Court of Justice and the Court of Auditors. The European Commission presently comprises 20 Commissioners. They are politicians nominated for a mandate of five years by the member state governments. Large member states nominate two Commissioners while small member states nominate one. The Parliament is directly elected for a corresponding period of five years. The Council of Ministers is presided over by each of the member states in a six-monthly rotation. During its presidency, a member state also organizes at least one European Council with the Heads of State and Government. The European Councils are the occasion for deciding and compromising on major political orientations.

The basic rule in preparing EU legislation is that the Commission, always acting as a team, makes a proposal, which can be amended by the Parliament and the Council and is decided upon by the Council. The member states have the obligation to integrate EU legislation into their own legal system. EU legislation takes precedence over national laws. Member states, companies, individuals and the Commission can go to the European Court of Justice if there are problems with the application of EU legislation. In addition to its fundamental 'right of initiative', the Commission is responsible for many aspects of implementation of EU legislation and for preparing the draft annual budget. The member states are involved in the decision-making process of the Commission through an elaborate system of committees meeting regularly. The Parliament has the power to modify the budget within certain limits set by the Council. The Court of Auditors is an independent body to verify regularly the use of budgetary resources.

At first sight it seems that NAFTA has no institutions at all, but this is not entirely true. NAFTA established a trilateral Commission, comprising cabinet-level representatives of the three countries, to administer the agreement and to settle disputes. There are also various committees and working groups dealing with specialized matters such as standardization, rules of origin and financial services. In addition, the side agreements on environment and labour led to the creation of two additional commissions (see Hufbauer and Schott, 1993). Nevertheless, an important distinction with the EU is that virtually all the work on NAFTA takes place *within* the national administrations.

An important part of the debate on institutional design is about *intergovernmentalism versus supranationalism.* Supranationalism implies the establishment of regional institutions that have specific powers of their own and that cannot be manipulated to serve the interest of a subset of member states. Supranationalism goes together with a system of regional legislation that prevails over national legislation. Under supranationalism, member states or companies that do not comply with regional legislation can be taken to a court that operates independently from the courts in the member states. Supranationalism is often seen by its supporters as a step in the direction of a confederation or even a federation of states. Those opposing supranationalism usually present it as a loss of state sovereignty. However, it is more correct to say that with supranationalism, states agree to exercise jointly some specific aspects of their sovereignty.[18] With intergovernmentalism, on the other hand, there is no regional legislation and each member state fully exercises its sovereignty. Intergovernmental institutions typically take the form of a secretariat that has no independent power. The main function of the secretariat is to facilitate the coordination and dialogue among the member states that must take all implementation decisions on their own.

Economic integration can be pursued both with supranational or intergovernmental institutions. Clearly, supranationalism is more demanding in terms of preconditions. Both approaches imply many practical differences. With the European Coal and Steel Community in 1951, the European countries chose, from the outset, a supranational path for the economic matters that are now referred to as the 'first pillar' of integration. The 'second and third pillars' that were only introduced in 1992 by the Maastricht Treaty deal respectively with justice and home affairs, and foreign and security policy and remain intergovernmental for the moment. Hence the EU presently comprises a mixture of intergovernmentalism and supranationalism. NAFTA, on the other hand, is purely intergovernmental. Even though the FTAA is only at a preliminary stage, the thinking is certainly not in the direction of supranationalism, which would be viewed with some suspicion in Latin America and the Caribbean. Integration initiatives among developing countries are virtually all intergovernmental. An exception is the West African Economic and Monetary Union.

Although there does not appear to be any research on this subject, it seems that intergovernmentalism can only work well when integration is rather shallow or when there are only a few member states with a clear common interest and not too much disparity. Typically, where deep integration and/or a grouping with a large number of diverse member states are involved, there will be calls for supranationalism to make progress. More commonly, such ventures will not get off the ground.[19] It is difficult to negotiate, implement and control policies when the number of member states is relatively large. Intergovernmentalism in principle requires unanimity for decisions and therefore a veto power for each member state on every issue. Supranationalism will introduce majority decision-making except for matters of vital interest to the member states. Supranationalism requires a strong political commitment.

The financial arrangements of regional integration will also be quite different in a supranational set-up in comparison to an intergovernmental one. Under supranationalism, it will be possible to install a system of 'own resources' to cover financial needs. Such own resources will be more or less automatically collected by the integration organization. A member state that does not transfer the necessary funds can be legally challenged and sanctions can be enforced. With intergovernmentalism, the member states are asked to make certain budgetary contributions, but the secretariat is typically weak *vis-à-vis* member states that do not fulfil their obligations. Many regional integration organizations covering small developing economies have been paralysed almost totally because member states fail to pay their contributions. In some cases these organizations have then become excessively dependent on outside donor funding. Needless to say, deep integration and supranationalism will usually lead to larger financing requirements to cover agreed common policies and activities.

There are some other useful concepts related to the design of regional integration: *subsidiarity, integration at different speeds and variable geometry*. Subsidiarity has been formally introduced in the EU only with the Maastricht Treaty.[20] As pointed out by Wallace (1994), the concept of subsidiarity has one of its roots in the Catholic social doctrine on the distribution of responsibilities between the individual, the family, the local community and the state within a just social order. It is directly related to the distribution of competence in federal states. The principle is thus present in the German Federal Constitution. According to Wallace, the Tenth Amendment to the American Constitution also expresses the same principle.[21] Subsidiarity implies that the responsibility for dealing with an issue should be kept as close as possible to the population concerned. Reference of an issue to an international organization requires that it can be more effectively dealt with at that level rather than at the national or local level. Subsidiarity has a strong intuitive appeal to civil society, because it implies that people should only hand over the right to decide when it is in their interest to do so. It can also offer some guidance in determining the division of labour among different layers of regional organizations.[22] However, the practical application of the principle may not always be easy.

Circumstances may differ considerably among members of a regional grouping so that it is difficult for all to move at the same speed. Under integration at variable speeds, those willing and able to implement a certain policy can go ahead and the others can catch up later. Multispeed integration avoids the situation where the pace of progress is determined by the slowest-moving member state. In the European context, the application of this principle can be traced back at least to the first enlargement of the European Community in the 1970s from six to nine member states. The transitional arrangements for accession of new member states are a form of multispeed integration. Multispeed integration is sometimes considered to be the same as variable geometry. However, it is possible to make a useful distinction between the two concepts. Variable geometry has a geographic connotation whereas multispeed integration has a time connotation. With a larger number of member states, views on many issues become more diverse. The capacity and willingness to implement new policies will generally be different across member states. Under variable speed, some member states can move faster on a certain issue than others, but there is nothing to stop the latter catching up when they are willing and ready.

Under variable geometry a subgroup of member states may wish to deepen integration on a more or less permanent basis. This can lead to groupings within groupings. With variable geometry, it is conceivable that a Free Trade Area contains a Customs and/or Monetary Union. The wider FTA may never plan to become a CU. Examples of subgroups with deeper integration are the OECS within the CARICOM in the Caribbean and the SACU within SADC in Southern Africa. Sometimes variable geometry is presented in terms of core and periphery. The core member states move further towards broad and deep integration and the periphery keeps to the basics of shallow integration.[23]

The prospective enlargement of the EU towards Eastern Europe has led to a renewed discussion on institutional design that is also relevant for the debate on economic integration among developing countries. The Eastern enlargement could possibly double the number of EU member states from the current 15 to almost 30. There is a consensus that the present institutional system needs adjustment in order to be workable with such enlargement. Variable geometry is one of the options. However, some observers fear that this may lead to a split of member states into a first, a second and maybe a third league (more or less arranged in concentric circles). Only the first league will enjoy the full benefits from membership.

Variable geometry and multispeed integration should not be confused with *à la carte* integration. Under multispeed integration, all the member states continue to share the same long-term objectives, but some will reach the objectives earlier than others. With variable geometry, the core members all have the same objectives to which members of the periphery can subscribe if they wish. An *à la carte* approach would allow member states to select the aspects of integration that they like most and reject the others. Each member state prepares its own menu.

Many analysts consider this approach as a recipe for disintegration. An interesting approach, called *flexible integration*, has been put forward by a group of researchers of the CEPR (1995). Flexible integration starts from a subset of policy areas rather than from a subset of countries. Certain policy areas are considered to constitute the *common base* to which all members are required to subscribe. In addition there would be *open partnerships* in which countries can participate on a voluntary basis. Flexible integration does not have the disadvantage of dividing the member states into a progressive core group and a lagging periphery. Still, a practical difficulty would be to determine whether all member states have an influence on the content of an open partnership or only those that actually subscribe to the partnership.[24]

Outcomes of regional integration arrangements

A review of the effects of regional economic integration arrangements invariably starts with the classic work of Jacob Viner (1950). Viner's analysis was triggered off by the remarkable fact that both free-traders and protectionists seemed to like regional integration. He therefore felt that something peculiar was going on when countries decided to form regional groupings. His conjecture was right. Even today, the peculiarities of regional economic integration continue to feed heated debates.

Starting with Viner, there is extensive literature on customs union theory. An interesting survey of the early literature was made by Krauss (1972), who focuses on the static effects. A recent thorough, more technical survey was prepared by Baldwin and Venables (1995). Most of the discussion below on gains and losses refers (implicitly) to CUs and FTAs because the bulk of the analysis was done for such arrangements. Only few references are made to deeper forms of economic integration.

A common distinction is between *static and dynamic effects* of customs unions. Static effects are the consequence of reallocations in production and consumption, following the formation of a CU. There is no generally accepted definition of dynamic effects, but it is understood that they are mostly related to phenomena such as economies of scale, increased competition, investment, growth and technical change. Two concepts, originating with Viner, can be considered the workhorses of customs union theory: *trade creation and trade diversion*. Trade creation occurs when less efficient national production is replaced by more efficient production from a partner country. Trade diversion takes place when more efficient production from the rest of the world is replaced by less efficient production from a partner country. Customs union theory examines the effects on the welfare of the integration partners as well as of the rest of the world. Recently, there has been increased attention for the systemic implications of regionalism. An important question in this respect is whether and how fast the spread of regionalism leads to multilateral liberalization. Bhagwati (1993) called this the 'dynamic time-path question'. The discussion below summarizes the theory of customs unions, with the aim of shedding light on the regional integration strategy of small developing countries. The dynamic time-path question is not examined here, because it is, in the first instance, related to the effects of integration involving 'hegemonic' trading powers. It is assumed that the partner countries implementing regional integration separately and together are small in the sense that they cannot influence prices on the world market. They do not have monopoly power so that restricting imports through tariffs will not improve their terms of trade.[25] They can buy or sell any desired quantity at the given world market price.

Together the static and dynamic effects are sometimes referred to as traditional effects. This is to distinguish them from the *non-traditional effects* that receive a lot of attention in recent literature (see for example Whalley, 1996 and Fernandez and Portes, 1998). The main non-traditional gains are the locking-in of policy reforms and the insurance against future protection. Both effects are particularly relevant when smaller countries are integrating with larger ones – which is likely to happen in the case of North–South integration which is dealt with in Chapter 6.

Last but not least, there are *non-economic* effects that may, in many cases, be the fundamental driving force towards regional integration. Greater security, consolidation of peace and increased political bargaining power are the most obvious non-economic effects. There is no agreed standard classification of the effects of regional integration. For easy reference, Table 4.2 lists the main effects that figure in the literature.

Except for the non-economic effects, which are a category apart, the order of the effects listed in Table 4.2 corresponds more or less to the historical evolution of the literature. Static effects were mainly studied following Viner (1950) during the 1950s and 1960s, the time of the creation of the European Community. During the same period, there was some work on economies of scale and competition, but the analysis of these themes became more prominent and more thorough during the 1980s when the European single market programme was being worked out. Investment and growth effects of regional integration also became an important subject around the same time. Finally, the non-traditional effects only entered the picture during the 1990s following Mexico's accession to NAFTA and the start of the thinking about the EU's widening towards the East European transition economies.

Static effects: trade creation and trade diversion (*)

The term 'static effects' is sometimes misinterpreted as if the effects do not need time or at least are quick. A more correct term would be 'comparative static effects', because essentially two equilibrium situa-

Table 4.2 Main effects of regional integration

Traditional effects
   Static
      Trade creation
      Trade diversion
      Tariff revenue
   Dynamic
      Economies of scale
      Increased competition
      Investment
      Growth rate

Non-traditional effects
   Locking-in of sound economic policies
   Insurance against future protection

Non-economic effects
   Security and consolidation of peace
   Political influence and bargaining power

---

tions are compared. The effects measure the differences between those situations. The theory does not shed light on how much time it takes or how much adjustment effort is needed to move from one equilibrium position to another.

Regional integration involves two kinds of changes in market conditions. First, price differences resulting from tariffs between the home and the partner country are eliminated. Second, new price differences are introduced between the partner country and the rest of the world. Partner country producers enjoy privileged access, and producers in the rest of the world are discriminated against. Both changes affect producers, consumers and the government (because of tariff revenue). The first type of change will increase efficiency through trade creation, while the second will tend to decrease efficiency by diverting trade. The static effects of regional trade liberalization can be illustrated with the same kind of graphs that were used to describe unilateral trade liberalization in Chapter 3. The illustration was developed by Cooper and Massell (1965). The explanations below follow those of Bhagwati and Panagariya (1996). In line with Schiff (1997), the analysis focuses on the import side, where both trade creation and trade diversion can occur and where the overall welfare effect is *a priori* ambiguous. It is assumed that there are three countries: the home country, the partner country and the rest of the world, denoted by subscripts h, p and row. According to Schiff, the welfare effects of changes on the export side are not subject to debate. Improved access of the home country's exports to the partner country's market generally raises welfare in the home country. The rest of this sub-section focuses on the import side.

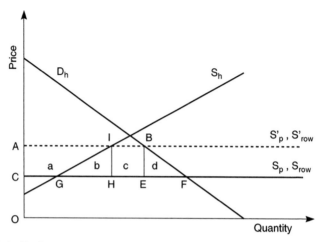

Figure 4.1 Trade creation

The trade-creating case is illustrated in Figure 4.1, which is similar to Figure 3.2 illustrating unilateral tariff liberalization. It is assumed that the partner country can supply the product at the cheapest price, which, by definition, must also be the supply price of the rest of the world.[26] Initially, the tariff rate is t per unit (t = AC) regardless of whether the imports come from the partner or from the rest of the world. If the home and partner country form a customs union, the supply price of the partner country decreases with the full tariff value. The partner country will replace part of the home country's production (GH). This is trade creation. In addition, the partner country will also supply an extra quantity (EF) resulting from increased demand at the lower price. Before the formation of the CU, the home country was indifferent about whether to import from the partner country or from the rest of the world. However, following the formation of the CU, all imports will come from the partner country.

Referring to areas a, b, c and d on Figure 4.1, the *net welfare effects* on the home country can be derived as follows:

increase in consumer surplus = a + b + c + d
minus decrease in producer surplus = a
minus decrease in tariff revenue = c.

Hence, the net welfare effect for the home country equals b + d, which must be positive. Tariff revenue (area c) is shifted from the government to consumers. In order to maintain the government budget balance at the same level, other taxes must be put in place. The size of the welfare effect depends on the elasticity of demand and supply and on the

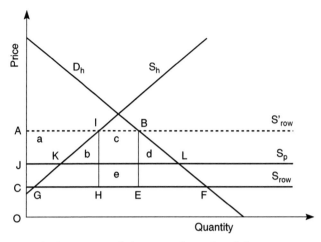

Figure 4.2 Trade diversion with horizontal supply of the partner country

original tariff level. There are no welfare effects on the partner country or on the rest of the world, because of the assumption of horizontal supply curves.

The trade diversion case is illustrated in Figure 4.2 where the partner country is no longer the cheapest source of supply. Its supply curve without tariffs S_p is still assumed to be horizontal over the range of possible imports of the home country, but now it is above the supply curve of the rest of the world S_{row}. The tariff level is again equal to AC. Before integration the tariff-inclusive supply curve of the rest of the world S'_{row} determines the import quantity IB and price OA. After integration, the partner country can supply imports at a price without tariff OJ. The latter price is above the supply price of the rest of the world without tariff, but below its tariff inclusive price OA. All imports before integration are now diverted to the partner country. However, because the price declines, imports now rise to KL, all coming from the partner country. The increase in imports can be split into a part due to demand increase and another because of supply decline. The latter part is, in fact, trade-creation because more efficient partner supplies replace home country production. Referring to areas a, b, c, d and e on Figure 4.2, the net effect on welfare of the home country can be derived as follows:

increase in consumer surplus = a + b + c + d
minus decrease in producer surplus = a
minus decrease in tariff revenue = c + e.

Hence, the net effect is b + d − e. The net effect can be positive or negative depending on the relative magnitude of b, d and e. There are

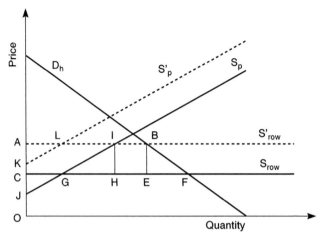

Figure 4.3 Trade diversion with upward-sloping supply of the partner country

no welfare effects on the partner country or on the rest of the world, because of the assumption of horizontal supply curves.

It is easy to demonstrate that in the situation represented by Figure 4.2 the home country could increase welfare unambiguously through unilateral trade liberalization, letting imports rise to GF at price OC.

A slightly different case of trade diversion is given in Figure 4.3, where it is assumed that the rest of the world still supplies at a constant price, but now the supply curve of the partner country has a positive slope. Without loss of generality, only the import demand curve of the home country is shown.[27] With an MFN tariff equal to t (AC or KJ), imports of the home country will be AB, at price OA. Some of the imports originate in the partner country (AL) while the remainder is supplied by the rest of the world (LB). The home country government obtains tariff revenue equal to rectangle ABEC. Figure 4.3 can be interpreted in two ways. The *first interpretation* assumes, as before, the formation of a CU between the home and the partner country. This implies discriminatory tariff reduction in favour of the partner country. The effective supply curve of the partner country now becomes S_p instead of S'_p. The crucial point is that the total imported quantity as well as the price remain unchanged, but some imports LI will be diverted to the partner country. A larger share of total imports will now be supplied by the partner country, AI instead of AL.

An additional striking change is that the home country's welfare is reduced by the full amount of tariff revenue on the imports from the partner, equal to rectangle AIHC. In other words, the home country loses from its own regional trade liberalization, at least in this particular market. The partner country gains, not only because it receives a higher price for the quantity sold before the formation of the CU, but also because it sells more now. Its welfare in the form of its producer surplus increases by area AIGC. However, together the home and partner country still lose an amount represented by triangle GHI, due to the fact that the partner country is a less efficient producer than the rest of the world, beyond a quantity CG.

A *second interpretation* of Figure 4.3 assumes that the home country forms a CU with the rest of the world rather than with the partner country. What happens in this case? The relevant supply curve of the rest of the world now becomes S_{row} instead of S'_{row}. Home country imports expand to CF and the price decreases to OC. Consumer surplus in the home country rises with area ABFC, which can be decomposed into what used to be tariff revenue represented by rectangle ABEC and a net welfare gain represented by triangle BEF. Because the supply curve of the rest of the world is horizontal, it neither gains nor loses as in the earlier interpretation. The original partner country is pushed out of the market and its welfare decreases with the part of the producer surplus represented by triangle CGJ.

Translating the two interpretations of Figure 4.3 into conclusions for the real world is tricky. First of all, there are many simplifying assumptions.[28] Bhagwati and Panagariya (1996) prefer the first interpretation and emphasize that the home country will lose its tariff revenue to its partner country. Because the loss of tariff revenue will not only be on the amount of trade diverted, but also on the original import quantity, it can be sizeable. Consequently, the common view that integration is beneficial if countries trade extensively with each other before integration is wrong at least from the point of view of the home country. Rather, the more pre-integration trade, the greater the tariff loss. The size of the loss to the home country depends on the original import quantity coming from the partner as well as on the elasticity of supply of the partner country (the more elastic, the greater the loss). Bhagwati and Panagariya warn about the situation where developing countries with relatively high tariff rates integrate with industrial countries, for example Mexico with the US or Tunisia with the EU. Such North–South integration is the subject of Chapter 6. They strongly criticize Summers (1991) for claiming that the effects of trade diversion are of secondary importance. In their view Summers only considers welfare triangles such as GHI in Figure 4.3 which will indeed be relatively small, but forgets about the loss in tariff revenue which will be represented by relatively large rectangles such as AIHC.[29]

Schiff (1997) provides a different account of the two cases described above. He concludes that a small country will lose from integration with another small country (interpretation 1), but will gain from integration with a large country (interpretation 2). In his view, the rest of the world in figure 4.3 can be considered to represent a large country. The difference in interpretation is related to the definition of a large country. For Bhagwati and Panagariya, the present 'trade hegemons' (US, EU and Japan) are, in fact, not *large* in the sense that they have a horizontal supply curve. They would consider Schiff's interpretation of a small country integrating with a large one to be unilateral trade liberalization, which they favour. Both interpretations can be reconciled by considering different product markets. In a wide range of products, large trading nations will normally be big, in the sense that they are among the most efficient producers. In a situation where the partner country supplies a large part of imports, preferential tariff reduction will reduce the price, opening the possibility for welfare gains in the home country. In addition, the home country also gains from increased access to the partner's country market for other products.

Even though trade creation and trade diversion are interesting concepts to shed light on the economic forces at work with economic integration, their actual estimation is not at all straightforward. Sawyer and Sprinkle (1989) consider that estimating these two effects is one of the more difficult problems in international economics. Empirical estimates have also been disappointingly low for the advocates of economic integration. While shifts in trade flows can be sizeable, aggregate welfare effects rarely exceed one or a few percentage points of GDP.[30] It is useful to outline briefly some of the complications that arise in measuring trade creation and trade diversion. This allows one to draw attention to a key assumption – whether or not products are homogeneous.

Empirical analysis can be divided into analysis using a computable general equilibrium (CGE) model and partial equilibrium analysis. A CGE model is the most advanced approach, but also the most demanding in terms of data collection and computations. It takes into account the interactions between different markets and represents the working of the economy as a whole. This makes it possible to include macroeconomic effects such as changes in inflation and the exchange rate. The partial equilibrium analysis has been most frequently used and comes in two varieties depending on whether products are considered to be homogeneous or differentiated. In partial equilibrium analysis, each product market is modeled separately. Agricultural and mineral primary commodities are, on the whole, more homogeneous whereas manufactures are usually more differentiated. With *homogeneous goods*, trade creation can completely wipe out national production and trade diversion can completely replace the previous source of imports. Effects on tariff receipts tend to be large. But these effects are dampened by the supply elasticity in the partner country, which is usually assumed to be relatively low. They are also dampened by the level of the tariff reduction. In the case of *differentiated goods*, the trade shifts are mainly constrained by the degree of substitutability of goods distinguished by geographic origin. The differentiated goods case is the more realistic, but it is difficult to obtain reasonable estimates of substitutability. In the case of differentiated goods, trade creation is more likely and consumers generally benefit from tariff reductions.

In summary, the static analysis of regional trade liberalization does not lead to general statements about the welfare effects for the participating countries or for the world as a whole. Trade creation will increase welfare, whereas trade diversion can have both welfare-increasing and welfare-decreasing effects. If this lack of clear conclusion is somewhat disappointing for those in favour of regional integration, it is worthwhile to recall an interesting result obtained by Kemp and Wan (1976). Their theorem demonstrates that a customs union is always *potentially* welfare-increasing, provided an appropriate common external tariff (CET) is chosen. The quantities traded with the rest of the world and their prices are assumed to be unchanged while trade within the CU is restructured to maximize the gains.[31] Expressed differently, if trade with the rest of the world remains unchanged, there can be no welfare loss resulting from trade diversion. At the same time the CU will allow some efficiency gains due to trade creation between the partner countries. The gains can be redistributed through lump-sum transfers so that no member of the CU is worse off. Even though the Kemp–Wan theorem is a nice theoretical insight, its practical value is limited, because it only indicates a possibility. It does not provide a rule on how to calculate the required CET. However, the presumption is that a relatively low CET will tend to limit trade diversion and ensure that a CU is welfare-increasing.

Dynamic effects

It was mentioned above that there is no agreed definition of dynamic effects. In some sense, all the effects that broaden the conventional static framework outlined above are considered dynamic. Referring to Table 4.2, the main dynamic effects figuring in the literature are related to scale economies, competition, investment and technical progress, and growth (see for example De La Torre and Kelly, 1992, as well as Holmes and Smith, 1997).

Larger markets offer opportunities for exploiting *scale economies*. This is more relevant for small countries than for large ones. Scale economies can be 'static' in the sense that, at any point in time, a change in the scale of production reduces costs, or 'dynamic' when they can only be realized over time (see Corden, 1974). They can also be internal to the firm or external. Internal economies typically derive from indivisibilities in production factors: for example, an assembly line must be complete. Often there is a minimum efficient size of a plant that exceeds the home market of small economies. External economies can occur, for example, when production leads to the formation of a pool of skilled labour or specialized service providers. Consider the case of static internal economies. Suppose two countries that both protect their market for a product with decreasing cost decide to form a CU. With a common external tariff, one of the countries can supply the union market and reduce its costs. Trade creation will take place. But now the welfare effects as described above will be augmented by the effect of cost-reduction. Economies of scale constitute an important argument for regional integration of small economies. But there are some limitations. Unexploited scale economies are not readily available. Moreover, there are often constraints caused by production factors that are fixed or cannot easily be increased, for example qualified technicians. If these are important, the cost-reduction effect is diminished. Furthermore, if the option is available to sell on the world market, even more economies of scale can be achieved.

A special category of scale economies arises for the provision of public goods such as transport and communication infrastructure, and specialized education. If resources can be pooled through regional arrangements, the cost of providing such goods can decrease substantially. This is especially relevant for developing countries.

It is frequently stated that a larger regional market stimulates *competition* and will force companies to become more efficient. Competition improves the functioning of the market system. It stimulates productivity and encourages adoption of technical innovations to cut costs. Competing on the regional market is generally easier than competing on the world market. Regional integration thus fits into a strategy first to achieve competitiveness in the regional market and later, when efficiency is increased, to move on to the world market. Regional integration improves competition by diminishing market segmentation that allows firms to make excessive profits. A related point that enhances competition is that lobbying by companies for a particular favour becomes more difficult and hence less likely to distort competition. Small economies tend to benefit more from the increased competition in regional arrangements than large ones.

Competition effects are sometimes explained with the concept of 'x-inefficiency'. If producers are not stimulated to be efficient there will be a lot of 'x-inefficiency' in the sense that the same resources could produce more. Regional integration will create pressure to reduce 'x-inefficiency' because otherwise foreign firms may easily capture the markets. This concept has been used to estimate the effects of completing the single European market.

An important dynamic effect is related to *investment*. Regional integration increases the size of the market and makes the member countries more attractive for investment, both foreign and domestic. If the regional market is sufficiently large, foreign investors may be encouraged to engage in 'tariff-wall jumping'. They invest within the Customs Union to avoid paying the tariffs. It is possible to distinguish between investment creation and diversion in analogy with trade creation and diversion. An important motive for small countries to try to join regional integration arrangements with large countries is to avoid investment diversion.

One of the recent trends in the literature on regional integration surveyed by Baldwin and Venables (1995) is the attention being paid to effects on *economic growth*. Even a modest effect on the growth rate is likely to lead, over time, to a large welfare effect. The literature on this subject is not very conclusive. One of the recently explored channels is the effect of regional integration on the rate of return of capital. If this rate of return is increased, there will be a continued attraction of capital. Another mechanism arises with technological spillovers. The increased trade and investment within a regional integration arrangement may facilitate the spread of technical progress leading to higher long-term economic growth.

In comparison to the static effects, the dynamic effects are generally considered to be much stronger especially in the case of (small) developing countries. At the same time, the understanding of these effects as well as their empirical measurement is quite imperfect. A key problem is that the dynamic effects are not exclusively linked to regional integration, but are a feature of an outward-oriented strategy in general. This leaves the possibility that they are exaggerated by the proponents of regional integration and minimized by the opponents.

Non-traditional effects

The theory of regional integration has been fluctuating between the views that it brings sizeable welfare gains – for example, trade creation, and the suggestion that these gains are small and can be achieved or surpassed by unilateral or multilateral trade liberalization. Why, given this difference of opinion, is regional integration so popular? Why has there been a second wave of regional integration that shows no sign of losing momentum? A number of interesting explanations have been put forward under the heading of non-traditional effects of regional integration arrangements.[32]

Regional groupings generally start with trade liberalization and move on towards freedom of factor movement. Gradually, there will also be calls for increased coordination and harmonization of macroeconomic policies. This includes fiscal policies as a prime target. A potentially very important effect of regionalism is the discipline of group action that increases the *credibility of policy reform*. Credibility is critical for private agents to enhance their confidence to make new investments. Another way of expressing the same idea is to say that integration helps to 'lock-in' sound economic policies. The effect of regional integration on policy credibility and the locking-in of sound policies is more relevant in explaining the widening of successful groupings, than in their initial formation. It is also relevant when small economies integrate with much larger ones. This is most likely to happen in the case of North–South integration (see Chapter 6).

The idea of lock-in can be applied not only to policies, but also to other issues such as technical standards. By joining a larger group, a country can take on board existing standards without going through the process of developing its own standards. With the latter approach, there can be problems over exports that are refused on technical grounds.

For a small developing economy, unilateral trade liberalization is not likely to be very credible to foreign investors. Membership of the WTO brings a number of disciplines that may help, but the enforcement capacity of the WTO is weak and developing countries can invoke special and differential treatment to justify policy reversals. On the other hand, membership of a strong regional integration arrangement may prevent policy reversals, because disciplines will be more strictly enforced. It was mentioned already that it is not straightforward for a small developing country to use the dispute settlement mechanism of the WTO, despite its improvements. Legal enforcement within a grouping can be faster, cheaper and more effective in settling problems than the WTO mechanism.

Another effect of regional integration is that it ensures access to the markets of the partner countries. This can be called the *insurance effect*. During the 1980s the spread of non-conventional forms of protection (for example anti-dumping measures, voluntary export restraints, inappropriate use of health standards), applied by major industrial countries, was a cause of concern among emerging economies that were starting to build up their export capacities. As mentioned above, there was a perception that the world economy might become divided into a small number of mutually hostile trading blocs. This provided a strong motive to look for a 'safe haven' and to integrate with one of the large trading blocs.[33] Membership of a trading bloc was seen as an insurance against the possibility of the bloc becoming protectionist in the future. Usually, but not always, integration arrangements exclude anti-dumping measures within the grouping. In order to deal with restrictive trading practices, a competition policy is then set up. Enforcing a competition policy within a regional grouping can be seen as a form of deep integration. A contentious issue is whether or not the smaller countries that join large blocs pay a kind of insurance premium. Perroni and

Whalley (1994) find that in some recent arrangements, small countries make significantly more concessions than large ones. These extra concessions (for example, in the area of intellectual property protection) can be seen as the premium to be paid by the small countries. Clearly, small countries should avoid paying too high an insurance premium.

Non-economic effects

Regional integration arrangements will generally have important non-economic effects. In fact, integration arrangements are often set up in the first instance to achieve non-economic objectives, such as the consolidation of peace and security, and greater bargaining power in international affairs. European integration was started following the Second World War to prevent a new war. One of the motives of setting up ASEAN was to contain the possibility of conflict between its member states and to be more united in view of outside security threats. More recently, MERCOSUR also has an element of reducing tension. Economic integration will increase interdependence through trade, investment and movement of persons. Rising interdependence constitutes a basis for the reduction of tensions and for closer political integration. Interdependence will be greater with deep integration rather than shallow. If political integration is an objective, this will often show up in calls for deepening and broadening the economic integration effort.

Several trade policy analysts, taking into account the ambiguity of the economic effects on welfare, and recalling the undoubtedly negative effects of a tariff war between large trading blocs, consider non-economic motives as the most important justifications for regional integration.

Even though the effect of regional integration arrangements on security has been recognized for a long time there has not been much systematic analysis of this relation. An interesting contribution of Schiff and Winters (1998) addresses this issue. They explore the economic implications of the notion that international trade can reduce tension between nations. The security effects of trade are external to individual agents, so that their incentives do not lead to their full exploitation. Hence, there is a case for subsidizing intra-regional trade or for the creation of a trading bloc. In this way, regional integration can be an element of an arrangement to increase security and reduce tension. Schiff and Winters demonstrate that the optimal external trade barriers tend to decline over time. However, they may increase again when new member states join the trading bloc.

Greater bargaining power can also be an important effect of regional trading arrangements. It can have payoffs of many kinds and constitutes an important motive for small countries to become part of a strong integration grouping. Andriamananjara and Schiff (1998) present a model in which the decision to form, expand or join a regional arrangement is based on bargaining power and negotiation costs. Their model is specifically relevant for small and very small economies. They consider that the savings in negotiation costs and enhanced bargaining power are the main benefits of integration among microstates. The model provides a nice explanation of why small countries tend to exchange support for specific issues in international negotiations. The model also illustrates the importance of the cost of entry. If membership is free, there is a tendency to form an inefficiently large group. The possibility for the newcomer to compensate the insiders would yield a socially optimal group size. Irrespective of entry conditions, the likelihood of integration between small countries as well as the group size increases with the number of issues to be tackled and with the degree of similarity between the countries. Adriamananjara and Schiff provide an interesting application of their analysis to CARICOM regional integration.

Adjustment costs

It is remarkable that the extensive literature on the effects of regional integration arrangements hardly touches on the issue of adjustment costs. The move from a pre- to a post-integration situation always implies rearrangements in production and consumption. There is a friction in moving from one equilibrium to another, leading to inefficiency and short-term costs. Adjustment is beneficial if the frictional welfare loss is more than compensated by future welfare gains. However, future welfare gains cannot be known in advance and with certainty. Helleiner (1996) underlines the importance of adjustment costs for small economies. Often small countries must adapt more than large ones, for example in the area of tariff reduction.

Adjustment concerns, in the first instance, producers, but also the government, because of tariff revenue decline. Adjustment costs of producers derive from closing production facilities and investing in new ones. There will be frictional unemployment and under-utilization of productive capacity. Common sense suggests that rapid adjustment will be more costly than slow, especially in terms of unemployment. Training schemes may help reduce frictional unemployment. It should be recognized, however, that trade liberalization is only one of several sources of adjustment costs. The process of economic development implies more or less continuous adjustment because of technical progress, changes in factor endowments or changes in institutions. Trade liberalization calls for a repositioning of the private sector. There are likely to be sizeable shifts in the distribution of income.[34] Regional trade liberalization tends to imply slower and cheaper adjustment than unilateral trade liberalization, because exposure to new competition is more limited and gradual.

There is also an adjustment problem for the government that must replace tariff revenue by other sources of income to maintain a satisfactory budget situation. Also for the government, regional liberalization will lead to slower and cheaper adjustment than unilateral liberalization.

Adjustment costs are related to what can be called the *political economy of trade creation and diversion*. Political economy considerations may turn some conclusions of economic analysis upside down. Trade diversion is politically easier to 'sell' than trade creation. With trade diversion, the partner country gains in market share at the expense of the original suppliers outside the region. The government in the home country will generally lose some tariff revenue, while, depending on the situation, consumers may or may not benefit through cheaper prices. However, producers in the home country are not affected by closures of production facilities. In the case of trade creation, the partner country also gains in market share and consumers benefit from lower prices. But now companies in the home country will have to close operations, because they cannot compete against cheaper imports from the partner country. Even though there should be trade creation in the other direction for other goods as well, leading to new investment, this may take time. Social disruption may occur before new production capacities have a positive effect on employment.

The political advantage of trade diversion has sometimes even led development analysts to consider it as the main objective of economic integration. 'I will divert your trade if you divert mine.' This paves the way for inward-looking integration and industrial planning at the regional level, which did not work in the past.

Free trade areas, customs unions and rules of origin

The regional integration initiatives of the first wave during the 1960s and early 1970s often had the objective of creating a CU or even a Common Market, perhaps because they were following European integration. Examples are CARICOM, CEAO, ECOWAS, CACM and UDEAC. Of the more recent initiatives during the second wave, many explicitly choose to become FTAs. Examples are NAFTA, ASEAN-FTA, SADC and the agreements between the EU and the Mediterranean countries. While the theoretical analysis of CUs and FTAs is not very different, the differences in practical implementation are substantial.

From an institutional point of view, a CU is much more demanding than an FTA because of the need to set up a mechanism to agree on the Common External Tariff (CET). This is not a once and for all matter, because the CU will be involved in multilateral negotiations. Hence a permanent structure is needed to establish the position of a CU in the multilateral system. This usually calls for very close collaboration or for a delegation of responsibilities to a supranational body.[35]

Trade policy analysts differ in their views on the advisability of FTAs in comparison to CUs. An advantage of an FTA could be that a member state can never be forced to accept trade diversion, because there is always the option of reducing MFN tariff rates so that no diversion can take place. Hence a free-trade-minded member of an FTA will not be constrained. But obviously, the same applies to a protectionist-minded member. The freedom of an FTA member to change tariffs towards the rest of the world is also a potential disadvantage. Lobbying for protection can still be done at the country level, whereas in a CU this needs to take place at the union level, which is likely to dilute the efforts.

The advantages of a CU and an FTA can be combined (or the disadvantages can be minimized) by moving towards a Harmonized External Tariff (HET). With an HET, members agree on a classification and on tariff bands with a maximum and a minimum allowing flexibility within these bands. This is attractive for developing countries where tariff revenues are an important component of the government budget. The specific decision on tariff levels within the bounds can reflect budgetary needs and does not require to be negotiated with all the members.[36]

It is worthwhile to recall that FTAs and CUs also differ as regards the possibility of overlapping arrangements. Overlapping FTAs are possible, but this is not the case for CUs. A member of a CU cannot join another CU, unless one creates a larger single CU. A CU member can also not join an FTA without 'breaking' the CET. The issue of overlapping CUs and FTAs has become an increasing concern for some groupings of developing countries. An example is COMESA which aims to become a CU by the year 2004, while several of its member states are also taking part in SADC which has the aim of becoming an FTA.

Under FTAs, countries keep their own level of protection towards third countries. Thus, it is necessary to avoid the situation where a product entering the FTA at the border with the lowest duty is shipped without duty to other members of the FTA. This phenomenon is called *trade deflection*. Rules of origin are the regulatory device to avoid trade deflection. In a CU, every entry point will apply the same tariff so that verification of origin is not needed to avoid trade deflection. Rules of origin are an administrative arrangement to determine which products are entitled preferential treatment, hence they are also required in one-sided preferential trading arrangements such as the Generalized System of Preferences (see Chapter 5).

An illustration can be made referring to NAFTA. Suppose that the United States charges 5 per cent duty on a product coming from outside NAFTA while Mexico charges 25 per cent. A trader can import goods into the US and pay the low rate and then transport them to Mexico claiming that they are an American product and make a profit of 20 per cent minus the extra cost of handling and transport. If the latter cost is high in relation to the tariff difference, trade deflection is unlikely. Rules of origin are specifically designed to avoid simple operations such as labelling, packaging or minor processing being used to convey origin status. The main difficulties arise in determining the origin of commodities that consist of a variety of materials and that are produced in various stages, such as cars. The globalization trend implies that, increasingly, production processes leading to a single end product take place in many different countries.

There is extensive literature on the implementation of *origin rules* (ORs). The main types of ORs are those based on a share of the value-added generated within a member country and those based on a change in tariff classification between the components and the final product. A change in tariff heading normally represents a substantial transformation (say from steel and other materials into a car). Sometimes, a list of processing operations that confer origin is specified. Another OR specifies that a minimum percentage of the value of purchased parts must be obtained within the FTA. In several cases, different rules are combined.[37] It is common in FTAs for the legal description of the rules of origin to be the largest and most tedious part of the agreement.

The value-added criterion has intuitive appeal. The cut-off point is usually situated between 25 and 50 per cent. The higher the cut-off point, the fewer products will be eligible for free trade. With a high cut-off point the free trade area can become quite hollow. The selection of a particular level is generally a delicate matter. The value-added criterion has also some obvious weaknesses. Actual measurement requires fairly sophisticated book-keeping. Furthermore, its application can easily be affected by circumstances such as a devaluation or a price shift in one of the inputs. This is likely to happen when the value-added share is close to the cut-off point, which would be difficult for companies because it would introduce uncertainty. The change in tariff classification is usually considered to be the criterion that is easiest to apply by customs officials. But, there are many complications, as described by Palmeter (1993). Tariff schedules are lengthy, complex and tedious documents. Sometimes they are only understood by specialists familiar with the details of certain industrial processes. They are not designed for the purpose of origin verification. There are various levels of classification. For example, the Harmonized System distinguishes two-digit chapters, four-digit headings, six-digit sub-headings and an eight-digit statistical level. The rule must specify the level at which a change in classification conveys origin status. According to Palmeter, there are frequent disputes about customs classifications.

In practice, the origin rules are never straightforward to apply and tend to complicate trade operations to the extent that they are considered to be a serious non-tariff barrier. Negotiations on origin rules frequently oppose business interests in different member states of a grouping. They can become complex and cumbersome, as in the case of NAFTA (see Hufbauer and Schott, 1993) and many other arrangements. Practical difficulties can increase because a trade bloc or country may apply a different set of rules depending on the geographical origin of the goods. The EU trade regime, for example, applies several different ORs depending on the trading partner.[38] Bhagwati and Panagariya (1996) warn about a 'spaghetti bowl' phenomenon when various protectionist-motivated rules of origin co-exist at a time when the local content and origin of a product become increasingly meaningless as a result of globalization.

There is not much analysis on the cost of compliance with origin rules. In the case of EFTA, the cost of complying with origin rules has been estimated to be at least 3 per cent of the trade value (Palmeter, 1993). In order to avoid the extra administrative burden of fulfilling ORs, around 25 per cent of eligible trade in EFTA is carried out under the MFN tariff regime. It is likely that the burden for developing-country trade is even higher, with the consequence that even more trade is carried out at non-preferential rates. It is also possible that strict origin rules are prohibitive, preventing trade altogether.

Despite their disadvantages, ORs will continue to be needed to implement preferential arrangements (whether or not they are reciprocal). There is a need to cut the cost of enforcing these rules, especially for developing countries. It is therefore desirable that rules of origin are harmonized as much as possible. Discussions in the context of the WTO are the best way to make progress in this direction. A start has been made with the understanding on rules of origin reached under the Uruguay Round (WTO, 1994), but much remains to be done.

Rules of origin may also be applied in relation to service trade. Origin of services can be established on the basis of criteria such as: place of incorporation of the provider, nationality of ownership, location of headquarters or principal place of business (WTO, 1995). In some cases regional groupings of developing countries have introduced similar requirements on the manufacturers of products. Preferences are granted for products only if they originated in a partner country and were manufactured by a company owned within the region. While the motivation of such rules is understandable, it is clear that they have a protectionist bias and are not conducive to an outward-oriented trading system.

ORs have been criticized on theoretical grounds by Anne Krueger (1993), who considers that they are mainly a protectionist device. Because finished products consist of various raw materials and components, ORs may lead to trade diversion in these materials or components. Some of her work is critical about NAFTA's rules of origin because of this.[39] Krueger therefore favours CUs rather than FTAs.

As was mentioned above, CUs do not need rules of origin to avoid trade deflection. However, a point sometimes overlooked is that a CU that does not pool the tariff revenue still needs to establish origin for the purpose of determining which country can keep the customs duty.[40] Even though, from the point of view of a private trader, it does not matter where his product enters the CU, from the country treasury's point of view, it does matter and therefore has to be checked. In most cases, the customs duty goes to the country where the product is consumed. Another reason for border controls in a CU (even though not of origin) is the existence of different levels of other indirect taxes such as VAT. To the extent that border controls always constitute non-tariff barriers and imply costly delays, CUs cannot fully eliminate them. In order to eliminate border controls, one needs deeper integration in the direction of an economic union, with harmonization of indirect taxation.

Assessment for small developing economies

Trade economists often do not share the enthusiasm of politicians about economic integration. They point to the negative aspects of trade diversion, the danger or even tendency of integration groupings to become inward-looking and the potentially large welfare loss in the event of a trade war. They are also concerned that regionalism will undermine the multilateral system. In addition, Bhagwati and Panagariya (1996) emphasize the loss of tariff revenue for developing countries and the complications and cost increase of rules of origin. To the extent that they recognize the static and dynamic benefits of regional integration, they find that these can be obtained through unilateral liberalization.

Despite these critical views, regionalism continues to be attractive for many developing countries. Baldwin (1995) observes that regionalism is spreading 'like wildfire'. While this may be exaggerated, it still appears that the second wave of regional integration is not weakening. The question arises as to what the effects listed in Table 4.2 and reviewed above add up to for small developing economies (SDEs). A related question is which kind of regionalism will maximize the potential benefits and minimize the potential costs for such countries.

When SDEs integrate, a point to be noted is that the grouping as a whole will still be small. This implies that the grouping cannot restrict trade in order to obtain terms of trade improvements. It also implies that regional integration should not be conceived as a strategy of regional import substitution behind high tariff barriers. Hence, regionalism of SDEs should always be outward-oriented. Barriers should be decreased towards the rest of the world at the same time, though not necessarily at the same speed as the barriers between the regional countries are being removed. This is a requirement that goes beyond the obligations of Article XXIV of the GATT and certainly beyond the Enabling Clause. The static effects of South–South integration of SDEs are likely to be rather modest. There is only limited scope for efficiency gains through trade creation, for example for light manufactures. At the same time, there is not much chance of costly trade diversion, because the preference margins will be relatively small, provided that trade liberalization towards the rest of the world indeed takes place. SDEs generally trade little with each other, so that the danger of large tariff losses is not present. On the whole, the static effects do not provide a strong argument in favour of South–South regionalism. At the same time they are not a reason for not integrating, as some analysts would say.

For small economies the dynamic effects are likely to be more significant than the static ones. Companies in SDEs will find it easier to compete in terms of quality on the regional market. It will be much harder to achieve competitiveness on the markets of industrial countries or more advanced large developing countries because of quality norms, technical standards and lack of information. Products that can most easily be exported by SDEs often still face protectionism (agriculture, apparel, light manufactures). Regional integration is a way to reduce x-inefficiency. It is also a way to increase the attractiveness of SDEs for inward investment.

Realizing the benefits from scale economies is another valid argument for SDEs to integrate more closely. This applies in the private sector, but it is also highly relevant for the provision of important public goods such as transport and communication infrastructure and education. Pooling resources in these areas can imply sizeable savings. Regionalism can also help SDEs to increase their negotiating and bargaining capacity. Regional groupings can represent the interests of their member states in multilateral forums such as the WTO. However, realization of these potential benefits typically calls for deep integration; they cannot all be achieved with shallow integration.

What about the non-traditional effects of increasing the credibility of policies through lock-in and providing insurance against future protection? Only limited benefits can be expected. It is unlikely that regional groupings of SDEs would be able and willing to apply tough sanctions to enforce compliance. Because of the limited size of their markets, the insurance effect can only be small. Clearly, the non-traditional effects occur in the first place when large economies are in the picture (see Chapter 6).

In conclusion, while there are potential benefits, that are by no means negligible, in regional integration of small developing countries, it should be stressed that the realization of these benefits is not straightforward. The earlier discussion on economic and non-economic preconditions and institutional design should be recalled. It is too early to assess the results of the more recent wave of regionalism among developing countries. The first wave that started in the 1960s produced very few results in terms of welfare and growth. Expectations about the current wave should be realistic. There is a lot of preparatory work to do in countries where political preconditions such as good governance, the rule of law, transparency and participation of civil society are not fulfilled. As regards the economic aspects, unlike what is sometimes advocated, regional integration is not an alternative for sound macroeconomic policies. In this respect, it should be recalled that fulfilment of the obligations of membership of the WTO and IMF provides a minimum basis for integration into the world economy. Many SDEs are implementing structural adjustment programmes. Such programmes generally contain reforms in economic policies that help put in place the basis for successful economic integration. Examples include good macroeconomic and monetary management, sound budgetary procedures and investment deregulation. In order for adjustment programmes to facilitate regional integration, they should be coordinated for countries in the same region. Regional institutions could play a key role in such coordination.

Even though, in principle, structural adjustment programmes can help put in place conditions for successful regionalism, in practice, adjustment programmes of countries within the same region are often not coordinated in terms of phasing and pace of liberalization measures. This may lead to increased economic distortions between neighbouring countries and disrupt regional trade. Adjustment programmes rarely pay attention to the promotion of *regional* trade and investment and to the facilitation of regional payments. The regional dimension should be part and parcel of the preparation of adjustment programmes.[41] This will improve the potential for beneficial regional integration.

An important aspect of regionalism concerns the *mitigation of adjustment costs* in comparison to unilateral liberalization. Repositioning of the private sector involving closure of production lines and creation of new ones is an unavoidable aspect of integration into the world economy. Regional integration can help to make repositioning socially and politically more sustainable.

5
Non-Reciprocal Arrangements with Industrial Countries

During the 1960s and 1970s developing countries pleaded strongly in favour of non-reciprocal trading arrangements with the industrial countries. Such arrangements were seen as a way to increase their exports and thus stimulate economic growth. It can be argued that the initial lukewarm response of many industrial countries strengthened the case for inward-looking strategies among developing countries. In fact, as argued in Chapter 3, the inward-looking strategy remained dominant well into the 1980s.

To some extent, the calls for special trading arrangements were also calls to preserve the market access of former colonies. Virtually all the former colonial powers had set up a system of imperial preferences. The United States, being the main architect of the GATT in 1947 and defender of an open, non-discriminatory trading system, was not in favour of special trading arrangements that conflicted with the GATT requirements.[1] One could also reason that the US did not wish to forgo trading opportunities in the newly independent states. It was anticipated that such opportunities would increase rapidly.

In the 1960s, a frequently mentioned argument in favour of preferences towards developing countries was the adjustment cost of abolishing imperial preferences. In many cases, a sizeable part of the economy of newly independent countries depended directly on the special trading link with the former colonial power. An example was the dependence of Senegal on groundnut exports to France at a price well above the world market level. Furthermore, many firms in the former colonial powers also depended on the business in the former colonies. This applied to firms using tropical raw materials, but also to companies selling finished products. There was thus a mutual interest in maintaining preferential relations or at least in phasing them out gradually.

The European Union has always maintained special trading relations with most of the former colonies of its member states. The Rome Treaty in 1957 foresaw *reciprocal* free trade between the European member states and the associated overseas countries and territories. The first and second Yaoundé Conventions (signed in 1963 and 1969 respectively) continued reciprocal trade arrangements between Europe and the newly independent states.[2]

Since its creation as a kind of alternative for the GATT, UNCTAD became the main forum for the trade demands of the developing countries.[3] Whereas the European states, partly because of their post-colonial linkages, were relatively quick to accept some of the demands of the developing countries, the United States maintained its objections longer. The European countries agreed to the principle of setting up a system of preferences for the developing countries as early as the first UNCTAD Conference in Geneva in 1964. As described by Langhammer and Sapir (1988), the US became isolated from both developing and other industrial countries on this issue and changed its position at the second UNCTAD Conference in New Delhi in 1968. At the latter Conference, the principle of setting up a *Generalized System of Preferences (GSP)* was unanimously accepted.

Despite this unanimous agreement, the practicalities of establishing the GSP took a long time to be worked out. Contrary to what developing countries had expected, the industrialized countries did not create a unified GSP scheme. Rather, each country or regional grouping such as the EC set up its own scheme, characterized by specific beneficiary countries, commodity coverage and exclusions, depth of preference margin, safeguard mechanism and rules of origin. The EC system became operational in 1971.[4] Most other OECD countries started their GSP soon afterwards. Canada initiated its programme in 1974 and the US only in 1976. Interestingly, according to Langhammer and Sapir (1988), the US linked its own GSP to the removal of discriminatory treatment of US exports in countries associated with the EC. As a result, in 1975, the EC replaced the *reciprocal* Yaoundé Convention by the *non-reciprocal* Lomé Convention. Under the Lomé Convention, the associated states were no longer supposed to accord preferential treatment to European imports.

In addition to general preferential tariff reductions, there are several commodity-specific European trade arrangements in favour of developing countries. For example, the sugar protocol permits import quotas from selected developing countries at the internally guaranteed European price. Because the European price generally exceeds the world price by a significant margin, the beneficiary countries receive a sizeable transfer on their export quota. There are also special arrangements for beef, rum and bananas. As it happens, these special commodity arrangements are strongly geared towards benefiting a number of small and very small developing economies.

The GSP arrangement constituted an obvious violation of the MFN principle of the GATT. For that reason, the GATT contracting parties agreed, in 1971, to a waiver from the MFN principle for ten years. Later on, in 1979, a permanent legal basis to cover the GSP, as well as other aspects of the treatment of developing countries, was agreed with the introduction of the 'Enabling Clause' (see also Chapter 2).

In 1983, the United States initiated the *Caribbean Basin Initiative (CBI)*, which provides preferential market access beyond GSP to most Caribbean countries. The Lomé Convention trade regime and the CBI are the main non-reciprocal arrangements in favour of developing countries that go beyond the GSP.[5]

To what extent can preferential trading arrangements be considered as part of a developing country strategy for integration into the world economy? This is the central question addressed in this chapter. One disadvantage for the developing countries is that the GSP modalities can be unilaterally modified by the industrial countries. Still, from the point of view of the developing countries, special and differential treatment, underlying arrangements such as GSP, has indeed been considered as an integration strategy. During the Uruguay Round, many developing countries bargained for the continuation of special and differential treatment. In this way, preferential trading arrangements might slow down multilateral trade liberalization, which is not necessarily in the long-term interest of the developing countries.

This chapter highlights the strategic aspects of preferential arrangements between developing and industrialized countries. Before describing some of the main arrangements (GSP, the Lomé Convention and the Caribbean Basin Initiative) the likely economic effects of non-reciprocal preferences are summarized. The final section assesses the advantages and disadvantages of non-reciprocal preferences for developing countries in general and specifically for small developing economies.

Effects of tariff preferences (*)

Tariff preferences can be analysed in the same way as unilateral tariff reductions or the formation of customs unions. There are again two main aspects. First, tariff preferences provide a price advantage to exporters of beneficiary countries. Second, they lead to discrimination against exporters of third countries. As with customs union theory, a distinction is made between static and dynamic effects. While the theoretical and empirical literature on tariff preferences deals largely with the static effects, the justifications of tariff preferences mostly refer to dynamic effects. The original appeal for tariff preferences in favour of developing countries, by Raoul Prebisch at the first UNCTAD Conference, emphasized dynamic effects such as the infant-industry argument. The markets of developing countries would be too small to allow in-

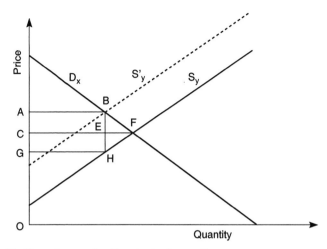

Figure 5.1 Tariff preference leading to trade creation

fant-industry protection to work at national level. Tariff preferences offered by the industrial countries would enlarge the market and strengthen the competitive edge of products from developing countries.

Referring to the *static effects* and considering the case of a market for a homogeneous product, two basic situations can be distinguished. In the first, the beneficiary developing country is an efficient supplier of the product (or a potentially efficient supplier that cannot produce at an efficient scale). The tariff preference will lead to increased demand to be supplied by the beneficiary country. This is trade creation. In the second situation, the beneficiary country is not an efficient supplier. However, with the tariff preference, it will be able to out-compete and replace part of the supplies that were delivered by third countries. This is the case of trade diversion.

The trade creation case is summarized in Figure 5.1 where it is assumed that the supply curve S of the beneficiary country is upward-sloping. The preference giving and receiving countries are referred to as countries X and Y. The supply curve that takes into account the tariff is represented as S'. Without a tariff preference, the excess demand curve of the preference donor country cuts the tariff-inclusive supply at point B, implying an imported quantity of AB at price OA that includes the tariff margin AG. While the beneficiary country only receives price OG, the consumers in X pay the tariff-inclusive price. Applying a tariff preference leads to a larger imported quantity CF and a lower price OC. It should be observed that the price goes down less than the tariff value in view of the elasticities of the demand and supply curves. The preference-

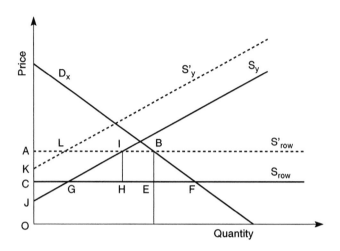

Figure 5.2 Tariff preference leading to trade diversion

receiving country clearly gains, its producer surplus increases with the area CFGH. Part of this increase (area CEHG) represents tariff revenue that previously went to the government in country X. In this case, the preference is an effective way to stimulate growth and exports in the preference-receiving country.

Whether or not the preference-giving country also gains depends on the circumstances. Its consumer surplus rises with area ABFC. Part of this gain comes at the expense of tariff revenue (ABCE). The rest is the welfare triangle BEF, resulting from lower prices. If the latter triangle is larger than the loss of tariff revenue, not recovered in the consumer surplus (CEHG), then there is also a net gain for country X. However, this is unlikely because the tariff revenue is lost on the total original import quantity, whereas the gain only applies to the increase in imports. For countries X and Y together, the trade creation of EF leads to a welfare gain represented by the triangles BEF and EFH.

The situation of trade diversion is illustrated in Figure 5.2, which is the same as Figure 4.3 in chapter 4. The difference with Figure 5.1 is the assumption of a country representing the rest of the world (row). It is assumed that the rest of the world is 'large' and can supply the product at a constant price OC. The tariff-inclusive price of the rest of the world is OA and the total imported quantity is AB. The supply curves of the beneficiary country without and with tariffs are S_y and S'_y respectively. Without tariff preferences, country Y delivers AL of the product, the balance being supplied by the rest of the world. Applying a tariff preference towards country Y will have no effect on the total quantity imported by country X, but will lead to a shift in supply from the rest of the world towards the country receiving preferences. Because Y no longer pays the tariff, it can increase its supply by LI at the expense of the rest of the world.

What are the welfare implications of this trade diversion? The rest of the world neither gains nor loses in this simplified representation because of the assumption of a horizontal supply curve. Country Y that benefits from trade preferences clearly gains because it no longer pays the tariff and therefore receives a higher price. The preference donor X loses the tariff revenue that it originally collected. Looking more closely at Figure 5.2, one can see that X's loss is not fully compensated by Y's gain. The overall net loss represented by triangle HGI is the result of producing the additional quantity GH in country Y at rising costs.

In the situation with trade diversion, trade preferences are nevertheless an effective tool to stimulate exports and thus growth in developing countries. In order to assess the effects of trade preferences more realistically, some simplifying assumptions should be recalled. Figures 5.1 and 5.2 only refer to a single market of a homogeneous product. Even within the same product category, goods are not homogeneous and therefore not perfect substitutes. For example, coffee from Colombia will not have the same characteristics as coffee from Kenya. A tariff preference in favour of Kenya will therefore not lead to a complete diversion in demand away from Colombian coffee. Empirical studies usually make assumptions about the substitutability of commodities depending on their origin. One disadvantage for the beneficiary country should be mentioned. If it can only export thanks to the higher price resulting from special preferences, it cannot be competitive towards the rest of the world, which may be the more rapidly expanding market. Referring to Figure 5.2, a shift in country Y's supply curve from S' to S could also be the result of technical progress that increases efficiency. This would lead to an improvement in every market, not just in the market where preferences are given. This is a much more beneficial situation for a developing country than receiving a tariff preference.

Markets for manufactured goods are much more differentiated than markets for primary commodities. In differentiated markets, it is difficult to know in advance whether tariff preferences will lead to trade creation or trade diversion. Both can occur at the same time: (inefficient) local production as well as (efficient) production in third countries can be replaced by imports from the beneficiary country.

Product differentiation is closely related to the structure of markets and thus the degree to which agents can exploit monopoly power. It may therefore not be possible to determine in advance which agent in the marketing chain will actually reap the benefits of trade preferences. From a development point of view, it is essential that the benefits reach the ultimate producer. However, partly because of uncertainty about specific preferences and the complications of compliance procedures (for example rules of origin), this may not be the case. Intermediary exporting agents in developing countries or even intermediary importing agents in the industrial countries may increase their profits, leaving no gain for the ultimate producer. If this is likely to happen, it might be preferable, from a development point of view, to maintain the tariff and arrange a direct transfer to assist the producers.

Further complications arise in moving from a partial analysis of one market to the general equilibrium analysis of many interrelated markets. Because trade with developing countries is only a small part of total trade of the industrial countries, general equilibrium considerations can be ignored in assessing the effect of trade preferences on these countries. However, this is not the case for developing countries that in fact carry out the bulk of their trade with industrial countries. If exports of commodities that receive preferences increase, adjustments have to be made in the rest of the economy. The net growth and employment effects derived in a general equilibrium analysis will tend to be smaller than the gross effects for a particular sector.

What about the *dynamic effects*? Again, there is a parallel with the general theory of tariffs and customs unions. In the context of tariff preferences, the most frequently mentioned dynamic effects are related to economies of scale, learning by doing and direct foreign investment. Preference-induced increases in production may help to achieve an efficient production scale. Countries benefiting from tariff preferences may therefore attract new investment. Tariff preferences will make investments more profitable.

The infant industry argument has often been used to justify one-sided tariff preferences.[6] Faber (1990) discusses the argument and presents a number of conditions that should be satisfied. For the infant industry argument to be valid, the preferences should be of limited duration, they should be transparent and reliable, and they should reach owners of production factors with a real potential to expand supply. In many situations, these conditions have not been fulfilled.

Experience with the main non-reciprocal arrangements

This section reviews some of the main non-reciprocal preferential trade arrangements that are implemented by the European Union and the United States.

The Lomé Convention: a special trade deal with the EU

Over time, the European Community, now the European Union, has built up an elaborate and arguably complex system of preferential

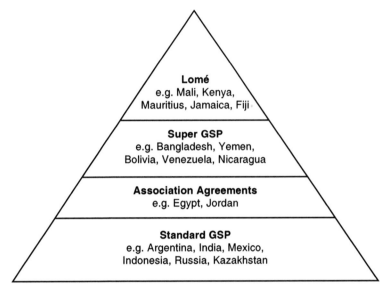

Figure 5.3 The EU 'pyramid of privilege'

arrangements.[7] Some analysts like to refer to this system as the 'pyramid' of EU preferences. Following Stevens *et al.* (1993), Figure 5.3 illustrates this pyramid of trade preferences towards developing countries.[8] The top, corresponding to the most preferred status, is occupied by the group of ACP states that adhered to the Lomé Convention. Slightly below this are some developing countries that benefit from the so-called 'Super GSP', an improvement over standard GSP. These are least-developed countries as well as some developing countries in Latin America (see the section on the GSP below). The Mediterranean countries with which association agreements have been signed occupy the middle part of the pyramid. The base is constituted by the remaining developing countries that benefit from the standard GSP.[9] This group comprises many large developing economies such as Brazil, India, Indonesia and Thailand. It also includes the transition economies that emerged from the break-up of the former Soviet Union.

The Lomé trade regime is non-reciprocal; in other words, the beneficiary countries have no obligation to accord preferences to imports from the EU. A non-reciprocal arrangement should be distinguished from a unilateral regime. The latter, also known as an autonomous regime, is a concession by one side that can be reversed. The Lomé Convention is not unilateral. It is an international treaty that can only be changed by agreement between both sides. The GSP, on the other hand, is non-reciprocal as well as unilateral, which means that it can be changed without the involvement of the beneficiary countries. In comparison to a unilateral regime, a contractual set-up such as Lomé is thought to boost the confidence of traders and investors. The Lomé Convention is governed by institutions with comparable representation from both sides. However, partly because of its limited duration (the current Convention will expire in the year 2000), and because of the way the system is managed, it is sometimes still perceived by the ACP side as a unilateral arrangement. It should be mentioned that Lomé also implies some restrictions on the ACP trade regime towards the EU. ACP countries cannot discriminate among EU member states and are obliged to offer trade access to the EU, which is no worse than that accorded to any other industrial country.

The Lomé Convention deals with development cooperation as well as trade and involves, at present, 71 states in Africa, the Caribbean and the Pacific (ACP). The ACP Group, as currently constituted, encompasses all of sub-Saharan Africa (48 states), most of the Caribbean (15 states) and most of the South Pacific islands (eight states).[10] With a few exceptions, the ACP states used to be colonies of the EU member states. The latest member to join, in 1997, was South Africa. However, South Africa has a special status and a number of key provisions, including the trade regime, do not apply to it. At present, that country benefits from the GSP, but negotiations have been concluded in early 1999 to establish gradually a Free Trade Area between the EU and South Africa. The current fourth Lomé Convention was signed in December 1989 with a validity of ten years until March 2000. Its first financial protocol comprising the financial resources for the cooperation part covered five years. The Convention was amended following a mid-term review in 1995. The revised text, including the financial protocol for the second five-year period, was signed in Mauritius in November 1995. Among the important revisions was a more stringent human rights clause.[11] In the trade field, access for agricultural commodities was improved.

Under the criterion used to define Small Developing Economies (SDEs) which was introduced in Chapter 1, all ACP states except the Dominican Republic, Nigeria and South Africa are small (GNP less than US$ 10 billion). In other words, 68 or four out of five of the world's SDEs are ACP states. It should be mentioned that least-developed, landlocked and island states receive special treatment in the Lomé Convention.

The trade preferences imply duty and non-tariff-barrier free access to the EU market for all mineral, industrial and tropical agricultural products that satisfy the origin requirements. Only a small proportion of the products covered by the Common Agricultural Policy (CAP) does not have free access. However, even for these products, ACP countries have privileged access in terms of reductions of import duties and import quotas. For some agricultural commodities, there are special arrangements called protocols that provide for free access up to a country-specific quota. The most important is the sugar protocol that provides for the import of approximately 1.3 million tonnes of cane sugar, raw or white, at the internally guaranteed EU price (see also note 14). There are other protocols for beef, rum and bananas.

An important aspect of the Lomé trade regime concerns the *rules of origin* that are more liberal than for the other EU preferential regimes.[12] These provide for full *cumulation* within the whole ACP group and with the EU. This implies that goods can contain unlimited components from other ACP countries or from the EU. Cumulation extends to Overseas Countries and Territories (OCTs), such as, for example New Caledonia and the Netherlands Antilles. Under certain circumstances, cumulation with non-ACP neighbouring developing countries 'belonging to a coherent geographical entity' is also permitted. Originating products must be 'wholly obtained' or 'sufficiently worked or processed' in the ACP states. The wholly obtained products such as minerals and agricultural products do not pose many difficulties.[13] The sufficiently worked or processed requirement is a lot more problematic. The basic rule is that origin status is obtained for a processed product if it falls in a tariff heading (four-digit level of the Harmonized System of tariff classification) that is different from the heading of all imported materials that are used as inputs. However, there are several qualifications. Some simple processing activities that may result in a change of tariff heading are always insufficient for origin status (for example, packaging, simple assembly, mixing or washing). A detailed list of activities that do not necessarily change the heading, but that are nevertheless considered sufficient processing is also provided (for example, some processes to preserve foodstuffs, assuming that the food ingredient is originating). There is also a provision for derogation through which ACP countries can obtain case-by-case exceptions on the origin rules, provided certain conditions are satisfied.

The fact that cumulation of origin is also allowed with the EU member states is considered a stimulus to EU *direct investment* in the ACP states. The exclusion of minimal processing activities to obtain origin status is justified as a way to avoid certain industries establishing simple assembly or packaging operations only to qualify for EU preferences. Such activities are not considered to be of lasting benefit to the ACP states, because of their limited employment creation and growth linkages. On the other hand it could be argued that sometimes, simple processing could be a first step on a learning curve paving the way for more sophisticated manufacturing.

Another key aspect of the Lomé trade regime is that it has always involved exemption from the requirements of the Multifibre Arrangement

(MFA). ACP countries have been able to export textiles and clothing without the stringent requirements of the MFA. However, there are still special limitations in terms of origin. Manufacturers must normally start from originating yarn rather than from fabric. In other words, exporting apparel requires 'double transformation', yarn into fabric and fabric into garment.

In terms of their general effects on ACP trade, the Lomé preferences are usually not considered a success. A frequently used overall indicator is the share of total ACP exports in the EU market. This declined from 7.4 per cent in 1975, to 4.8 per cent in 1990 and only 3.3 per cent in 1993. From 1994 to 1996 the share went up slightly and stabilized at around 3.8 per cent. These percentages do not include imports from South Africa. It should be recalled that a significant component in the initial decline and in subsequent fluctuations is due to the changing value of oil exports from Nigeria. In contrast, the import share of Asia's newly industrialized economies on the EU market increased rapidly from only 2.4 per cent in 1975 to 7 per cent in 1996. Between 1988 and 1996 the share of ASEAN also went up quickly from 3.5 to 6.6 per cent. Over the same period, there was a small rise in imports from the Mediterranean region reaching 8.5 per cent in 1996, while imports from Latin America declined slightly to 5.2 per cent. The largest absolute change over that period was the fall in imports from the (old) industrialized countries down from 53 to 46 per cent.

Despite their low share of the EU market, ACP countries continue to depend very heavily on it. For 1990–92, about 41 per cent of ACP exports went to the EU. The proportion for the sub-Saharan Africa subgroup was even higher at 46 per cent. Surprisingly at first sight, the US also takes a relatively high share of the ACP group's exports: 29 per cent over the same 1990–92 period. This high share is explained by the extreme dependence of the Caribbean sub-group on exports to the US (57 per cent). Together, the EU and US absorb an astonishing 70 per cent of the ACP exports (see Davenport, Hewitt and Koning 1995). The high shares of African exports to the EU and of Caribbean exports to the US partly follow from historical connections and geographical proximity, but they are also, undoubtedly, a result of the preferential arrangements of Lomé and the Caribbean Basin Initiative.

The assessment of the effect of ACP preferences is more varied and positive at the level of specific countries and products. Mauritius, for example, has increased its exports of manufactures, especially clothing, in a spectacular way over the past two decades. From a negligible amount in the early 1970s, manufactured exports rose to more than US$ 1 billion in 1995, representing 65 per cent of total exports. Mauritius was probably the country that took most advantage of the absence of the restrictions of the Multifibre Arrangement. Some investors from Hong Kong, who faced clothing export restrictions to the EU market, decided to invest in the Mauritius export processing zone. Local investors followed. A few other countries have recently increased their clothing exports to the EU: Zimbabwe, Jamaica, Côte d'Ivoire, Namibia and Madagascar. According to an evaluation study by Imani Development (1995), several ACP countries have successfully developed new non-traditional exports including processed rubber (Côte d'Ivoire), cut flowers (Ethiopia, Kenya, Mauritius, Zambia and Zimbabwe), cotton yarn (Kenya, Zambia and Zimbabwe) and timber products (Côte d'Ivoire, Ghana and Cameroon).

The relatively generous cumulation of origin provisions, that are considered a stimulus for regional integration among ACP countries, did not lead to any significant increase in intra-ACP trade. In other words, it is rare for ACP states to procure materials for further processing in other ACP countries in order to qualify for duty-free access to the EU market. An explanation could be that Lomé does not require ACP countries to reduce barriers between each other. Moreover, implementation of trade liberalization within ACP economic integration arrangements has moved very slowly (see the discussion in Chapter 4 and Appendix A). More effective regional integration within the ACP group would probably trigger better use of the origin cumulation provisions.

It is also important to mention that several of the smaller ACP states receive transfers through the Lomé trade system that are very large in relation to the size of their economy. This is particularly true for the beneficiaries of commodity protocols. For example, for Mauritius and Guyana, the average benefits of the sugar protocol amount to 4.6 and 9.1 per cent of their respective GDP.[14] The very small economies of the Windward Islands such as Dominica, St Lucia, and St Vincent & the Grenadines depend very much on the protection offered by the special banana regime. Several other Caribbean countries benefit from the rum protocol. There is a lot of debate about the long-term effect of the commodity protocols on diversification. Often, the beneficiary countries are extremely dependent on one export product and diversification is a recognized priority. The benefits of the commodity protocols can be compared to pure transfers. But implementing transfers through commodity exports may not be the most cost-effective way to promote diversification. Nevertheless, diversification depends in the first instance on the policies in the beneficiary country. It has been demonstrated, for example, that the beneficiaries of the sugar protocol in Mauritius did invest in new product lines in the export processing zone.

A matter of increasing attention and controversy is the WTO status of special trade arrangements such as Lomé. The discriminatory aspects of the EU's banana regime triggered a complaint by some Latin American producers (Ecuador and Guatemala), supported by the United States as a result of the lobbying of US companies involved in exporting Latin

American bananas to the EU. The dispute led to an examination of the legality of the Lomé trade regime. It concluded that this was not compatible with the WTO legal framework. Because of non-reciprocity, the Lomé regime cannot be seen to fulfil the requirements of Article XXIV on Free Trade Areas (see discussion in Chapter 4). Furthermore, because the Lomé regime discriminates among developing countries, it cannot be seen as acceptable under the 'Enabling Clause'. Notwithstanding these problems, a waiver has been obtained from GATT article I (application of MFN) until the end of the current Convention in the year 2000.[15]

The Caribbean Basin Initiative

The Caribbean Basin Initiative (CBI) was launched in 1984 following approval of the Caribbean Basin Economic Recovery Act. The CBI provides non-reciprocal preferential access to the United States market as well as economic assistance for most of the small Caribbean states except Cuba and Suriname. This represents all the member states of CARICOM (apart from Suriname that became a member only in 1996) and the Central American Common Market (CACM), plus the Dominican Republic, Aruba, the Netherlands Antilles and the British Virgin Islands, altogether 28 countries. The initiative was improved and extended for an indefinite period by the 1990 Caribbean Basin Economic Recovery Act.[16] The revision is sometimes referred to as CBI II. An important aspect of the CBI is the promotion of US private investment in the beneficiary countries.

The CBI represents a considerable improvement over the standard American GSP. It covers a wider product range and is not subject to the yearly reviews of competitive needs limitations and graduation thresholds (see the section below on GSP). The rules of origin are easier: substantial transformation is interpreted as a shift in customs classification and 35 per cent value added contributed by the exporting country. The value added can even be lowered to 20 per cent if the difference is made up by materials imported from the US. Origin can be cumulated over beneficiary countries, which is seen as a boost for CARICOM and CACM integration. Even though fewer products are excluded than under GSP, the list of exclusions still covers several important items that typically would constitute strong export products for the region: textiles and clothing, footwear and agricultural products. However, since 1986 improvements have been made for the access of textiles and clothing through bilateral General Access Level agreements.

The overall results for the CBI are not very different from those of Lomé. The combined share of CBI countries' imports in the US market declined from 2.7 per cent in 1984 to 1.8 per cent in 1993. This overall figure conceals sizeable differences across the beneficiary countries and over the time period. The Dominican Republic and, to a lesser extent, Central America did quite well. Trade with Haiti was subject to sanctions and thus declined. CARICOM exports fell sharply during the second half of the 1980s, to a large extent because of the declining value of petroleum products, but recovered in the first half of the 1990s with increased clothing exports.[17] The empirical studies of the early CBI, as reported by Brown (1988) show only very modest results. Exports of covered products went up by around 15 per cent, but total exports from CBI countries only increased by 1.5 per cent. Brown concludes that direct aid was a much more significant component of CBI than trade preferences. The bilateral access level agreements on textiles and clothing, outside the CBI led to a rapid increase in apparel exports from CARICOM and the Dominican Republic. The graduation of some newly industrialized countries from the GSP in 1989 (Hong Kong, South Korea, Taiwan and Singapore) led to some investment diversion towards the CBI countries especially in the clothing sector.

The CBI has not yet led to the same controversy about its WTO compatibility as the Lomé Convention. Nevertheless, the arguments against Lomé are equally valid against CBI.[18] Presently, the CBI has been granted a WTO waiver until the year 2005.

Generalized system of preferences

Unlike the Caribbean Basin Initiative (CBI) or the Lomé Convention, the Generalized System of Preferences (GSP) is universal, in the sense that, in principle, all developing countries and more recently all transition economies are eligible (there are a few exceptions as mentioned below). It is also the only system that explicitly resulted from the demands of the developing countries in UNCTAD. It is legally covered by the 'Enabling Clause' of the GATT, which was agreed following the Tokyo Round and which has been integrated into the WTO.

There is an extensive body of literature describing the Generalized System of Preferences and analysing its effects.[19] However, most of the analysis was done for the 1980s and does not take into account the new developments during the 1990s. This section reviews some aspects of the GSP in order to assess its possible role as part of a strategy of integration into the world economy for small developing countries. Only the European and American schemes are outlined, which together account for the bulk of the GSP.

The European scheme started in 1971. Originally set up for a period of ten years, it was renewed and revised several times. The revisions in 1995 for industrial products and in 1996 for agricultural products have considerably simplified and improved the regulations.[20] The system provides full tariff exemption for most manufactures and full or partial tariff exemption for processed agricultural products. However, there are certain conditions such as the rules-of-origin requirements that are more stringent than under the Lomé trade regime. Anti-dumping measures can be applied towards beneficiaries of the GSP system. Products are divided into four categories: *non-sensitive, semi-sensitive, sensitive* and *very sensitive*. Non-sensitive items are completely exempt from tariffs. For semi-sensitive, sensitive and very sensitive items, the applied tariffs are 35, 70 and 85 per cent respectively of the applied MFN tariff. Industrial products, except textiles and clothing, are generally non-sensitive. The list of very sensitive agricultural products is still quite long, including, for example, cut flowers, bananas, citrus fruit, grapes, apples, pears and strawberries. Non-sensitive agricultural items include mostly tropical products such as coffee, tea and pistachios.

In terms of country coverage, the EU's GSP is available to all developing countries that are members of the group of 77. Thus, Taiwan has always been excluded. South Korea has been temporarily excluded because of a disagreement on intellectual property rights. China, Romania and the former Yugoslavia have always been included. Several other Central and East European countries were briefly in the system from 1989 until they signed, mostly between 1991 and 1993, the 'Europe agreements', that are reciprocal and prepare for full EU membership. The newly independent states of the former Soviet Union are also included and since 1994, following its democratic transition, South Africa takes part as well. The GSP is also available to the ACP countries, but because of the more advantageous Lomé regime, it is not used.

An important modification of the standard GSP is the regime for the *least-developed countries (LDCs)* that was initiated around the mid-1980s. This so-called *super-GSP* provides deeper preferences (almost like those under Lomé, except for agriculture) and simplified procedures. However, rules of origin are more stringent than under Lomé. Since 1990, four Andean Pact countries (Bolivia, Colombia, Ecuador and Peru) also receive super-GSP. Venezuela was added in 1995. The grant of super-GSP to the latter group of countries was considered a gesture to encourage and support a stricter drug-control policy. Better export opportunities to Europe were seen as a substitute for drug production. Since 1992, the members of the Central American Common Market and Panama also receive super-GSP treatment.

In 1997, it was agreed to equalise the Lomé trade regime and the super-GSP for the least-developed countries. In other words, all least-developed nations, whether they are members of Lomé or not, will receive the same trade preferences.[21] This was done in view of the plan of action in favour of the least-developed countries approved at the December 1997 Singapore ministerial meeting of the WTO.

Recent discussions on the European GSP have focused on the concept of *graduation* as well as on encouraging good social, environmental and human rights behaviour. Since the inception of the GSP in the early 1970s, MFN tariff reductions have considerably eroded the GSP preference margins. The Uruguay Round agreement implies a significant further erosion. The reasoning is that, by graduating the successful newly industrialized economies, that should now be able to comply fully with the standard WTO requirements, it is possible to target the remaining preferences towards the countries that most need them. The view behind this is a rather static one of a limited 'cake' of preference benefits to be allocated. Successful exporters are often able to expand the market through quality improvement or product differentiation. Recent graduates are Hong Kong, Singapore and South Korea. The human rights requirement, excluding, for example, products made by forced labour, reflects an important shift in development cooperation in general. It was applied in 1997 to withdraw GSP for Myanmar. Environmental requirements, such as sustainability of forest management, come in the wake of increased worldwide attention on ecological issues.

The United States launched its GSP in 1976. Right from the start, country coverage reflected a compromise between development concerns, protectionism and, more than in the European case, political considerations. Eligible countries could neither be communist nor members of commodity cartels such as OPEC. Beneficiaries were expected to cooperate on preventing drugs from entering the US. As mentioned above, similar considerations much later led the EU to grant super-GSP to several Latin American countries. Protectionist pressures led to an important list of excluded products including textiles and clothing, footwear and import-sensitive electronic articles. The regulations provided for the possibility for interested parties, such as import competing companies, to petition for the exemption of additional products. The US system also uses rules of origin to determine eligibility (35 per cent of value added). From the beginning, there was also a peculiar 'competitive need limitation', implying that a country exporting a product to the US beyond a certain value would lose duty-free treatment for that product. The US was a lot earlier than the EU in the application of graduation criteria. As early as 1989, graduation excluded Hong Kong, South Korea, Singapore and Taiwan from further participation.

According to Langhammer and Sapir (1988), while in theory the original EU system was more comprehensive in country and product coverage, in practice the US system was more effective. This is because the European administrative rules at that time were much more complex, especially due to the management of quantitative restrictions at the level of EU member states. Later on these rules were simplified.

The empirical evidence of the welfare effects of GSP appears inconclusive.[22] On the whole, research demonstrates that the systems have been more trade-creating than trade-diverting. The increase of exports of preferred products has been estimated to be between 10 and 30 per cent (Brown, 1988). However, because of various exclusions, preferred products are only a small part of total exports. Hence, the overall effects have been small, leading perhaps to an expansion of only 1 to 2 per cent of total exports of beneficiary countries. Nevertheless, Davenport (1986, p. 126), analysing the ASEAN countries, concludes that 'for certain products in certain countries, the GSP has been of considerable importance in stimulating exports'. One thing that clearly emerges from the empirical analysis is the concentration of GSP-induced exports on a small number of eligible countries, mostly newly industrialized economies. The principal beneficiaries have been India, Thailand, Brazil, China (for the EU), Taiwan (for the US), Mexico, Indonesia, Hong Kong, Singapore, Malaysia and South Korea. The smaller and least-developed countries did not benefit significantly from the American or European GSP.[23] One of the implications of the complexity of the rules appears to have been that benefits sometimes went to intermediaries in importing countries, who understood the tricks, rather than to third-world producers.

While recognizing the erosion in the margin of preferences as a result of MFN-based tariff reductions in the Uruguay Round, the 1996 UNCTAD Conference in South Africa nevertheless called for a continuation of the GSP as an instrument to foster industrialization and integration into the world economy. However, the final declaration of the UNCTAD Conference underlined the need for a better distribution of GSP benefits among beneficiaries. It also contained a reference to the great concern among beneficiaries about linking the eligibility to non-trade considerations (i.e. labour and environment).

Non-reciprocal arrangements and small developing economies

There is no straightforward answer to the question about the relevance of preferential arrangements in the post-Uruguay Round world trading system. The MFN tariff reductions agreed in the Uruguay Round further erode the preference margins that have already become quite small in any case. The inclusion of agriculture in trade liberalization and the agreement to dismantle the Multifibre Arrangement will gradually remove old areas of dispute between developing and industrialized countries.[24] The new areas of contention are of a very different nature, for example services liberalization, social and environmental clauses, investment regulations, intellectual property, quality standards, and sanitary and phytosanitary regulations.

Before turning to the situation and strategies of small developing economies, it is helpful to assess the overall interests of the developing countries in relation to non-reciprocal trade preferences. Whereas in the 1960s, trade preferences, together with other aspects of special and differential treatment, were virtually seen as a complete alternative to the mutual obligations approach under the GATT system, this has no longer been the case since the Uruguay Round. Three decades after the first UNCTAD Conference, the benefits and costs for the developing countries as well as for the (old) industrial countries seem quite different from the original assessment. The benefits in terms of trade expansion have been limited. Some countries that were successful in terms of export growth, such as those in East Asia and Chile, made good use of the preferential regimes. There is no doubt, however, that their success derives much more from domestic policies than from external preferences. The small and poor countries that needed the assistance most were the least able to benefit. Even some countries that did not receive tariff preferences could still be very successful in exporting to the industrial countries. For example, Taiwan was excluded from the European GSP, but nevertheless rapidly increased its exports to Europe.

For the developing countries as a group, the non-reciprocal arrangements have had some hidden costs. Special and differential treatment made it easy for the industrial countries to ignore the specific trade liberalization needs of the developing countries. Because developing countries did not have to make 'concessions' in the GATT sense, the industrial countries did not feel obliged to liberalize their markets in the areas most relevant for the developing countries such as agriculture, textiles, clothing and other labour-intensive manufactures. There have always been strong lobbies defending the interests of these sectors in the industrial countries. It is conceivable that, in the absence of special and differential treatment, progress on liberalization in these sectors would have been more rapid, leading to important growth incentives in developing countries. Another point, especially relevant for the least-developed countries, is the high cost of compliance with the complex administrative arrangements such as rules of origin (that are different for each preference donor), contrary to what developing countries had requested. The lack of predictability of the arrangements has shifted part of the benefits towards the importing countries. This could also explain why the anticipated dynamic effects in terms of new investment have been disappointing.

On the side of the preference donors, the costs in terms of increased competition and forgone tariff revenues have been quite small. MFN tariff reductions and progressive economic integration among industrial countries themselves (especially in Europe) reduced the budgetary effects of non-reciprocal tariff concessions and very much limited the possibilities for trade diversion. It should be recalled that, for developing countries, trade diversion taking place in the industrial countries was generally desirable, especially combined with the infant-industry argument. Another aspect from the preference donor's side is that it is not necessary to make budgetary outlays. This tends to facilitate the political approval process, as budgetary authorities may be less concerned.

It is unlikely that the recent reforms of the European GSP will significantly increase the benefits for the least-developed countries. The graduation of the more advanced developing countries will take place over the period when the Uruguay Round tariff reductions are implemented. Furthermore, the EU is committed to extending implementation of *reciprocal* liberalization towards most of the Central and East European, and Mediterranean countries. Further reciprocal liberalization is being prepared with a number of other countries and groupings (South Africa, Mexico and MERCOSUR). For all the countries involved, these reciprocal arrangements will lead to access to the EU market that is comparable to Lomé or super-GSP.

The EU's renewed GSP scheme foresees incentive mechanisms in the areas of social, environmental and human rights policies. With the likely benefits going down from a level that already did not have a great impact, it seems difficult to add such broad-ranging objectives to the GSP. This does not at all mean that these objectives are not important for their own sake, but the issue is whether a trade policy instrument that showed limited success in the past, and that is anyhow declining in importance, is a suitable one to promote these objectives.

In the Western Hemisphere, the formation of NAFTA has fundamentally changed the competitive position of the Caribbean Basin countries in the US and Canadian markets. The plans for a Free Trade Area of the Americas (FTAA) may further erode the tariff advantages of the CBI and GSP. The FTAA is discussed under the heading of North–South integration in Chapter 6.

While the larger and especially the more dynamic developing countries received most of the standard GSP benefits in an absolute sense, the smaller, poorer and more vulnerable countries did obtain sizeable benefits from the other more specialized schemes such as Lomé, CBI and super-GSP. The spectacular growth in exports of East and South-East Asia and a few other economies such as Chile obscures a reasonable export evolution in many small developing economies. For sub-Saharan Africa, the average trade performance is not a good indicator. It combines many situations of conflict, civil strife and sometimes a complete breakdown of the state, together with examples of impressive economic progress over the recent past (Botswana, Côte d'Ivoire, Ghana, Mauritius, Namibia and Uganda).

Mauritius stands out as an example of a small developing economy that made good use of the special trade preferences. It does not enjoy sizeable natural resources, nor does it have the advantage of a strategic location such as Hong Kong or Singapore. Despite this, it made a transition from a single export economy (sugar cane) in 1975 to a progressively diversified economy. The export share of manufactures went up from just above 15 per cent in 1975 to around 65 per cent in 1993. Services exports, mainly tourism and, increasingly, financial services, became important sources of foreign exchange. Per capita GNP grew by 5.8 per cent per year between 1985 and 1994, putting Mauritius in the same growth league as East Asia and Chile. Within SADC, Mauritius now has the highest per capita income (US$ 3380 in 1995), above the level of South Africa.

The sizeable benefits of the sugar protocol for Mauritius were partly channeled to the Export Processing Zone (EPZ), fostering diversification. Foreign investment from Hong Kong and Europe also went into the EPZ. What has been the overall contribution of non-reciprocal trade arrangements to Mauritius's success? Pierre Yin (1993), a Mauritian economist, provides the following view: 'Foreign investors were no doubt attracted by the advantages which the free zone offered and particularly the large supply of cheap labour, the tax benefits and the infrastructure. What tipped the balance, however, was the possibility of free access to the EC.' In other words, Mauritius did take advantage of trade preferences because other complementary conditions were satisfied as well. In fact, since the late 1970s Mauritius had implemented a successful economic adjustment operation with liberalization in the areas of trade (mainly non-tariff barriers) and investment, with a market-determined exchange rate and a cautious monetary policy.

In contrast to large developing economies with a sizeable export potential, increased exports from small economies do not influence the prices that they receive. Non-reciprocal preferences will usually increase the export price for small economies and can be compared to an income transfer. This is not the case when market imperfections lead to increased profit margins for exporters or importers and there is no effect on producers. In such cases the benefits amount to poorly targeted subsidies. Hence it is important for small developing economies to insist on clarity and predictability of procedures.

Some preferential arrangements, such as the EC's commodity protocols, are almost equivalent to a pure transfer. A good strategy for small developing economies is to treat such transfers as windfall gains and to make the best use of them, as long as they last. The success of Mauritius illustrates that such a strategy can work. The challenge is to avoid the situation where the preferences are simply absorbed as extra profits for exporters. The consequence of this is that it becomes almost impossible to compete in markets without such preferences. In fact, Mauritius has been able to increase exports not only to the EU, but also to non-EU markets such as the US and recently the Southern Africa region. This double diversification over products and markets will determine the sustainability of the export success.

As observed above, many small developing economies are least-developed countries (LDCs). In the EU market, those that do not participate in Lomé receive super GSP rather than standard GSP. Other industrial countries also apply special measures in favour of the LDCs. The implementation of the Uruguay Round will make the preference margins of the standard GSP almost negligible. At the same time, the pace of graduation from the GSP is expected to increase. In order to maintain a significant preference margin for the LDCs and to simplify and consolidate the world trading system, it is desirable to phase out the standard GSP.

What about the future of the trade arrangements that go beyond the standard GSP and that almost exclusively benefit small developing economies? A distinction should be made between least-developed and other developing countries. The efforts of the WTO Secretariat led to the adoption of a special action programme for the LDCs at the December 1996 ministerial meeting. The follow-up meeting in October 1997 endorsed a favourable trade regime for the LDCs in combination with enhanced capacity-building on trade-related matters. An innovative and welcome aspect is that emerging trading economies also start granting privileged access to the LDCs. As a concrete step, the EU started to equalize at the beginning of 1998 its super GSP benefiting the LDCs and the trade regime of the ACP countries. In other words, the top two layers in the pyramid represented in Figure 5.3 will gradually be merged.

But what about the small developing economies, which are not LDCs? As mentioned above, these typically benefit greatly from the special trade regimes including the EU's commodity protocols. These regimes have been increasingly criticized by some developing and industrial countries. An example is the EU's banana regime, which has been the subject of a dispute settlement procedure and found to be incompatible with the WTO rules. The banana regime provides advantages to a few very small economies in the Caribbean and some others in Africa (for example Cameroon). Bananas are the main export of Dominica, St Lucia and St Vincent, accounting for about half of their export revenue. Efforts towards diversification are under way. The best strategy for these Windward Islands would be to invest the profit of the special EU banana regime in new economic activities, perhaps in the services area. But politically and socially, such a transition process will not be easy. It is fair to say that because of their small economic size and physical characteristics (see Chapter 1), this group of countries is confronted by a high degree of vulnerability. Any change in the preferential regimes should be gradual so as to avoid, as far as possible, the social and political disruption that would result from a forced and speedy adjustment process.

The EU and the ACP countries are involved in discussions on the future of the Lomé Convention beyond the year 2000. On the ACP side, initial views emphasized the *status quo* and maintaining as much of the special preferences as possible. The EU is committed to respond to the development imperatives of the ACP countries, but it is equally committed to full compliance with the WTO system. One of the avenues to maintain the preferential access of the ACP countries is to move towards reciprocity in the form of Free Trade Areas sanctioned under Article XXIV of the GATT. This amounts to a form of North–South integration and will be further examined in Chapter 6.

An alternative possibility, that would not imply any inconsistency with WTO rules, would be to convert some parts of the special trade advantages into explicit grants or transfers. As mentioned above, for small developing economies, these advantages can be often considered comparable or sometimes even equivalent to pure grants. A grant has the advantage of simplicity and transparency, it would facilitate an equitable distribution over beneficiary countries and should not lead to any market distortions. For the industrial countries, these grants would not be purely altruistic. They would contribute to a smooth integration process of vulnerable states into the world economy. Increased instability in such states could backfire to the detriment of the industrial countries, for example in the form of drug-trafficking, money laundering or illegal environmental deals. However, there could also be some disadvantages in transforming trade preferences into transfers. Grants would generally lead to certain conditionalities as is the case with structural adjustment. Small developing countries may prefer an implicit grant resulting from a trade concession with few strings attached to it.

6
North–South Regionalism

In order to be better integrated into the world economy, small developing economies can follow a unilateral strategy or they can take part in a regional arrangement together with other countries. The most common regional strategy is partnership with other developing countries. This is the case of 'South–South' regionalism, which was the subject of Chapter 4. It is also possible that the partner countries or grouping are from the North. This is 'North–South' regionalism, which is the subject of the present chapter.

Following the creation of NAFTA in 1993, putting Mexico in an economic integration grouping with the United States and Canada, the idea of North–South economic integration has been much debated. From the beginning of NAFTA, there has been speculation about its enlargement, which would bring in more developing countries. Chile has been put forward as the most likely fourth member state. Any widening of NAFTA would necessarily involve developing countries. In contrast to arrangements such as the Caribbean Basin Initiative (CBI) or the Lomé Convention, NAFTA is a *reciprocal* agreement. In other words, the same mutual obligations apply to all the member states, whether or not they are developing countries. However, there can be some asymmetry, for example on the length of the transition period. It might be argued that NAFTA was not the first North–South arrangement. The widening of the European Community towards the South with Greece, Portugal and Spain during the 1980s was in some respects comparable. A usual characteristic of North–South integration is the large degree of economic disparity between the partners.[1]

The December 1994 Miami Summit of the Americas launched the idea of a Free Trade Area of the Americas (FTAA) from 'Alaska to Tierra del Fuego'. The FTAA is another North–South arrangement. It contains a large number of small developing economies at its centre in the Caribbean basin. As argued by Bernal (1994b), the creation of NAFTA had a strong negative effect on the economic prospects of the small developing economies in the Caribbean region. Mexican goods became more competitive on the US and Canadian markets in comparison to Caribbean products. American or Canadian investment was diverted from the Caribbean towards Mexico. The small countries also lost advantages in services such as tourism. The FTAA offers the prospect for the Caribbean countries to undo some of the negative effects of NAFTA. From the outset the FTAA process recognized the special situation of the smaller economies by creating a working group to discuss their problems.

The United States, together with Canada, Australia and Japan, take part in the Asia Pacific Economic Cooperation (APEC) which is another kind of North–South arrangement. A characteristic of APEC is that it comprises predominantly large and very large developing economies such as China, Indonesia, Malaysia, Mexico, Thailand and the Philippines. Only one member, Papua New Guinea is a small developing country.[2] APEC is committed to a form of open regionalism whereby the member states together apply MFN trade liberalization. There are no plans for APEC to become a Free Trade Area or a Customs Union. Certainly, with NAFTA, the FTAA and in a different sense APEC, North–South integration will remain high on the international trade policy agenda for the US.

The European Union is also deeply involved in North–South economic integration.[3] The December 1995 Euro-Mediterranean Conference in Barcelona between the EU and 12 Southern and Eastern Mediterranean countries agreed on the objective of creating a Free Trade Area by around the year 2010. The new generation of association agreements between the EU and these countries contains FTAs as a main element. By the end of 1998, agreements have been reached for Tunisia, Morocco, Israel and the Palestinian Authority. Negotiations are under way with most of the other countries. In the same region, a Customs Union between the EU and Turkey came into effect in 1996. The negotiations for the creation of a Free Trade Area between the EU and South Africa were concluded during the first quarter of 1999. Moreover, there are discussions on an FTA with the Gulf Cooperation Council (GCC), with MERCOSUR and with Mexico. Finally, the future trade regime between the EU and the ACP countries could also be oriented towards achieving FTAs between the EU and groupings of ACP countries.

The first and second sections of this chapter discuss the motives of industrial and developing countries for engaging in North–South economic integration. The third section examines the participation of small developing economies in the FTAA. The fourth section looks at the relation between the EU and the African, Caribbean and Pacific countries. An assessment of North–South integration as a strategy for small developing countries is made in the final section.

Motives for industrial countries

Why should industrial countries prefer North–South regional integration arrangements rather than multilateralism, integration *within* the North and non-reciprocal preferences for developing countries? Altruism or solidarity may play a role, but this would tend to be reflected in the extension of unilateral concessions, rather than in demands for greater reciprocity. North–South integration is often thought to require difficult economic adjustment in the South, which could not easily be justified by the motive of solidarity, unless mitigated by far-reaching compensatory assistance, which generally only takes place with deep integration. Enlightened self-interest, represented by both economic and non-economic motives, appears to be a more plausible motive. The debate on North–South integration is typically focused on near neighbours such as the Caribbean Basin for the US and the Mediterranean region for the EU. A connection can be made to what is sometimes called 'new interdependence'. New forms of interdependence between the North and the South have become much more prominent recently. They arise in relation to cross-border problems such as drug-trafficking, money-laundering, international terrorism and illegal migration.

The globalization process in general facilitates communication of all sorts, while at the same time population growth and poor economic prospects increase the incidence of some of the above-mentioned problems in many vulnerable developing countries. The possibility of containing the problems of new interdependence provides a strong political motive for North–South integration. If Mexico or North Africa can achieve equitable and sustainable economic growth thanks to better trade opportunities with their northern neighbours, the attractiveness of illegal cross-border activities is likely to diminish. This is a kind of 'insurance' motive for the North. The trade concessions may affect some production activities in the North, but that may be a price worth paying for enhanced security and stability. The question arises why more traditional development assistance would not be preferred. An explanation is that in the past, traditional development assistance does not seem to have tackled the growing problems posed by the new interdependence.[4] Economic integration with reciprocal obligations could have more leverage on the policies of the South than classic development assistance. Reciprocity could, in fact, constitute a credible threat to prevent policy reversal in the South.

Even though non-economic motives are prominent in the public debate on North–South integration, economic motives are also important. A number of developing countries have experienced rapid economic growth and are becoming ever more interesting export markets and investment locations. North–South integration can greatly facilitate profitable trade flows. It may give some northern countries a competitive advantage over other industrial and developing countries in the markets of emerging economies. Moreover, it will provide better protection for investment and intellectual property rights than is presently offered by the multilateral system. Economic motives explain why the private sector in the North is usually strongly in favour of North–South integration.

Both the non-economic and economic motives appear to account reasonably well for the positive reception of North–South integration in the North. However, most of the analysis of the subject concerns the motives of the developing countries, to which we now turn.

Motives for developing countries

At first sight, North–South integration does not seem attractive from the point of view of the South. Because of the Generalized System of Preferences (GSP) and other non-reciprocal arrangements such as the Lomé Convention and the Caribbean Basin Initiative, access to the markets of the North should not pose a fundamental problem. Furthermore, the implementation of the Uruguay Round agreement reduces protection in agriculture and textiles, the two sectors that were traditionally the most contentious for the developing countries. Further reduction of agricultural protection is on the agenda for the 'millennium' round. As WTO members, developing countries can take part in the multilateral rule-based system that guarantees against discrimination and unfair practices. If necessary they can, with technical assistance from the WTO, invoke the dispute settlement mechanism, even though the discussion in Chapter 2 demonstrated that this might not be so easy for small countries. They can also unilaterally lower tariffs to ensure cheap supplies of raw materials and capital goods for investors and to keep consumer prices low. Tariff reductions can be made irreversible through bindings in the WTO, so that a newly-elected government that respects the rules cannot undo them. So, why are developing countries interested in North–South integration?

There are two main explanations. One motive is usually referred to as the *locking-in of policies*. A binding North–South agreement will make it costly for the governments in the South to reverse policy decisions. The reasoning goes that if policy reversal carries real penalties for the government, it will think twice before reversing. Another motive is *reducing uncertainty of future trade access*. A binding agreement with an 'anchor' economy in the North will provide a kind of *insurance* for developing countries that they will not become victims of increased protection in the future. This applies particularly to anti-dumping measures.

North–South integration implies reciprocal obligations and rights. It

Table 6.1   Comparison of non-reciprocal and reciprocal trade arrangements for developing countries

Non-reciprocity	Reciprocity
No effect on policy credibility.	Helps locking-in policies and increases credibility.
Market access is not secured; contingent protection such as anti-dumping measures remains possible.	Market access is guaranteed; contingent protection is not allowed or is more difficult.
Tariff revenue is not affected.	Tariff revenue is reduced significantly because trade with a Northern anchor economy typically covers a high share of total trade.
Almost full freedom of trade policy; infant industry protection is possible.	Trade policy is restricted by the terms of the agreement; infant industry protection is not possible or restricted; another industrial policy must be worked out.
Negotiation is not necessarily required.	Negotiated arrangement; calls for adequate negotiating capacity.

is strategically quite different from the non-reciprocal arrangements between the North and South that have dominated the scene for the past few decades. Table 6.1 summarizes the main differences between non-reciprocal and reciprocal North–South trade arrangements.

Past efforts at trade policy reform by developing countries have frequently been reversed (see for example Gunning, 1994). A survey by the African Economic Research Consortium of trade liberalization in ten African countries demonstrated that only two did not experience policy reversal.[5] In many developing countries, unilateral trade liberalization has been encouraged through structural adjustment assistance. According to Collier (1995), trade liberalization purely in exchange for structural adjustment lending is likely to lack credibility. The assistance offered is always temporary, and when it runs out, the government has a tendency to fall back into its old habits, leading to a reversal of reforms. A new round of aid and temporary reform is then possible. What is missing is a strong *agency of restraint* or anchor to keep policy reform on track. A reciprocal agreement with a strong economy can increase the credibility of reforms. For small developing economies in sub-Saharan Africa and the Caribbean, such an anchor economy cannot be found in the region, hence the argument in favour of North–South integration.[6]

One explanation of the beneficial effects of locking-in policies with those of an anchor economy is linked to the importance of local interest groups. In a small economy, policy decisions can be strongly influenced by a single company or pressure group. In a large economy, interest groups will be more diverse and may keep each other in balance. Locking in the policies of a small economy may diminish the negative effects of interest groups on these policies.

A famous example of North–South integration in the African context is the CFA monetary zone. Fourteen African countries, all of them small economies, use the CFA franc, which is linked with a fixed parity to the French franc and since 1 January 1999 to the euro. Monetary policy decisions are determined jointly by the CFA zone countries and France. In this case, France clearly acts as a monetary policy anchor providing guaranteed convertibility, but also requiring strict rules on reserve pooling and management, and on financing of government budget deficits. Whereas many African countries have experienced monetary volatility, rapid inflation and massively overvalued currencies, the CFA zone has maintained price stability. The CFA zone countries experienced low inflation and relatively strong economic growth during the 1970s and the first half of the 1980s. However, mainly because France and the African countries were exposed to asymmetric macroeconomic shocks in (agricultural) commodity prices, the CFA franc became increasingly overvalued during the late 1980s and early 1990s. This was a key reason for the economic stagnation in the CFA zone. The situation was only corrected at the beginning of 1994 with a 50 per cent devaluation of the CFA franc. Economic growth has since resumed in many CFA countries, especially in Côte d'Ivoire. However, growth did not resume in some of them, illustrating that, while monetary stability is necessary, it is not the sole determinant of growth.

The locking-in motive can also be seen as a way of *reducing time-inconsistency of policies*, as discussed by Fernandez and Portes (1998). A government may have embarked on the implementation of an optimal policy in the area of trade and investment. However, without a sufficiently strong restraint, it might give in to pressure groups and change the policy. Investors and traders, in fact, anticipate that the government will give in and therefore do not base their decisions on the optimal policy. This, in turn, makes it more difficult for the government to maintain the optimal policy. Integration with the North could increase the confidence of investors and traders and therefore reduce the problem of time-inconsistency of policies. A requirement is that there should be a significant penalty for leaving the regional arrangement or deviating from the agreed policy. Hence, the arrangement cannot be too loose or shallow.[7] Fernandez and Portes (1998) also discuss 'signaling' as a motive for joining a regional trading arrangement. By joining an arrangement with a good reputation, a government can provide a signal that it is committed to similar policies. Signaling could be an important advantage of North–South integration especially in relation to attracting foreign investment. Signaling is a way for developing countries to enhance the credibility of their policies.

While the locking-in motive is concerned mainly with the internal economic policy situation, the insurance motive is more about the external policy environment. Especially during the 1980s there has been an increased incidence of protection in the form of voluntary export restraints (VERs) and anti-dumping measures. Several developing countries, which achieved successful growth combined with unilateral trade liberalization have been affected by this (for example, Taiwan and Thailand). These measures are forms of contingent protection, i.e. protection that depends on circumstances. With the general decline in tariff rates, the relative importance of contingent protection has rapidly increased. This provides a strong motive for export-oriented economies in the South to look for a 'safe haven' in the North. Perroni and Whalley (1994) emphasize the insurance motive when smaller economies integrate with larger ones, which is generally the case with North–South integration. In their view, 'the large country–small country arrangements which dominate the new regionalism have to be seen as insurance-based arrangements with side payments, not as reciprocity driven'.

It is interesting to consider the above points in the context of Mexico's accession to NAFTA. According to Francois (1997), the main advantages for Mexico relate to the reduction of uncertainty about future access to the US market and the role of the US as an external policy anchor for domestic economic and, to a lesser extent, political reform. Market access as such was not the issue, because prior to NAFTA, Mexico already had preferential access through GSP. However, this access was not guaranteed. As De Long *et al.* (1996, p. 9) observe: 'NAFTA made Mexican businesses and investors a solemn promise that they would not be bankrupted by a sudden wave of US protectionism.' One may also wonder whether, without NAFTA, there would have been the large-scale rescue plan that was set up mainly by the US in collaboration with the IMF to cope with the peso crisis at the end of 1994. Mexico's economy still experienced a very severe recession during 1995, but before the end of that year, recovery was underway and growth resumed in 1996. At the beginning of 1997, Mexico arranged early repayment of most of the rescue loans. The rescue plan provided access to liquidity (not free assistance) to avert a serious depression in Mexico. Such a depression would very probably have led to a slowdown of economic activity in California and Texas and a rise in illegal immigration into the US. It might well have spread to other developing countries in the region (De Long *et al.* 1996). The rescue package allowed Mexico to sustain its policy reforms in the areas of trade, investment and monetary management. According to Whalley (1996), the locking-in motive was important for Mexico to join NAFTA. He considers that increasing the credibility of domestic reforms was a key part of the Mexican negotiation strategy. Pursuit of this objective explains why the concessions within NAFTA were asymmetric in favour of the US.

North–South integration may also involve risks and disadvantages for developing countries. Northern economies tend to be more open and less protected than those in the South. Dismantling tariff barriers to create a free trade area implies much larger reductions and thus adjustment costs in the South than in the North. It should be added that the potential efficiency gains will also be larger in the South, but it will take time before these are realized. Fiscal adjustment often has to be substantial in the South to replace declining tariff revenue.

Bhagwati and Panagariya (1996) argue that developing countries may incur important *tariff redistribution losses* as a result of North–South integration.[8] They consider this a very serious risk for developing countries engaging in integration with 'hegemonic' partners in the North and recommend relying instead on multilateral trade liberalization. A lot depends on how efficient the northern anchor economy is. Bhagwati and Panagariya also refer to the example of Mexico *vis-à-vis* the United States. For them, it cannot be assumed that the US is the most efficient producer for many industrial products, otherwise there would not have been an increase in US anti-dumping measures. If Mexico lowers its tariffs for such products only towards its NAFTA partners, domestic prices will continue to be determined by the prices of the most efficient producer in the rest of the world plus the tariff. Assuming that Mexico imports both from NAFTA and the rest of the world, American and Canadian exporters may capture the tariff revenue at the expense of the Mexican treasury. This applies even if their market share is unchanged, and more so if their market share increases, as can be expected. However, there is a counter-argument. Mexico is not obliged to simply forgo cheap imports from the rest of the world to the extent that it can still reduce its tariffs unilaterally – because NAFTA is a Free Trade Area and not a Customs Union. The argument of tariff revenue redistribution in favour of the North applies more in the case of a Customs Union. Most of the contemplated North–South arrangements are, in fact, Free Trade Areas. It should be added that a large anchor economy is likely to be an efficient producer of a wide range of products anyhow. In that case, the decline in tariff revenue will be offset by an increase in consumer welfare for the partner in the South.

A potential disadvantage of reciprocal North–South arrangements is the restrictions they imply on the autonomous use of policy instruments in trade-related areas (for example, intellectual property, sanitary and phytosanitary measures, investment regulations). The smaller country generally has to accept the regulations of the larger country. Helleiner

(1996) considers the loss of policy autonomy as a serious risk for small countries. In a non-reciprocal arrangement, developing countries retain almost full freedom to use trade policy instruments, for example infant industry protection. WTO membership implies a number of restrictions, but these are softened through special and differential treatment. However, there is another side to this argument. Many economists, referring to past experience in a lot of developing countries, would consider that freedom in trade policy has often not been used wisely, leading to growth-reducing political decisions. Harmonizing trade policy with a partner in the North generally helps to prevent trade policy failures (for example unsustainable subsidies) and makes it easier for the government to focus on fundamental issues such as education, health, basic infrastructure, the legal system and security. A small country can save resources by adopting the regulations of large countries (for example, industrial standards), rather than developing its own.

Reciprocal arrangements must be negotiated, unlike non-reciprocal ones such as GSP.[9] In a negotiation, the parties are expected in the first place to pursue their own interests. This will put small developing countries at a great disadvantage, which underlines the need for building adequate negotiating capacity in the South. This capacity is required anyhow if developing countries are genuinely to take part in the WTO machinery. Capacity-building for small economies can be more (cost-) effective if they work together in a South–South integration arrangement.

North–South integration, probably more than other forms of economic integration, may lead to what has been called a *hub-and-spoke system*. This results when a dominant economy enters into agreements with several other smaller trading partners, that do not establish an agreement among themselves. The likely effects of hub-and-spoke systems have been studied by Wonnacott (1996). The spoke economies face a disadvantage, especially in terms of attractiveness as investment locations. Firms will have an incentive to locate in the hub, which provides easy access to all the spokes. The spoke economies have the option to integrate among themselves and diminish the hub-and-spoke effect, but this may not be easy over a short period. For a single-spoke economy, a deal with the hub will be more attractive than an arrangement with one or more of the other spokes. Wonnacott (1996) argues that even for the hub, the hub-and-spoke system may not be advantageous because it implies various costs that reduce efficiency. A particular complication for companies, even in the hub, is the need for the verification of import origin. A hub-and-spoke system would result in the case where NAFTA makes separate deals with other Latin American and Caribbean economies. The EU already constitutes a hub, with an increasing number of spokes such as the Central and East European economies. The North African economies, South Africa and possibly

MERCOSUR could also become spokes of the EU. The disadvantages of becoming a spoke economy of a northern hub is an important stimulus for economic integration among 'spoke' countries prior to North–South integration.

Small economies and the FTAA

The idea of establishing a Free Trade Area of the Americas (FTAA) was launched by President Clinton at the first Summit of the Americas in Miami in December 1994.[10] Of the 35 independent nations in the Americas, only Cuba does not participate in the discussions. A democratic system is a condition for participation. The main objective is to reach agreement no later than in the year 2005 on establishing a Free Trade Area in the Americas. Background work has been carried out by the Inter-American Development Bank (IDB), the Organization of American States (OAS) and the United Nations Economic Commission for Latin America and the Caribbean (ECLAC). The groundwork for the actual negotiations is prepared in a system of working groups. The Trade Ministers' meeting in June 1995 in Denver established seven working groups including one to deal with the specific problems of smaller economies. The other working groups cover: market access; customs procedures and rules of origin; investment; standards and technical barriers to trade; sanitary and phytosanitary measures; and subsidies, anti-dumping and countervailing duties. Four additional working groups were established at the Cartagena Trade Ministers' meeting in March 1996: government procurement; intellectual property; competition policy; and trade in services. The third meeting of Trade Ministers in Belo Horizonte in May 1997 created a twelfth working group on dispute settlement.

It should be underlined that, even though the establishment of free trade is the key objective of the FTAA, it is the intention to move significantly beyond a textbook Free Trade Area concept by including subjects such as: standardization, competition, services, intellectual property, subsidies, government procurement, anti-dumping and dispute settlement.

The likely process for achieving the FTAA is not yet clear. Several alternative paths have been suggested. Three frequently mentioned ones are the gradual widening of NAFTA, convergence of the principal sub-regional trading groups and hemispheric negotiations. The gradual enlargement of NAFTA may no longer be credible, because, more than five years after its creation, no new member has been admitted. Convergence of the regional trading groups is politically attractive for most of the Latin American and Caribbean economies, especially the smaller ones. The existing regional trading groups would then become the building blocks of the FTAA. The five main regional groups are NAFTA, CARICOM,

CACM, the Andean Community and MERCOSUR. Only three countries are not (yet) full members of any of these groups: Chile, the Dominican Republic and Panama. However, Chile made an agreement with MERCOSUR, while the Dominican Republic and Panama collaborate with CACM. The Dominican Republic is also negotiating with CARICOM. A variant to this path would be the gradual widening of both NAFTA and MERCOSUR and later on, as Bernal (1995) calls it, a bi-polar amalgamation. The agreements of Chile and Bolivia with MERCOSUR in 1996 go in that direction. Brazil is likely to favour such an approach, which would first enlarge MERCOSUR into a South American Free Trade Area (SAFTA). The third path of hemispheric negotiations should lead to an overall agreement to which all the individual countries can subscribe when they are ready and willing. Such negotiations would be comparable to a hemispheric Uruguay Round, except that undertakings in the various trade policy domains would go much further.

What about the smaller countries in the FTAA process? There is no single agreed criterion to define small economies in this context. In terms of population, 23 of the 34 participating states can be considered as small with a population under 10 million. In terms of economic size, the criterion introduced in Chapter 1, there are 21 small economies with a GNP of less than US$ 10 billion. The group of 23 countries with a population under 10 million comprises all member states of CARICOM and CACM except Guatemala, as well as Bolivia, the Dominican Republic, Panama, Paraguay and Uruguay. The group with GDP less than US$ 10 billion is the same, but without the Dominican Republic and Uruguay. The Trade Unit of the OAS (1996a) carried out a study on the characteristics of 'small and relatively less developed economies' which could affect the process of hemispheric integration. The main findings of this study are:

- there is no direct correlation between different size indicators (population, land area or national income) and indicators of level of development (income per capita, economic diversity or human development index);
- small and relatively less developed economies are particularly vulnerable to external fluctuations in output and demand, because of the limited size of their domestic markets, high dependence on international trade, non-diversified economic structures, narrow tax base and high costs of infrastructure and public administration.

Another study of the Trade Unit of the OAS (1996b) analyses measures to facilitate the participation of smaller economies in the FTAA. The reasoning takes into account that the FTAA will represent a 'single undertaking of mutual rights and obligations' rather than an *à la carte* menu. All adherents should agree to the full negotiated text. In other words, smaller economies cannot assume less demanding obligations.

The study recommends that smaller countries should be allowed longer periods for implementing obligations and greater flexibility in the implementation of agreements and procedures. Moreover, they should be provided assistance aimed at capacity-building to help them meet their commitments. This approach is in line with the thinking described in Chapter 2 on moving away from a two-tiered trading system (a preferential tier with limited obligations for developing countries and another tier with full obligations for industrial countries).[11] The OAS study recommends some further options for helping smaller economies. The rules of origin should certainly foresee regional cumulation among smaller economies. Smaller economies should be provided with technical assistance to help them deal with issues such as subsidies, anti-dumping and countervailing measures, and intellectual property rights. There should also be help for small economies on the design and implementation of national legislation on competition, and on the establishment of national standardizing bodies and participation in international standardizing bodies. In the area of sanitary and phytosanitary measures, the suggested modalities include allowing longer time frames for compliance, time-limited exceptions and technical assistance.

The second Summit of the Americas, which took place in Santiago, Chile in April 1998, established the framework of commencing negotiations. The summit also endorsed a number of principles that had been agreed one month earlier at a trade-ministerial meeting in San José, Costa Rica. These principles can be summarized as follows:

• decisions in the negotiating process will be made by consensus;
• the agreement will be consistent with the rules of the WTO, in particular with article XXIV of the GATT and article V of the GATS;
• the FTAA should improve upon WTO disciplines wherever possible and appropriate;
• the agreement will constitute a single undertaking of mutually agreed rights and obligations;
• countries may negotiate and accept the obligations of the FTAA individually or as members of a sub-regional integration group negotiating as a unit;
• special attention shall be given to the needs, economic conditions and opportunities of smaller economies, to ensure their full participation;
• technical assistance in specific areas and longer periods for implementing the obligations could be included on a case by case basis, in order to facilitate the adjustment of smaller economies.

It is interesting to see that the recommendations outlined above on taking into account the special characteristics of smaller economies are well reflected in these principles. It is particularly relevant that countries can negotiate as a sub-regional group. This can be seen as a political achievement for the smaller countries. Nevertheless, just as the readiness of individual countries cannot be taken for granted, the same applies to the sub-regional groups. The secretariats of the sub-regional groups will have a difficult task. Not only will they have to negotiate the FTAA, but they must also achieve consensus among their member states. They should be given help to carry out this double negotiation. But it can still be argued that assistance at the level of sub-regional groups will be more cost-effective than at the level of individual countries.

More generally, variable geometry and variable speed are recognized aspects of the FTAA process.[12] This is not only relevant for smaller economies, but also, for example, for Argentina and Brazil as members of MERCOSUR. The Ministerial Declaration of San José states: 'The FTAA can co-exist with bilateral and sub-regional agreements, to the extent that the rights and obligations under these agreements are not covered or go beyond the rights and obligations of the FTAA.'

It is also important to mention that the FTAA process is not just about economic integration. It is also a forum to discuss and exert peer pressure in relation to the whole array of new interdependence problems. In addition to trade, the plan of action adopted at the second summit comprises a wide variety of themes such as education, democracy and human rights, migration, corruption, drug-trafficking, terrorism, security, the justice system and regional infrastructure. This clearly reflects the (northern) motive of coping with the new interdependence problems.

The FTAA process will require some difficult choices on the part of the smaller economies, especially those that have a preferential trade arrangement with the EU. The Caribbean states that are members of the ACP group enjoy extensive trade privileges on the EU market (see Chapter 5). The current rules of the Lomé Convention cannot be reconciled with the FTAA or for that matter with membership of NAFTA. There is a requirement that ACP trade provisions *vis-à-vis* the EU should be *no less* favourable than those applied to any other industrial country (including the US). Participation in the FTAA would thus require free trade with the EU as well. In order to deal with this situation, Bernal (1995) suggests the possibility of associate membership. Smaller economies that are not yet ready for full FTAA membership or that are committed to trade arrangements with groups outside the hemisphere could opt for associate membership and keep their other privileges. This could be an attractive alternative for CARICOM member states. It might also be worthwhile for other small economies in Central America.

The EU and the ACP countries: ready for reciprocity?

The ACP group, comprising sub-Saharan Africa, the Caribbean and the Pacific consists almost wholly of small developing economies.[13] The trade relations between the EU and the ACP group are determined by the Lomé Convention (see Chapter 5). As mentioned above the predecessor arrangement until 1975, the Yaoundé Convention was, in principle, a reciprocal agreement. For some time there have been discussions about modifying the Lomé trade regime again in the direction of more reciprocity. The most frequently mentioned reasons are the widely perceived lack of success of the non-reciprocal regime in terms of trade performance of the beneficiary states and the criticism that it does not fully respect the requirements of the WTO.[14] Most of the discussions refer to the African countries. The situation in the Caribbean and the Pacific is significantly different.

Sub-Saharan Africa

Collier and Gunning (1995) make a strong plea for reciprocal arrangements between African groupings and the European Union. They do not consider the classic trade-creation effects to be very important for Africa. However, they provide five other arguments why, in their view, an African grouping tied to the EU market would dominate unilateral liberalization:

> it would achieve as much as Africa can expect to gain from global liberalization; it would establish credibility of trade reform; it would serve a defensive purpose, avoiding that Africa would be left out in a world of trade blocs with GATT rules insufficiently enforced; it might be politically easier to achieve than unilateral reform; and, finally, it might facilitate the adoption of useful institutions by the regional union (p. 400).

Several of these arguments echo the above discussion on the motives of developing countries for North–South integration.

Rather than having a large number of bilateral arrangements between the EU and countries in sub-Saharan Africa, which they consider impractical, Collier and Gunning recommend arrangements between the EU and viable African integration groupings. Agreements between the EU and groups of countries would also diminish the negative hub-and-spoke effects mentioned above. The monetary arrangements between the African countries of the CFA zone and France provide a prototype of this kind of North–South arrangement. Collier and Gunning do not say much about the type of arrangement and refer to CUs and FTAs more or less interchangeably. However, there are reasons for North–South integration to be limited to an FTA rather than a CU. A CU would imply that the Southern partner group gives up its own trade policy towards the rest of the world. This would put severe constraints on the trade policy of the South.

Oyejide (1996), reporting on a large-scale research programme on regional integration and trade liberalization in sub-Saharan Africa, considers three ways for African countries to find an effective 'agency of restraint' to ensure credibility and sustainability of trade reform. The first is an African regional organization. Oyejide, however, finds it unlikely that an African regional integration scheme can serve as an effective agency of restraint. A more viable option for him would be to use the World Trade Organization. However, as mentioned in Chapter 2, African countries have made few efforts to establish effective tariff bindings. But the opportunity continues to exist and is worth pursuing through more active participation of the African countries in the WTO. The third option for Oyejide is North–South integration between African groupings and the EU. For this option, he recommends a careful examination of its viability. Such an arrangement even risks being considered as a kind of re-colonization. It might also impose an excessively high adjustment cost on the African countries. In the light of the discussion in the preceding chapters, the first and second options suggested by Oyejide are not really alternatives, but are fully complementary. The best chances for the success of African regional integration schemes are when they can be implemented in the context of the WTO provisions on regional groupings.

Caribbean and Pacific

In comparison to Africa, the main difference affecting the possibility of North–South integration between the EU and the Caribbean or Pacific countries is the lesser importance of trade with the EU. The EU's share of the Caribbean and Pacific total imports is only around 18 and 5 per cent respectively. Meanwhile the EU is the destination for 24 and 19 per cent respectively of Caribbean and Pacific ACP exports. The latter figures are higher because of the preferential trade regime. Hence in both sub-regions, the EU is a significant trading partner, but it is far from dominant as is the case for Africa. Almost half of African imports originate in the EU and a comparable share of exports is destined for the EU. In the Caribbean and Pacific, the relatively low share of imports from the EU increases the likelihood that tariff reductions could benefit EU exporters rather than local businesses.

There are other problems as well. The Caribbean countries continue to benefit from the Caribbean Basin Initiative, but these advantages require that no competitor of the US receives a better import regime. This requirement mirrors a similar provision in the Lomé Convention mentioned already in the discussion of the FTAA. For the Caribbean ACP countries, especially for the Dominican Republic, the US is the dominant trading partner. The situation is comparable in the Pacific. Even though trade with the Asian economies is rising, Australia and

New Zealand remain the main trading partners. It is unlikely that the latter countries would accept improved access for EU goods with no comparable benefits for their own products.

The future of the Lomé trade regime

The fourth Lomé Convention will end in the year 2000. In 1996, the European Commission launched a broad debate on the future of the Lomé system by publishing a 'Green Paper on the Relations between the EU and the ACP Countries on the Eve of the 21st Century'. The paper covers trade and development cooperation as well as political aspects.[15] Only the trade aspects are dealt with here. The Green Paper presented four main options:

1. *status quo*, i.e. continuation of non-reciprocal preferences;
2. integration of Lomé preferences into the Generalized System of Preferences (GSP);
3. uniform reciprocity and
4. differentiated reciprocity.

Options 1 and 2 fall under the heading of preferential arrangements (the subject of Chapter 5). There are two main differences between these options. With option 2, countries that are *not* least-developed (31 ACP states) would experience a significant deterioration in their access to the EU market. Their access will be made equivalent to the GSP, which brings them into the same league as emerging economies such as Chile and Malaysia. The margin of preference between the standard MFN and the GSP regime is smaller than the difference between GSP and Lomé. For the 39 least-developed ACP states, there is no difference between options 1 and 2, because the EU decided in 1997 to extend the equivalent of the Lomé trade regime to all the LDCs. The other main difference is that the second option would be automatically compatible with the provisions of the WTO, while the first option would require an extension of the WTO waiver that is currently applicable to the Lomé trade regime. This is considered to be difficult because, according to Article IX of the WTO agreement, the Ministerial Conference may decide to waive an obligation only in exceptional circumstances. This requires backing of a three-fourths majority of the members. Moreover, a waiver granted for a period of more than one year must be reviewed annually until it terminates. The EU and ACP states together represent more than half of the WTO members, but less than the three-fourths needed for a waiver.[16] Other WTO members would have to support it. But, even if a waiver were to be obtained, the annual review process would diminish the security of the arrangement for traders and investors.

Options 3 and 4 can be considered as forms of North–South integration. They are comparable to the FTAA, except that in the FTAA, there are several large developing economies (for example Argentina, Brazil,

Colombia and Mexico), which is not the case in the ACP group, with the exceptions of Nigeria and South Africa. Another difference is that the FTAA countries constitute a geographical bloc while the EU–ACP state parties are much more dispersed. Option 3, uniform reciprocity, would require that all ACP countries, in line with WTO rules and after a common transition period, remove tariffs on EU exports. Option 4, differentiated reciprocity, would be a system of separate trade arrangements between the EU and regional groupings of ACP countries or individual ACP states.

There has been extensive debate on the trade regime options of the Green Paper.[17] Discussions have focused on the North–South options, which would represent a fundamental reorientation. Options 1, 2 and 3 are all considered problematic. For the first option, a WTO waiver needs to be obtained, which must be reviewed every year. The second option is very unattractive for the non-LDC countries, which would lose substantial advantages in comparison to large emerging economies. The third option of uniform reciprocity with all the ACP countries in conformity with WTO rules is unrealistic because of the large differences between ACP countries. The reactions to the Green Paper on the ACP side have generally been in favour of maintaining the *status quo* as much and as long as possible.

Taking into account the discussions on the Green Paper, the EU adopted a negotiating mandate in June 1998. The mandate is largely based on option 4 of differentiated reciprocity, but contains elements of the other options as well. The mandate can be summarized as follows. It proposes the preparation and negotiation of a *framework agreement* to which all the ACP states should subscribe, preferably by the year 2000. This agreement would set a number of parameters for the negotiation of a series of *regional economic partnership agreements* (REPAs) between the EU and sub-groups of ACP states that are ready and willing to do so. During the negotiation period, estimated to be from the year 2000 to 2005, the present Lomé trade regime would continue. Hence, a WTO waiver is needed for that period. The REPAs would be set up as FTAs within the meaning of Article XXIV of GATT. In principle, services will also be covered in conformity with Article V of GATS. Implementation of these FTAs would begin from 2005 onwards. Implementation can be asymmetric, taking place over a longer period on the ACP side and excluding more of their sensitive products.[18] It should be stressed that there would be no transition period on the EU side, because the present trade regime would continue as it is. In fact, some additional liberalization of agricultural imports is envisaged. It is suggested that the REPAs could be subsequently extended, harmonized and merged in the light of further integration of the ACP countries into the world economy.

For countries that are not in a position to join a REPA, a distinction must be made between least-developed and other developing countries. Least-developed countries can opt for the *status quo*. This is in conformity with WTO rules, because *all* least-developed countries, whether or not part of the ACP group, will have the same regime. The other countries might conclude an FTA on their own with the EU. Alternatively, these countries would end up with option 2 of the Green Paper; this is integration into the GSP.[19] A bilateral FTA is only considered realistic with a few relatively large ACP countries (for example, Nigeria).

Implementation of the framework agreement and the regional partnerships would be combined with increased EU support for the adjustment efforts at national level on the ACP side. Fiscal adjustment would be necessary to compensate for the reduction in tariff revenue. Industrial restructuring might also be required. In addition, EU support for regional integration efforts in the ACP groupings will be stepped up. This would involve capacity-building in the increasingly important trade-related areas (for example, intellectual property, standardization, competition policy and investment security).

Initial reactions on the ACP side have demonstrated only limited readiness and willingness to move towards REPAs. The idea raises a lot of controversy. What are the main arguments for and against REPAs? The general positive argument is that the REPAs will foster integration of the ACP countries into the world economy. They liberalize the economy towards a key trade and economic partner, which should raise efficiency. Technical progress will be stimulated. Another favourable argument is the boost for regional integration among the ACP countries. As mentioned earlier, virtually all ACP countries are small and very small economies. Their long-run economic viability without progressive regional integration is doubtful. Regional integration could strengthen their competitiveness, increase their bargaining power, save resources and make them a better investment location. Another point is that REPAs are probably the only way for the more advanced ACP countries to keep their preferential margin on the EU market *vis-à-vis* many emerging economies.[20]

But there are also arguments against the REPAs. For the ACP countries, the most important is the need to accord preferences to the EU and hence discriminate against imports from other industrial and emerging economies. The possible effects of this could be trade diversion and loss of tariff revenue. Moreover, for a REPA to work, ACP countries will have to check the origin of imports, which amounts to a new administrative burden. The REPAs will also lead to adjustment problems for the private sector and the government. A practical argument against REPAs is the lack of progress towards regional integration within ACP sub-groups. REPAs are only justified if there is adequate progress towards regional integration. Preferably they should reach the stage of a Customs

Union like the EU itself. If the ACP integration grouping constitutes only a Free Trade Area, bilateral agreements will have to be negotiated between the EU and all individual ACP members. This is clearly a complicated process.

It is important to mention that the arguments against the REPAs between the EU and ACP sub-groups also apply to the participation of the countries that benefit from the Caribbean Basin Initiative in the FTAA.

An issue that emerged from the initial discussions on the REPA proposal is the divergence of interest of the least-developed and the other ACP countries. Virtually all the ACP sub-groupings that could consider REPAs contain both types of countries (for example, CARICOM, UEMOA, SADC, EAC, COMESA, Pacific ACP states). And both types face a difficult choice about whether or not to participate in a REPA. The least-developed countries have the option of not taking part and still keeping the same access to the EU market. However, if they do opt out, the integration process within their ACP sub-group is damaged. But if they decide to take part in the REPA they are bound to face adjustment problems. As regards the non-least developed states, if they do not join a REPA they lose preferential access to the EU market. On the other hand, if they join a REPA, they will (gradually) have to compete with EU products in their 'own' regional market. A divergence of interest could apply, for example, in the EAC (Kenya versus Tanzania and Uganda) or in UEMOA (Côte d'Ivoire and Senegal versus Mali and Burkina Faso).

During 1998 the European Commission organized a number of studies on the likely effects of REPAs for some groupings of ACP countries. The following groupings were included: UEMOA, CEMAC, EAC, SADC, CARICOM and the Pacific ACP states. The UEMOA study also dealt with Ghana, and the CARICOM study covered the Dominican Republic. It was made clear that the selection of the groupings studied did not imply any view of the EU about which groupings would be the most plausible candidates for REPAs. It is up to the ACP countries and groupings to indicate, in due time, whether or not they wish to move towards REPAs. McQueen (1999) presents a brief summary of the six studies. The quantitative results are influenced by the assumptions that had to be made and by the incompleteness of the data. Two assumptions strongly affect the results: the degree of substitutability between EU and third-country products and the relation between theoretical and actual tariff revenue. On the whole, the quantitative results demonstrate relatively small welfare gains. But in many cases there are sizeable downward effects on government tariff revenue. The least-developed countries have not much to gain because they can continue benefiting from non-reciprocal preferences anyhow. For many other countries the effects are dominated by what will happen to the special commodity protocols (bananas, sugar, rum and beef). The qualitative results on the dynamic and non-traditional effects are considered to be positive for the REPAs, even though there is no standard methodology for their assessment. The REPAs are expected to improve the macroeconomic policy environment and the investment climate. Several studies pointed to the limited negotiation capacity of the ACP groupings and the lack of progress with their own integration. If REPAs would be implemented, they recommend a long transition period.

It may be useful to illustrate the issue further by considering the situation in Southern Africa. With the accession of South Africa, SADC has become the largest economic integration grouping in terms of GDP in sub-Saharan Africa. Within SADC, there is a sub-group: the Southern African Customs Union (SACU), comprising South Africa, Botswana, Lesotho, Namibia and Swaziland. In 1995, South Africa began negotiations on establishing a Free Trade Area with the EU. The negotiations were concluded at the beginning of 1999 and implementation is expected to start in the year 2000. Both the EU and South Africa indicated all along that their planned arrangement must be fully consistent with economic integration at the Southern African level. An FTA between the EU and South Africa *not* involving the rest of SADC makes it more difficult for the latter to compete on the South African market. This would also increase the attractiveness of South Africa as an investment location in comparison to the rest of SADC. A European investor could buy EU inputs and spare parts without customs duty only in South Africa. A wider FTA between the EU and SADC would diminish that effect, but would lead to significant (short-run) adjustment costs for the SADC economies. Fiscal adjustment would be necessary to compensate for the reduction in tariff revenue. Industrial restructuring, with its associated costs in terms of frictional unemployment, would also be required. But restructuring is needed in order to capture the benefits from trade-creation. SADC countries outside South Africa would not gain in market access to the EU, in contrast to South Africa itself. The EU has indicated its readiness to support the adjustment process in the Southern African countries resulting from the changes in the EU trade regime. Potentially the most important gain of the EU–South Africa Free Trade Area for the rest of Southern Africa, although an uncertain one, would come from a higher growth rate in South Africa. Higher growth could result from improvements in the investment climate and political stability. More growth in South Africa would increase imports from the rest of the region, which are presently at a low level.

North–South integration and small developing economies

Following the general discussion on the motivations of North–South integration and an examination of the FTAA process and the future of the Lomé Convention, it is useful to assess North–South integration more explicitly as a strategy for small developing economies. There are certainly potential benefits, but there are also important risks.

What would be the expected benefits of North–South economic integration? *A priori*, because the divergences in factor endowments and income between the North and the South are generally larger than within the South, the traditional static and dynamic effects should be more important for North–South integration than for South–South integration. However, most small developing countries have already obtained preferential access to the North. Integration with the North will hardly improve their market access. Sensitive products that are partly excluded from the current non-reciprocal arrangements (clothing and agriculture) would probably still be restricted with reciprocal arrangements.[21] For small economies, unilateral liberalization towards the North provides them with most of the potential gains from North–South integration, with the advantage that they can determine freely the pace of their own liberalization. It is also an advantage for small developing countries when they do not have to discriminate between trading partners in the North or emerging economies. This avoids trade diversion and tariff revenue losses. It also avoids setting up the administrative machinery to determine the origin of imports. As long as the North does not *reverse* its current level of preferential access, the traditional gains from integration are not a strong motive for small developing countries to demand integration with the North.

What about the insurance motive for North–South integration? In contrast to large developing countries, especially the newly industrialized ones, contingent protection towards small developing countries has not been an important limitation. The problem of increased market penetration of small developing economies in the North is not so much a problem of new forms of protection, but rather of the possibility to produce at a competitive price and quality and to set up an adequate marketing chain. The insurance or 'safe haven' motive to avoid contingent protection is not particularly strong for small developing countries. However, there is another aspect of insurance that is relevant for small developing countries: this is, to prevent a reversal of current preferential arrangements. As described above, such a reversal is certainly possible for the non-least-developed ACP countries that do not join an FTA with the EU. The participation of Mexico in NAFTA does not imply a reversal of US trade concessions, but it still undermines the advantages of the Caribbean Basin Initiative. If other large countries were to join NAFTA, this effect would increase and the smaller economies would again suffer. If joining a North–South scheme is the only way for small developing economies to be sure to avoid reversal, it may be a valid motive. But it could be questioned whether it is good development policy on the part of the North to encourage small developing countries to join an integration arrangement with the North under the threat of policy reversal.

The other main argument for North–South integration is the locking-in of sound economic policies. The locking-in effect depends on the credibility of the threat of sanctions in the event of non-respect of policy obligations. Two questions arise here. Is the developing country likely to maintain sound policies because of the threat of sanctions and is the Northern country actually prepared to apply sanctions? If the answer to both questions is yes, then North–South integration has good prospects of success. In practice, the answer may be positive only in some cases. Moreover, the effectiveness of sanctions should not be overestimated. Probably more important is the signalling effect. Foreign investors need the right kind of information on which to base their decisions. In the case of small developing economies, it may be hard to obtain relevant information. Participation in a North–South integration scheme could be a powerful signal. It would make it easier to access information about such economies and would increase confidence in them. This would most strongly apply to investors from the Northern partner.

The assessment of the benefits of North–South integration so far assumes that this integration will only be shallow, basically taking the form of an FTA, albeit with some important added elements in services and trade-related areas. This is the agenda of the FTAA and the planned partnerships between the EU and sub-groups of ACP states. It can be argued that becoming part of a *shallow integration* arrangement with the North is indeed risky, because transition or adjustment costs are likely to be sizeable. The profitability of companies may be affected. In small economies, social stability can depend on the success of a single company. There will also be a need for large fiscal adjustment because of dependence on customs revenue.[22] A lot will depend on the length of the transition period. If the Northern partner provides substantial assistance to cope with the adjustment and transition costs, integration is likely to be a beneficial strategy. Adjustment assistance from the North is more likely to be sizeable with *deep integration* than with the shallow variety. But deep North–South integration will tend to be exceptional, because of its political implications.

There is another aspect that should be taken into account. North–South integration with individual small developing economies is not very likely. From the Northern perspective, integration with a cohesive regional grouping of small economies in the South is more attractive than with small developing countries separately. This is in fact the position of the EU in relation to the future of the Lomé trade regime. At the same time, the countries in the South have an interest in negotiating as a group in order to have more bargaining power and to benefit from the pooling of resources. But integration among developing countries needs to be sufficiently advanced for North–South integration to have a good chance of success.

Integration in the South is not likely to accelerate much in the near future because of the inherent difficulties (see Chapter 4). This could be problematic for the EU's intention to negotiate FTAs with groupings of ACP countries, because these may not yet be sufficiently advanced towards their own integration. Small economies that are not least-developed and not members of an integration grouping might see their preferential access to the EU market reversed. However, many such economies still face the problem of high vulnerability. It would not be fair to penalize these countries for the lack of progress towards South–South integration, which is a slow process that depends on many partners. If the continuation of Lomé type of preferences is uncertain, because of the need for a WTO waiver, a possibility could be to introduce economic size as an explicit criterion of differentiation in the GSP. This would still require an agreement at the WTO level. But a reasonable case can be made. Based on objective criteria, small economies could be given a regime that in some respects would be comparable to that of the least-developed countries. In this way, small economies would keep an edge over the (large) emerging economies. Regional integration between least developed and other small economies would be stimulated. Such a differentiation would not be a disadvantage for the least-developed countries, because the export capacity of small economies will anyhow remain limited.

In conclusion, the benefits of shallow North–South integration for small developing economies on their own are limited. Such integration can be beneficial for small developing countries if the Northern partner is prepared to engage in deep integration and provide sizeable assistance to cope with transitional costs. This situation will only arise in a limited number of cases. In other cases, individual small developing countries, which become part of a reciprocal arrangement with the North, will face the risk of a difficult adjustment. The prospects for North–South integration are much better if small developing countries first achieve regional economic integration among themselves. Regional groups are also more attractive partners given the North's own political objectives. The macroeconomic transition costs are likely to be smaller, hub-and-spoke effects are diminished and there will be less risk of polarization. Regional integration is a way to diminish vulnerability. However, it will take time before regional integration of small developing countries is sufficiently advanced to engage in reciprocal North–South integration. In the meantime, it would be fair to recognize the vulnerability of small developing economies in general, not only when they are also least developed, and maintain their access to the markets in the North. For the United States, this would mean agreeing to NAFTA parity for the Caribbean countries, before the FTAA negotiations are concluded. For the European Union, it would imply maintaining preferential access for the ACP countries that are not least-developed.

7
Summary and Conclusions

By integrating into the world economy, developing countries can take advantage of the current globalization trend. Participation in the world economy calls for openness; in other words, barriers to international trade, investment and payments should be reduced. There is overwhelming evidence that lack of openness or autarky prevents the achievement of optimal results. However, there are different strategies towards openness. And there are risks as well as opportunities. Small developing economies face extra problems because of their lack of economic diversification and vulnerability. Opening up the economy will lead to adjustment costs that can be very high and socially disruptive. How should openness best be achieved in the case of small developing countries? Should they move towards openness in a unilateral way or in a regionally coordinated way? How should regional partners be selected? What is the contribution of non-reciprocal preferences granted by the North? Are they still worth the trouble? Should there be more attention for reciprocal North–South arrangements? This chapter suggests some answers to these questions.

Subscribing to the benefits of the multilateral trading system

Membership of the World Trade Organization (WTO) and the International Monetary Fund (IMF) are among the logical first steps towards openness and integration into the world economy. IMF membership should go beyond the minimum requirement and comprise current account convertibility and also *some* liberalization of capital movements. The key purpose of IMF membership is to participate in an orderly exchange and payments arrangement. The IMF helps countries to maintain a stable monetary system. It also carries out regular macroeconomic surveillance under its Article IV. To help assist countries cope with balance-of-payments problems, the IMF can provide short-term loans that are

openness and integration into the world economy, there are limitations. From a political economy perspective unilateral trade liberalization is difficult to implement. Unilateral trade liberalization does not increase market access in any direct way. Companies will not lobby to reduce tariffs on import-competing goods that they produce. The new companies that will become profitable in the liberalized economic environment cannot *yet* lobby because they must still grow. Governments in small developing economies will have difficulties making unilateral trade liberalization credible. There is always a temptation to reverse policies if an industry is hurt and no alternative is in place. Unilateral liberalization can be time-inconsistent. In practice, despite the sanctioning of structural adjustment programmes, unilateral liberalization in small developing countries has often been reversed. Because of these limitations, it is worthwhile to see whether regional arrangements can make a contribution.

South–South regionalism when preconditions are fulfilled

In a context where certain basic political preconditions (peace, stability, prevalence of the rule of law, accountability and transparency of governance) are fulfilled and where a sound macroeconomic framework is in place, small developing countries should explore the possibilities for using regional arrangements to facilitate their integration into the world economy. This does not mean that there should be a rapid multiplication of regional arrangements. The analysis in Chapter 4 demonstrated that the potential for successful regionalism is limited. There are regional arrangements that will lead in the first place to non-economic benefits such as enhanced security. The non-economic benefits may influence the potential for economic benefits, at a later stage. This reasoning implies caution against setting up an apparatus to deal prematurely with economic integration. A better use of resources in such a situation would be to consolidate first the political and security aspects of regional arrangements and to address the economics when possible.

Small developing countries are advised to evaluate critically the costs and benefits of membership of regional organizations. A careful analysis is also needed to establish the appropriate level or 'depth' of integration. Shallow integration will usually precede deep integration. Many integration arrangements of developing countries have suffered from putting forward too quickly an agenda of deep integration that could not be realistically implemented and that led to waste of resources and frustration.

Regional integration should not be conceived as a form of collective autarky, but rather as *a coordinated policy of openness of like-minded countries.*

Provided that small developing economies combine their integration with gradual multilateral liberalization, there should not be much fear about trade diversion. On the other hand, there is a risk of trade diversion losses when small economies integrate with large economies, whether or not they are developing countries, and when protection towards third countries is not reduced.

The main arguments for regional integration of small developing economies can be summarized as follows:

- increased bargaining power (even though a grouping of small developing economies will not create a large entity, any increase is welcome)
- cheaper provision of public goods such as social and physical infrastructure, but also non-tangible ones such as negotiation capacity in international forums;
- avoidance of distortions resulting from uncoordinated unilateral liberalization of neighbouring countries;
- efficiency gains in the regional market;
- more manageable adjustment process than with unilateral reforms;
- some themes can be handled regionally which cannot (yet) be covered multilaterally (for example investment regulations and competition policy);
- trade liberalization within the region can be faster than is required by the multilateral agreements.

Regional integration agreements are permitted in the multilateral system provided certain conditions are fulfilled. The most important requirements for Free Trade Areas and Customs Unions, set out in Article XXIV of the GATT are: *complete* elimination of tariff and non-tariff barriers on *substantially all trade* and protection towards third parties that is *not on the whole higher* than before. 'Substantially all trade' is often interpreted as representing at least 90 per cent. The Uruguay Round Understanding added that the transition period should exceed 10 years 'only in exceptional circumstances' and that the tariffs of Customs Unions that should 'not on the whole be higher' are the *applied* tariffs rather than the *bound* tariffs. It is also understood that no major sector should be left out from liberalization. For example, agriculture should not be excluded. Developing countries are not obliged to fulfil the conditions of Article XXIV, but can implement regional integration under the 'Enabling Clause'. However, regional integration under the Enabling Clause, because it lacks the disciplines of Article XXIV, may not provide a very strong signal towards investors. Developing countries that wish to make genuine progress on regional integration have an interest in accepting the obligations of Article XXIV.

In the past, the GATT was criticized for being very weak in enforcing the rules applicable to regional arrangements. It is the intention of the WTO to tighten the follow-up of such arrangements. In 1996, a Committee on Regional Trade Agreements was established for this purpose. The increased attention of the WTO for the endorsement of regional arrangements is to be welcomed. Clear guidelines should be established and agreed on matters such as sectoral coverage, protection towards third parties, public procurement and rules of origin. Groupings involving small developing countries should be able to rely on WTO assistance. Regional groupings should be allowed to represent their member states in the WTO on a wide range of themes. This would save resources and ensure a better representation of the interests of small developing countries.

The *level of integration* should reflect a careful analysis of potential problems and benefits. The decision to move from a Free Trade Area to a Customs Union is trickier than is often thought. In an FTA, unilateral trade policy towards the rest of the world is still possible, whereas it is excluded in a CU. The implementation of an FTA already requires considerable administrative capacity. For example, the verification of origin can lead to delays at the borders and increased possibilities for corruption. Documents need to be prepared and understood in different languages. Contrary to what is sometimes assumed, a CU still needs verification of origin for the purpose of collection of duties. Only a CU that also has pooling of customs duties does not need origin verification. For small developing countries, customs duties are typically a large share of government revenue, and an agreement to split the revenue from a common pool is bound to be politically very delicate.[3] Another point to be noted in comparing FTAs and CUs is that a country can be a member of different FTAs. Although overlapping membership of regional organizations is not desirable, it is at least possible. This is not the case however, for CUs or indeed, for any other form of integration that implies a *common* policy. Overlapping membership should not be confused with variable geometry, where a sub-group pursues deeper integration than the wider group. For example, some members of an FTA can form a CU, a Common Market or an Economic Union. When a large economy enters into FTAs with several smaller economies, we speak of a hub-and-spoke system (see Chapter 6). Such a system is not in the interest of the spoke countries.

It is not necessary for regional integration to proceed according to the textbook sequence FTA, CU, Common Market, Economic Union. Depending on the specific circumstances, topics should be addressed when there are anticipated benefits. For example, it may be beneficial to agree on mutual recognition of diplomas and on the free movement of professional staff, before there is a CU. It will often be useful to address some aspects of macroeconomic policy coordination at an early stage, even though, in the textbooks, these are considered to be topics for an Economic Union, the ultimate stage of regional integration. A minimum requirement would be exchange of economic information using compatible statistics and concepts. Gradually macroeconomic cooperation can be deepened to move towards harmonization. The lack of macroeconomic harmonization will become increasingly disturbing with progress towards full market integration. A system of joint macroeconomic surveillance can be helpful. Such a system can build on the multilateral surveillance that is already in place via the IMF and the WTO.

The success of regional integration arrangements will not only depend on economic conditions, but also very much on the *institutional design*. This is a subject that has been neglected in relation to developing countries. Appropriate institutions have simply been taken for granted. In the European context, there has been a lot of discussion and experimentation on institutional design. The European design is often misunderstood, and as such may not be applicable to other parts of the world, even though it constitutes a useful reference. In some cases, the European design has been wrongly copied, inviting failure from the beginning. The choice between an intergovernmental or supranational institutional design will have important implications. Experience demonstrates that *deep* integration will typically require supranationalism except perhaps in the case where there are very few partner countries. On the whole, developing countries will prefer intergovernmentalism.[4] This should be reflected in putting forward realistic goals. Countries that have a lot in common may be willing to accept some supranationalism as a way to pool their sovereignty in well-defined areas. Whatever approach is adopted, an effectively functioning regional body is indispensable for real progress towards integration.

Application of the principles of *variable geometry and variable speed* may help practical progress towards regional integration. Variable speed is a pragmatic principle that recognizes the fact that partners in a regional grouping may not always be *able* and *ready* to implement a certain provision at the same time. Rather than let the pace of integration be determined by the slowest member state, under variable speed some member states are allowed to move faster, while the others can catch up later. Whereas variable speed refers to time, variable geometry has a spatial connotation. Within a wider grouping, sub-groups may pursue deeper integration. Variable geometry is relevant in cases where a group of small developing countries are part of a wider regional integration initiative. An example is the Organization of Eastern Caribbean States (OECS) whose members are all also in CARICOM. The OECS constitutes a monetary union, a form of deep integration, whereas the CARICOM does not. In Southern Africa, there is the example of the Southern African Customs Union (SACU) completely within the wider SADC, which plans to become a Free Trade Area.

In assessing the prospects of beneficial regional integration, small developing economies should be careful with the *selection of partner countries*. Even though there is no blueprint, on the whole, the prospective partners should be 'like-minded' in economic policies and have a comparable political and legal system. Progress will be easier between countries of comparable economic size and development and with a common history. Large disparities in the development level can make things difficult, partly because of the demand for *compensation* of the weaker partners. The compensation issue has the tendency to derail integration initiatives, sometimes even before they get properly started, so that there are no gains. Compensation should not receive excessive attention during the early stages of integration. In the European context, compensation through regional and cohesion funds only came after more than twenty years of successful cooperation practice and it became really sizeable another ten years later following the accession of Portugal and Spain. In the context of South–South integration, it is better to refrain from direct budgetary compensation during the early stages. It is still advisable to take account of differences in industrialization through asymmetric transition arrangements and exclusion of sensitive products. However, exclusions need to be limited and their phasing-out should be planned from the start in order not to undo the integration effects. Successful integration into the regional and world economy will, by itself, bring forces into play that will gradually lead to convergence. In cases where cohesion is sufficiently strong at the outset, it may be possible to speed up convergence through explicit compensation policies.[5] Even if compensation is not part of the integration policy within a group of developing countries, *outside* partners should pay attention to the issue of unequal distribution of the gains in the context of development cooperation programmes.

Preparing the phasing-out of non-reciprocal arrangements

During the Uruguay Round negotiations, many small developing countries lobbied in favour of the continuation of non-reciprocal preferences and special trade arrangements granted by the industrial economies. Examples are the Generalized System of Preferences (GSP), the trade regime accorded by the European Union under the Lomé Convention and the Caribbean Basin Initiative of the United States. Under the Lomé regime, many small developing economies also benefit from special commodity arrangements (for example sugar, beef and bananas) allowing imports into the EU at prices well above the world market level. The question arises whether these non-reciprocal preferences and special arrangements can be considered a useful strategy to help small developing economies with better integration into the world economy.

Multilateral trade liberalization has already eroded considerably the non-reciprocal preferences granted to developing countries. This process will continue with the implementation of the Uruguay Round and with future multilateral trade liberalization. Preparations are under way for the 'Millennium Round' that will certainly cover agriculture. Notwithstanding this trend, it should be recognized that small developing economies tend to receive a disproportionate share of the benefits of special preferential arrangements of industrialized countries. This can be explained by political factors. It is politically easier for industrialized countries to justify favours to small developing countries that, even if they are very successful, will not constitute a threat in terms of market share. The political factor will also be present within the beneficiary countries, leading to lobbying in favour of maintaining preferential deals.

Many economists have argued strongly that non-reciprocal trade preferences are not in the (long-term) interest of the beneficiary countries. Examples are Hudec (1987) and Langhammer (1992). There are three frequently mentioned arguments against such arrangements. First, because they are non-reciprocal, they can be easily reversed, making any industry that depends on them relatively vulnerable. Second, developing countries whose exports depend on special preferences in a particular market will find it extra hard to penetrate new markets, which may be precisely the ones growing faster. In other words, beneficiary countries may lose in terms of competitiveness. Privileged access to the European market virtually implies exclusion from the East Asian market. Third, special preferences may weaken the bargaining capacity of developing countries in the multilateral negotiations in areas where they have a comparative advantage. The first and second arguments are weakened if one allows for the possibility of learning by doing. Any new industry is vulnerable, but with learning, its competitiveness increases so that it may not be hurt by a preference reversal. This counter-argument implies that special preferences should be temporary. The question then arises for how long special preferences are needed. For developing countries as a whole, though not for the smaller ones, the third argument is perhaps the most important. It has been observed that, for industrialized countries, non-reciprocity provided a justification to maintain protection in sensitive products (especially clothing, agriculture and labour-intensive manufacturing). In this way, developing countries, in fact, paid a price for the preferential arrangements. Another practical aspect that diminishes the real value of non-reciprocity is the need to fulfil rules of origin requirements that tend to be costly.

Empirical calculations measuring the actual benefits of preferences usually lead to positive but limited results. The title of Davenport's article summarizes his analysis: 'Africa and the Unimportance of Being

Preferred' (1992). Some of the empirical analysis shows that preferences may have an initial positive effect that is gradually eroded in the form of rent-seeking behaviour in the marketing chain. However, it is easy to find examples of small developing countries that obtain very sizeable benefits from the special arrangements (for example Fiji, Guyana and Mauritius) or that strongly depend on them because of lack of diversification (for example, some of the Windward Islands as regards banana exports to the EU).

Given the theoretical analysis and the mixed results of the empirical studies, it is not easy to make a general recommendation on preferential arrangements. Still, it is safe to argue that small developing countries should not unilaterally refuse the benefits of specific arrangements, especially when these are substantial in relation to GDP or exports. What they should attempt, however, is to neutralize the distortions that may result from the arrangements and to foster diversification whenever possible. This might be done through fiscal measures. Small developing economies have an interest in treating the special deals as windfall gains that cannot be taken for granted and that should not affect long-term investment decisions.

The evaluation of preferential arrangements should also be made from the side of the industrialized countries. Such arrangements have a cost in terms of customs revenue forgone, extra administrative requirements to verify origin and quotas and, on occasion, budgetary outlays for specific deals.[6] While there are economic arguments for phasing out preferential deals, there could still be political arguments for providing additional support to small developing countries. In order to cater for the political justifications, the replacement of the special arrangements by an equivalent amount of budgetary support should be examined. Adequate attention should certainly be given to the difficult transition problems facing countries strongly dependent on particular commodities (for example, bananas in the Windward Islands).

North–South arrangements may be beneficial in some cases

The decision of Mexico in 1993 to join Canada and the United States to form NAFTA stimulated a lot of debate on the benefits of *North–South integration*. Of course, before NAFTA, there was already the Southern enlargement of the EU, in 1981 with Greece and in 1986 with Portugal and Spain. While these three countries were never considered to be part of the South, their economic development level at the time of accession to the EU was below the EU average. Anne Krueger (1995) considers the integration of Portugal and Spain in the EU a real success. She concludes that the transition in Spain from relatively high protection to low protection within the EU went much more smoothly than had been anticipated. Since 1995, the EU has become deeply involved with North–South integration. In 1996, a Customs Union between the EU and Turkey was established. The EU is also in the process of negotiating new regional agreements, including Free Trade Areas, with the Mediterranean countries. Agreements have already been reached with Morocco, Tunisia, Israel and the Palestinian Authority. Another negotiation, with South Africa, came to a conclusion at the beginning of 1999. Both the United States and the European Union are considering even wider forms of North–South integration. For the US, this takes place most strikingly in the initiative to create a Free Trade Area of the Americas. But the new Africa initiative launched in the wake of President Clinton's visit to the continent in 1998 also foresees Free Trade Areas with selected countries. The EU's position for the future trade regime with countries that take part in the Lomé Convention foresees the negotiation of Free Trade Areas with sub-groups of countries that are ready and willing to do so. Unlike the North–South arrangements mentioned earlier, the latter initiatives involve small developing economies, which are the focus of this book. The interest of the North in such arrangements is influenced by a political motive to get a better grip on the new interdependence problems that are a rising concern (e.g. money laundering, drug and arms trafficking, illegal migration).

Collier and Gunning (1995) make a strong plea for integration arrangements between the EU and groupings of African countries. As an example, they point to the positive aspects of the monetary union between France and the CFA franc zone, in terms of monetary stability. They specifically argue that the non-reciprocal preferential arrangements of the EU in favour of Africa should be replaced by reciprocal trade arrangements. Their main argument for such a change is the enhanced credibility of macroeconomic reform in the African countries. Another argument used frequently in favour of North–South integration is the fact that a North–South arrangement implies a kind of insurance against future contingent protection in the North. Such protection usually takes the form of anti-dumping measures. The use of such measures has increased over the past decade. The latter argument is particularly relevant for larger developing countries that are successfully beginning to export manufactured products. Small developing economies have not been greatly affected by anti-dumping measures.

Other authors such as Bhagwati and Panagariya (1996) are sceptical about North–South arrangements. They argue that such arrangements may lead to a sizeable loss of tariff revenue and costly trade diversion for the Southern countries that must reduce their protection much *more* than that of Northern countries. Referring specifically to the case of smaller developing countries, Helleiner (1996) warns about some disadvantages of North–South integration. In his view, there will not only be relatively large adjustment costs, but small economies may also have to give up too much policy autonomy. He concludes that there is a significant risk for small countries that integrate with large ones.

Except in special situations (for example, the possible accession of Cyprus and Malta to the European Union), the likelihood of *deep* North–South integration in the near future seems small. The initiatives presently being considered are generally about *shallow* integration in the form of Free Trade Areas, albeit with added features in trade-related areas. Deep integration between small developing countries and countries in the North will be determined much more by political than by economic factors. Deep integration is likely to be beneficial for small countries, as it would involve cohesion policies, adoption of useful institutions and locking-in of sound economic management. The negative side for small developing economies is the loss of sovereignty.[7] For such economies, the assessment of shallow integration is quite different from deep integration. It is unlikely that the locking-in of sound economic policies will be very effective in the case of shallow North–South integration. The main implication for small developing countries will be the phasing-out of the non-reciprocal preferential arrangements. Taking into account the economic arguments against non-reciprocal preferences discussed above and allowing for possible compensation in the form of untied budgetary support, it can be in the best interests of small developing countries to *gradually* establish reciprocal arrangements with the North. However, this should not divert attention from wider liberalization in the context of the WTO. It would not be helpful, for example, to arrive at a situation where small developing countries in Africa reach free trade with the EU and keep sizeable tariff restrictions for their trade with Latin America, Asia and other countries in the North. This may, in some cases, imply a transfer of tariff revenue from the South to the North. This would not only aggravate fiscal problems, but would be hard to justify in the North as a way of helping the South.

There is another aspect that should be considered. Integration between trading partners in the North and a dispersed group of small developing economies is not a very manageable option. In the absence of integration between the countries in the South, it will create hub-and-spoke systems benefiting particularly the Northern countries. In order for North–South integration to be manageable and beneficial for the South, it should take place between groupings of smaller developing countries and groupings in the North. But the groupings in the South need to be sufficiently mature and indeed ready to start negotiations with the North. If the small developing countries can negotiate as groups, they will have more bargaining power and may be able to avoid the generation of hub-and-spoke situations. If small developing countries do not effectively cooperate among themselves, North–South integration will be a risky strategy for them. It is doubtful whether many groupings in the South are sufficiently advanced.

In summary, small developing countries should not refuse deep integration with the North, at least not on economic grounds. However, it is unlikely that such an integration option will be available to many small developing economies. Shallow North–South integration may be beneficial, but there are important risks in the form of trade diversion and tariff revenue losses. As long as the North does not reverse its unilateral preferences, the net gains for small developing countries will be limited. The best chances for small economies are to strengthen and deepen their own integration before gradually moving towards reciprocal trade liberalization with the North.

Finding the right strategy mix

The strategies elaborated in the preceding chapters and summarized above are not mutually exclusive; in fact, they complement each other to a large extent so that they can be seen as elements of the wider strategy of integrating into the world economy. How far a country should go for each of these elements will depend on the specific circumstances. Smaller developing countries cannot escape from the effects of globalization. Trying to insulate themselves from globalization is certainly not viable; the cost in terms of economic growth will be high. They are also profoundly affected by increased regionalization in the North and need to respond. WTO membership, complemented by unilateral liberalization in a number of key areas, is necessary for integration into the world economy. However, unilateral liberalization often lacks credibility, because protectionist lobbies may cause policy reversals. It also does not directly improve market access. In addition, it still leaves small developing economies vulnerable to shocks and trade policy actions of large countries or trading blocs. Closer integration with larger developing economies or trade blocs of industrialized countries has the potential to deal with these problems, but there are also significant risks. There is no incentive for the larger country or trading bloc to give much consideration to the special situation of smaller economies. Hence the logic for smaller developing economies first to strengthen their hand through South–South integration. In this way, they can benefit from dynamic efficiency gains beyond what can be achieved with a unilateral strategy, but more importantly they can increase their bargaining power and avoid becoming spokes of a large economic hub. Still, expectations about South–South integration should be realistic. The possibilities for success are less extensive than is frequently assumed. Successful regional integration among small developing countries will take time. A ten-year transition period would not be excessive in most situations. South–South regionalism should certainly not be conceived as a defensive or autarkic strategy, but should be outward-oriented.

What can be said about the non-reciprocal arrangements with the North? These are neither an alternative to South–South integration nor to unilateral liberalization. However, they can have an important economic impact on smaller developing economies and sometimes involve a sizeable transfer of resources. But it should not be forgotten that non-reciprocal arrangements have not been completely free of charge in the past. In the future as well, they could restrict the bargaining potential of the beneficiaries in areas that tend to become increasingly important (for example, services and intellectual property). It is also expected that the non-reciprocal arrangements will continue to be eroded through multilateral liberalization. Small developing economies are not capable of reversing or even delaying this process, nor would this be in their interest. For the beneficiaries, the trick would be to make as good use of the non-reciprocal arrangements as possible, as long as they last, while at the same time preparing for their phasing out. It would be wise to treat the advantages as much as possible as neutral transfers. As these special favours are often politically motivated, it would make sense for smaller developing countries to request compensation for their phasing out.

With the right strategy mix, there are certainly possibilities for successful repositioning of smaller developing countries in the face of globalization and increasing regionalization. The best approach beyond the base line strategy of participation in the multilateral trading system, combined with unilateral liberalization in key areas, will be to move gradually towards larger regional entities in the South. Such South–South regionalism will diminish the adjustment cost of integration into the world economy. It will also prepare the ground for smaller developing countries to take advantage of North–South regionalism. With the right strategy mix, small developing economies can successfully compete in the big league.

Appendix A: Regional Integration Arrangements Involving Developing Countries

This review provides some background information on the main regional groupings involving (small) developing economies. It serves to clarify the references made in the main text. The organizations covered are those with a regional economic integration mandate, though, in most cases, they also cover other matters. There are also many regional organizations dealing only with a specific type of functional cooperation, for example, transport, education and finance. These are not included in the review. Groupings that have not been very active recently are also not included. Bilateral arrangements are not covered, as this would be beyond the scope of a brief review. For each regional arrangement, its origin, main objectives and main achievements are summarized together with an appreciation of its general prospects. Table A1 contains a few basic figures on the main regional integration arrangements involving small developing countries.

There is extensive literature on most of the organizations covered. A detailed overview has been prepared by UNCTAD (1996). Brief overviews, also covering arrangements between industrial countries, are contained in IMF (1994), Lawrence (1996) and Frankel (1997).

Africa

Regional integration in Africa was stimulated by the founding, in 1963, of the Organization for African Unity (OAU). At present all African states are members of the OAU, with the exception of Morocco. South Africa became a member shortly after its first democratic election in 1994. Its headquarters is in Addis Ababa, Ethiopia, where the seat of the United Nations Economic Commission for Africa (UNECA) is also located. Even though the OAU's activities lie mainly in the political area, it has been at the origin of the idea of pan-African economic integration. This led first to the Lagos Plan of Action, approved in 1980, on which the OAU collaborated closely with UNECA. In 1991, it led to the Treaty on the African Economic Community (AEC) that was signed in Abuja, Nigeria. The AEC foresees gradual deepening of economic integration over a period of 35 years leading eventually to a pan-African economic and monetary union. The first stages involve the consolidation of the existing regional communities (see discussion below). Although the Abuja Treaty has been ratified by more than the required two-thirds of the African states, its practical significance

Table A1 Basic data of regional integration arrangements involving small developing countries

	GNP 1996 (US$ billion)	Population 1996 (million)	Number of members	Exports 1996 (US$ billion)	Intra-trade (%)[1]
Sub-Saharan Africa					
ECOWAS	65.0	213.8	16	26.3	8.9
UEMOA	24.6	63.7	8	8.5	9.5
ECCAS	25.0	86.2	10	9.2	2.1
CEMAC	16.8	27.8	6	7.0	2.2
COMESA	135.2	344.3	20	20.8	7.7
SADC	175.0	180.0	14	48.7	11.4
SACU	142.9	43.6	5	35.1	–
EAC	19.7	77.5	3	5.1	–
Latin America and the Caribbean					
CACM	40.7	30.7	5	11.1	15.7
Andean Com.	230.0	103.4	5	54.2	10.4
CARICOM	20.1	13.6	15	6.2	13.2
OECS	2.1	0.6	7	–	–
MERCOSUR	1032.4	204.8	4	87.4	22.7
Asia and the Pacific					
ASEAN	687.9	478.9	9	398.9	22.9
SAARC	471.4	1241.6	7	63.4	4.3
ECO	412.7	345.3	10	70.6	7.1
GCC	229.3	27.0	6	–	–
FIC	8.3	6.3	14	3.8	–
MSG	7.2	5.4	3	3.6	–

Notes
– = not available.
Data are generally for 1996, but membership is for 1998. For several small developing countries no comparable data could be found, so that the aggregate figures are an approximation. Exports are the total for goods and services. For the GCC, the GNP figure is for 1997.
1. This is the percentage of total exports within the bloc. For SACU there are no regular statistics, but the dependence of Botswana, Lesotho, Namibia and Swaziland on imports from South Africa is estimated to be above 80 per cent. Taking into account the high intra-SACU trade, the figure for intra-SADC trade would rise to around 20 per cent. For the FIC, intra-trade is estimated to be around 2 per cent.
Source: World Bank.

so far is limited. Over the past few years, the OAU has stepped up its activities related to conflict prevention and peace-making. The latter subjects are outside the scope of this review.

Regional integration in Africa is characterized by a multitude of partly overlapping arrangements. Sometimes there is rivalry between different regional organizations. The OAU, together with UNECA, have been involved for a long time in efforts towards rationalization and harmonization of regional organizations, but progress is very slow. African regional organizations are on the whole weak and their activities are hampered because of low political commitment of many member states and limited resources.[1]

Economic Community of West African States (ECOWAS)

Creation: The ECOWAS Treaty was signed in 1975 and revised in 1993.

Membership: Benin, Burkina Faso, Cape Verde, Côte d'Ivoire, Gambia, Ghana, Guinea, Guinea-Bissau, Liberia, Mali, Mauritania, Niger, Nigeria, Senegal, Sierra Leone and Togo.[2]

Background and main objectives

ECOWAS is part of the first integration wave in Africa, probably inspired by the success of European integration. It is considered to be one of the main building-blocks of the AEC. It was set up shortly after the first oil price shock. Nigeria is the dominant member state, accounting in 1996 for approximately 53 per cent of the population and 43 per cent of GNP. During the 1970s and 1980s, when oil prices were high, Nigeria's economic weight in the region was even greater.

The original ECOWAS Treaty called for achieving a Customs Union over a period of 15 years. The revised Treaty of 1993 envisages an economic union. The trade liberalization schedule has been modified and postponed several times. The present schedule provides for elimination of all tariffs on *originating* industrial products by the year 2000. The more industrialized member states (Ghana, Côte d'Ivoire, Nigeria and Senegal) are expected to liberalize faster than the others.

In 1979, a Protocol on free movement of persons, right of residence and establishment in ECOWAS was adopted, to be implemented over 15 years.

The West Africa Clearing House (WACH) was set up in 1975 as an affiliated organization. After an initial successful period, activities of the WACH gradually declined, following the accumulation of arrears mostly owed to the members of the CFA franc zone. In 1992, the WACH was transformed into the West African Monetary Agency (WAMA), an autonomous specialized agency of ECOWAS. One of the tasks of WAMA is to oversee the achievement of a monetary union.

Main achievements and assessment

ECOWAS has made only limited progress towards its core integration agenda of trade liberalization. Despite its objective of becoming a Customs Union or even an Economic Union, origin rules were put in place restricting trade liberalization to industrial products of companies owned within West Africa. This caused problems, particularly for French-owned companies in countries such as Côte d'Ivoire. Closer cooperation in the monetary field has not succeeded. Significant progress has been made on the movement of persons and in functional cooperation (telecommunications and transport infrastructure). Member states do not attach great importance to the implementation of agreed measures. Deadlines have not been met. ECOWAS has tried to set up a fund to compensate member states for revenue losses, but this has not worked well. The Secretariat, since 1998 based in Abuja in Nigeria, has been weak and under-resourced. On the whole, economic and non-economic preconditions for success have been lacking. Several member states have been or still are affected by civil strife and instability that frequently spills over to neighbouring countries.

Future progress will be constrained by factors such as the relatively large number of member states and the wide disparities between them. Despite its lack of achievements, ECOWAS has a clear appeal to civil society and the private sector in the West African region. There is scope for gradually implementing a realistic, but shallow, integration agenda. There is also potential and need for increased collaboration in areas such as trade facilitation, transport, communications, education and research. ECOWAS could also play a useful role in relation to the participation of its member states in the WTO. If the UEMOA, a subgroup of ECOWAS, is successful, it could become a stimulus for integration at ECOWAS level. But this view appears not to be widely shared in non-UEMOA member states, where UEMOA is sometimes seen as a threat for ECOWAS. The progress of economic stabilization and adjustment programmes has certainly improved the outlook for ECOWAS. The future of the organization will, to an important extent, depend on the stability and leadership of Nigeria. The democratic transition in Nigeria in 1998 could provide a window of opportunity.

It should be mentioned that, over the recent past, ECOWAS's most prominent and effective role has been through the peace-making operations in Liberia and Sierra Leone of the ECOWAS Monitoring Group (ECOMOG).

West African Economic and Monetary Union (WAEMU)

Creation: The Treaty to establish the WAEMU, better known in French as the 'Union Economique et Monétaire Ouest Africaine' (UEMOA) was signed in 1994.

Membership: Benin, Burkina Faso, Côte d'Ivoire, Guinea-Bissau (1997), Mali, Niger, Senegal, and Togo. All members are also members of ECOWAS.

Background and main objectives

The UEMOA is the successor of the West African Economic Community or in French 'Communauté Economique de l'Afrique de l'Ouest' (CEAO), which was created in 1973, around the same time as ECOWAS. UEMOA combines the economic responsibilities of CEAO with the West African Monetary Union. But the membership of CEAO was slightly different, comprising Mauritania, but not Togo. UEMOA was created immediately following the long-overdue 50 per cent devaluation of the CFA franc that took place at the beginning of 1994.

The members of UEMOA are all small economies. In 1996, the combined GNP and population were only US$ 25 billion and 64 million respectively. Because of their size and remoteness, transport costs are high for the three landlocked countries (Burkina Faso, Mali and Niger). Disparities within the region are important, but not excessive. Except for Guinea-Bissau, the most recent new member, the common language and institutions resulting from the colonial past are a favourable factor for integration. Again, except for Guinea-Bissau, the political stability and security situation has been reasonable, even though there have been some tensions in most member states.

UEMOA's objectives are ambitious: achieving a full economic union in addition to the existing monetary union. This implies eliminating all intra-regional tariff and non-tariff barriers, putting in place a Common External Tariff, liberalizing factor movement and harmonizing fiscal and macroeconomic policies. Policy harmonization involves installing a system of macroeconomic surveillance.

An aspect that contrasts UEMOA from virtually all other South–South integration initiatives is the setting-up of supra-national institutions, including the Council of Ministers, the Commission, the Court of Justice and the Court of Auditors. Under the Treaty, UEMOA legislation prevails over national legislation. The institutional set-up is similar to the EU system. However, for some critics, the UEMOA copies too much from the EU.

Main achievements and assessment

The CEAO, the predecessor of UEMOA, was generally considered as one of the more successful regional integration initiatives in Africa. Until the second half of the 1980s, economic growth in the sub-region was reasonably high. Côte d'Ivoire and, to a lesser extent, Senegal were the engines of this growth. Côte d'Ivoire developed a significant manufacturing production capacity that partly supplied the rest of the region. Other member states, particularly Burkina Faso, benefited because of important labour migration into Côte d'Ivoire. Benin and, to a lesser extent Togo, are in a special situation because of their closeness to Nigeria. The extent of informal trade is sizeable throughout the region. Being part of the CFA franc zone, the region benefited from monetary stability at a time when the exchange rates of other West African countries became massively overvalued and unstable. Towards the end of the 1980s and during the early 1990s the economic parameters changed drastically. Commodity prices declined, the CFA franc became seriously overvalued and manufacturing exports lost competitiveness. The CFA zone became an important destination for smuggling, benefiting mainly the non-UEMOA members of ECOWAS. This was one of the factors leading to the CFA franc devaluation (halving its value) at the beginning of 1994. The CEAO had not succeeded in establishing its planned Customs Union. The tariff system remained excessively complex partly due to restrictive origin requirements. The compensation mechanism did not work satisfactorily.

It is too early to judge the success of UEMOA because implementation is only beginning. The economic performance of most of the UEMOA member states, particularly Côte d'Ivoire, has improved significantly since 1995, as a result of the devaluation and a rise in commodity prices. The UEMOA has made rapid progress towards tariff liberalization. This implies agreements on commodity classification, speed of internal tariff reduction and movement towards the Common External Tariff (CET). But the details for temporary exclusions, commodity valuation and verification of origin continue to be controversial.

In contrast to most of the earlier integration initiatives in the region, the discussions in UEMOA involve the IMF and the World Bank as well as France and the EU. In this way, the UEMOA programme is made fully consistent with the national structural adjustment programmes. For example, these programmes take into account the fiscal consequences of the UEMOA. A start has been made with the macroeconomic surveillance mechanism. A tight deadline has been agreed to achieve a CET by the year 2000, comprising three non-zero rates: 5 per cent, 10 per cent and 20 per cent.

The coming few years will be critical to see whether UEMOA will make genuine progress towards regional integration. It was mentioned above that the institutional set-up of UEMOA is supranational. But it remains to be demonstrated whether the national governments will play by the rules if, at some stage, national interests may have to be subordinated to regional ones.

Economic Community of Central African States (ECCAS)
Creation: The Treaty to establish ECCAS was signed in 1983.

Membership: Burundi, Cameroon, Central African Republic, Chad, Congo, Equatorial Guinea, Gabon, Rwanda, Sao Tomé & Principe, and the Democratic Republic of Congo.

Background and main objectives
ECCAS has been mainly promoted by the OAU and UNECA as one of the sub-regional organizations that would become building-blocks for pan-African integration. Its objectives are the same as those of ECOWAS: to achieve free movement of goods, services, people and capital, to harmonize national policies and to engage in functional cooperation.

Main achievements and assessment
If a number of preconditions for successful integration have not been fulfilled in the case of ECOWAS, this applies with even more force to ECCAS. Many of its member states have been confronted by severe political instability, widespread insecurity and civil conflict. Disparities within the region are very large. The member states are only weakly connected due to lack of cross-border infrastructure. Macroeconomic management has been deficient in several member states. Given these circumstances it comes as no surprise that ECCAS has not made progress towards its integration objectives. Notwithstanding this lack of progress, Angola has recently reiterated its interest, indicating that ECCAS has a certain appeal as a political forum for the sub-region. In fact, Angola was a participant in the original discussions leading to the creation of ECCAS, but there was no follow-up because of its civil war.

Central African Economic and Monetary Union (CAEMU)
Creation: The Treaty to establish the Central African Economic and Monetary Union (CAEMU), better known in French as the 'Communauté Economique et Monétaire de l'Afrique Centrale' (CEMAC) was signed in 1994.

Membership: Cameroon, Central African Republic, Chad, Congo (Brazzaville), Equatorial Guinea and Gabon. All members are also members of ECCAS.

Background and main objectives
CEMAC replaced the Central African Economic and Customs Union, known in French as the 'Union Douanière et Economique de l'Afrique Centrale' (UDEAC), which was created in 1964. UDEAC belonged to the early-wave African integration initiatives. Equatorial Guinea became a member in 1983. All the members of UDEAC are also in the CFA franc zone. The UDEAC states are all small economies and their combined GNP and population amount only to US$ 17 billion and 28 million respectively. Cameroon dominates the grouping, accounting for about half of its GNP and population. The economies of Gabon, Congo, Cameroon (to a

lesser extent) and Equatorial Guinea (increasingly) are dominated by oil exports.

While the CEMAC Treaty was signed in 1994, around the same time as the UEMOA Treaty, its full ratification and entry into force was delayed until 1999. The objectives of CEMAC are comparable to those of UEMOA; in other words, the creation of a fully-fledged economic and monetary union. The monetary union already exists in the context of the CFA franc zone.

Main achievements and assessment

Despite a number of favourable conditions for integration, such as the monetary union and the common history of its member states, achievements have been very limited. UDEAC did not develop into a real Customs Union. A complex system of border taxes, rules of origin and transit regulations prevented this. Enterprises were admitted to a system of reduced intra-regional taxation on a case-by-case basis. Unlike in the case of CEAO there was no meaningful increase in intra-regional trade. Cameroon developed some manufacturing capacity, but its exports to partner countries did not increase significantly. Economic development in Gabon and Congo was dominated by oil exports, which financed infrastructure and some import-substituting industries. Recurrent internal problems, especially in the landlocked member states of Chad and the Central African Republic, hampered progress.

In 1991, a renewed effort was made to achieve a Common External Tariff. With involvement of the Bretton Woods institutions, agreement was reached on the simplification of the customs regime. Products were classified in four categories with tariff rates ranging from 5 to 50 per cent. Around the same time a new system for transit traffic was elaborated.

The region was affected by the devaluation of the CFA franc in 1994, but the UDEAC member states did not show a growth response comparable to the UEMOA members. Likely explanations include the decline in oil prices since 1995 and civil unrest in some member states. Again in contrast to the UEMOA case, the signing of the CEMAC Treaty has not resulted in a renewed integration effort.

Common Market for Eastern and Southern Africa (COMESA)

Creation: The Treaty establishing COMESA was signed in 1993.

Membership: Angola, Burundi, Comoros, Djibouti, Democratic Republic Congo (1995), Egypt (1998), Eritrea, Ethiopia, Kenya, Madagascar, Malawi, Mauritius, Namibia, Rwanda, Seychelles (1997), Sudan, Swaziland, Tanzania, Uganda, Zambia and Zimbabwe.

Background and main objectives

COMESA is the successor to the Preferential Trade Area for Eastern and Southern Africa (PTA) whose Treaty was signed in 1981. The COMESA Treaty of 1993 broadened and deepened the integration foreseen under the PTA. There has been full continuity between PTA and COMESA activities. COMESA is seen as one of the main building-blocks of the African Economic Community. In contrast to ECOWAS, for example, both PTA and COMESA have paid a lot of attention to bringing in new member states. The likely explanation is its rivalry with SADC (see below). It is sometimes difficult to know how many member states COMESA has. One of the original PTA countries has not (yet) signed the COMESA

Treaty (Somalia). Some signatories have given notice to withdraw (Tanzania) or have effectively done so (Lesotho and Mozambique). The most recent new member state is Egypt. One of Egypt's motivations appears to be its adherence to the African Economic Community, which implies the requirement to take part in one of the sub-regional organizations. Egypt may also wish to benefit from tariff-free access to the COMESA market.

Of the regional groupings in Africa, COMESA is the largest in terms of population (around 345 million, including Egypt) and number of member states (presently 21). But the large number of member states also implies certain limitations. Within COMESA, divergences of various kinds are extreme. Per capita GNP ranges from US$ 3700 in Mauritius and US$ 6800 in the Seychelles to less than US$ 100 in Mozambique and US$ 170 in Tanzania. Population ranges from 58 million in Ethiopia to only 80 000 in Seychelles. In other areas, such as culture and the political system, divergences are also large. Many countries in the region have been or still are confronted by internal conflicts. Recently, there has been an increase in difficulties and conflicts involving several member states in the Great Lakes and Horn of Africa areas. Clearly, the circumstances do not point to rapid progress towards integration at the COMESA-wide level. The COMESA Treaty acknowledged the difficulties of countries with very different circumstances moving ahead together, by allowing multiple speed and variable geometry. Hence, progress is bound to take place at the level of sub-groups.

The agenda foreseen in the COMESA Treaty calls not only for a Customs Union and a Common Market, but also for an economic and monetary union. In addition, the Treaty stipulates collaboration in a large number of sectors and themes. The targets for the trade liberalization, which have been postponed, are currently to achieve intra-regional free trade during the year 2000 and a Common External Tariff in 2004. The CET foresees three non-zero tariff rates with a maximum of 30 per cent. The planned rates are 0, 5, 15 and 30 per cent respectively on investment goods, raw materials, intermediate goods and final products. Other key objectives in the Treaty are trade facilitation and free movement of persons. In the monetary field, the PTA Clearing House was established in 1984.

Main achievements and assessment

It is clear from the brief description of the context that rapid progress towards regional integration at the COMESA-wide level cannot be expected. Notwithstanding these unfavourable factors, there has been significant progress in a number of areas. The main advance has been on trade facilitation. Implementation has proceeded well in matters such as harmonization of road transit charges, simplification of customs and transit documentation, insurance coverage and the trade information network. COMESA has also worked out a customs bond guarantee scheme, which would cut the cost of transit traffic, but implementation is delayed.

Satisfactory progress has been made in the area of trade liberalization. Most member states apply significant tariff preferences (between 60 and 90 per cent) on intra-regional trade. Some member states have rapidly increased their regional exports (for example, Kenya, Zimbabwe and Mauritius). There has been some progress towards the planned CET, but the 2004 objective will be difficult to reach. In fact, progress towards the CET has been mostly an aspect of unilateral trade liberalization of the kind promoted under structural adjustment programmes. Progress on trade liberalization was also part of the move towards a *Harmonized External Tariff (HET)* agreed by the countries that participate in the *Cross-Border Initiative* to facilitate trade, investment and payments in Eastern and Southern Africa. This initiative is co-sponsored by the African Development Bank, the European Commission, the IMF and the World Bank and has contributed to the consistency between national adjustment programmes and regional integration policies (regional dimension of adjustment). The HET implies three non-zero tariff *bands* and does not require identical tariffs, leaving countries free to take account of fiscal considerations. It is generally recognized that fiscal problems have hampered trade liberalization in other parts of Africa (for example, ECOWAS). Compensation mechanisms to redistribute fiscal revenues have typically not been successful. The COMESA Secretariat has been closely involved in this initiative, which also addresses the lack of capacity to formulate and implement trade and integration policies.

Like most other African arrangements, COMESA started its trade liberalization with very restrictive rules of origin. Countries had to negotiate which goods would be put on a *common list*, for which preferences would be granted. Agreeing on such a common list turned out to be a slow and ineffective process. The common list approach was abolished in 1994. The current rules of origin of COMESA are reasonably straightforward (see note 37 in Chapter 4). However, their practical application continues to pose problems, thereby diminishing the benefits of regional trade liberalization.

In the monetary cooperation area, the COMESA Clearing House, in contrast to its West African counterpart, functioned quite well until the early 1990s. Around that time, the clearing volume started to decline. Because many countries achieved current-account currency convertibility, the demand for clearing services diminished. The Clearing House is being transformed into an agency to improve financial services for cross-border economic activities. There has been no progress yet towards the objective of monetary union. However, the objectives of the monetary harmonization programme have been scaled down so that they are more realistic.

Southern African Development Community (SADC)

Creation: The Treaty establishing SADC was signed in 1992 in Windhoek, Namibia.

Membership: Angola, Botswana, Lesotho, Malawi, Mauritius (1995), Mozambique, Namibia, Seychelles (1997), South Africa (1994), Swaziland, Tanzania, Democratic Republic Congo (1997), Zambia and Zimbabwe.

Background and main objectives

SADC's predecessor, the Southern African Development Coordination Conference (SADCC) was founded in 1981, shortly after Zimbabwe's independence. SADCC's origin is the movement of the front-line states and its main objective was to reduce economic dependence on South Africa. Until the Windhoek Treaty in 1992, SADCC's objectives related to functional cooperation, focusing on areas such as: transport, food security, human resource development, energy and industry. In the area of transport, SADCC promoted investment in the corridors connecting landlocked countries to the sea without passing through South Africa.

The transformation of SADCC into SADC coincided with a reorientation of objectives in the direction of regional economic integration. Following its democratic election in 1994, South Africa joined SADC.

A majority of the SADC member states are also members of COMESA. The original exception was Botswana that apparently never considered PTA or COMESA membership. This may be related to the fact that the SADC Secretariat is located in Gaborone, Botswana. South Africa also did not join COMESA and more recently Lesotho and Mozambique pulled out, while Tanzania indicated its wish to leave. Following South Africa, Mauritius joined SADC in 1995. With 10 out of 14 SADC members also in COMESA, there is a very substantial overlap. This would not pose many problems if the subjects handled by both organizations were different, or in the event that they deal with similar subjects, that the objectives were at least consistent. But SADC's policy orientation after 1992 moved straight into COMESA's economic integration mandate. This is probably the main reason for some rivalry between the two organizations. In 1996, SADC approved its *Trade Protocol* whose main aim is to achieve free trade among SADC members over a period of eight years following ratification. For the many SADC members that also subscribe to COMESA, it is clearly not possible to implement the CET foreseen under COMESA together with the FTA under SADC. Moreover, the Trade Protocol also contains certain regulations on issues such as transit, trade defence measures and rules of origin that deviate from the COMESA trade regime.

The SADC Secretariat has only a general coordinating role. Each member state is responsible for one or more specific sectors or themes. There are *sector coordinating units,* which are usually part of the relevant ministry in the host country. For example, Zimbabwe is responsible for food security and the sector coordinating unit is in the Ministry of Agriculture. This set-up dates from the time of SADCC where functional cooperation was the main task. There are also sectors with a more horizontal responsibility, such as the finance and investment sector that is handled by South Africa.

Right from its origin, SADCC had an important political dimension, which was continued by SADC. South Africa's decision to join not only drastically increased its economic size, but also enhanced SADC's prominence as a political and security forum.

Main achievements and assessment

SADC is one of the best-known regional organizations in Africa. Its role in promoting and coordinating functional cooperation, especially in transport and food security, is generally recognized and appreciated. Its role as a political forum is also recognized. With South Africa taking part since 1994, SADC is the largest economic bloc in Africa, with a GNP of around US$ 175 billion. But it should be recalled that South Africa alone represents 75 per cent of this figure. Accordingly, the economic dominance of South Africa within SADC is even more pronounced than the weight of Nigeria in ECOWAS or Cameroon in CEMAC. Apart from South Africa, all SADC members are in fact small and very small economies.

As an organization for regional economic integration, SADC still has to prove its value. Since the signing of the Trade Protocol in 1996 progress has been slow. Three years after its signing, the Protocol has not yet been ratified by the required two-thirds of the member states for entering into force. Negotiations about practical implementation of the Protocol are tedious and frequently oppose some of the old SADC members to South Africa. A source of contention is the fact that several member states, including Malawi and Zambia, have implemented rapid *unilateral* trade liberalization in the context of structural adjustment programmes. In combination with the normalization of trade with South Africa, this has led to large and rising bilateral trade deficits between such member states and South Africa. Countries such as Malawi, Zambia and Zimbabwe have not been able to compensate for this through increased exports to the rest of the world. South Africa has not yet implemented much *additional* preferential trade liberalization, even though it is implementing the 'across the board' tariff reductions it agreed to under the Uruguay Round.[3] Partly stimulated by its growing regional trade surplus, South Africa has become an important investor in the SADC region. This should be to the advantage of the receiving countries at least in the medium and long run. But in the short term, these investments may force closure of companies previously sheltered by protection. As a result, there is a significant adjustment cost for these countries. To complicate matters further and underline the policy dilemmas, all this is taking place when unemployment in South Africa is increasing.

The fact that SADC is moving slowly on its integration agenda should not be considered as negative. The failure of virtually all other African integration arrangements to implement their agreed objectives suggests that, in fact, more preparation and longer transition periods may be desirable. Because of its weight, South Africa will determine the pace of integration in SADC. Complicating factors for South Africa, such as its negotiation on an FTA with the EU and the revision of the SACU regime (see below) may help explain why movement at the SADC level is slow.

Southern African Customs Union (SACU)

Creation: SACU was formed in 1910. The agreement was renegotiated in 1969 and again in 1990.

Membership: Botswana, Lesotho, Namibia, South Africa and Swaziland.

Background and main objectives

SACU is, in many respects, different from the other groupings in Africa. It predates all the other arrangements and is, in fact, *more* than its name would indicate. It is a Customs Union with also a pooling of excise duties and with reasonably free movement of labour and capital. On the other hand, there is no SACU Secretariat. The practical operation of the system is mostly handled by South Africa. At independence in 1990, Namibia chose to remain in SACU. Botswana, Lesotho, Namibia and Swaziland, referred to as the *BLNS countries,* represent only 15 per cent of the population and less than 10 per cent of the GNP of SACU. All the SACU member states are also members of SADC.

Customs and excise duties are pooled and shared according to an agreed formula. For South Africa, fund transfers to the BLNS are compensated for by the fact that the CET mostly protects South African industry that also supplies the BLNS. For Lesotho and Swaziland almost half of government revenue comes from the common pool. The shares for Namibia and Botswana are much lower, but remain sizeable at 30 per cent and 20 per cent respectively. During the apartheid period until 1994, the BLNS, especially Swaziland received inward investment because of the sanctions against South Africa.

All SACU members apart from Botswana belong to the Common Monetary Area (CMA) known also as the rand zone.

Main achievements and assessment

SACU's main achievement is that it clearly works to the benefit of its five member states. SACU constitutes an integrated economic area, with all the benefits that this implies in terms of scale and competitiveness. Furthermore, the CMA is a stable monetary zone. For the BLNS countries, a special advantage of SACU is that it is a convenient system for the collection of government revenue. For South Africa, an important benefit is the guaranteed BLNS market for consumer goods.

Despite the benefits of SACU, there has been increasing dissatisfaction with the system. A widespread view in South Africa is that the payments from the common pool to the BLNS are too high. At the same time, the size of the common pool is diminishing because of the implementation of SACU's tariff dismantling offer under the Uruguay Round. For their part, the BLNS want a greater role in the management of the system and would like to transform SACU into an institution in which they have a real say. Discussions on the reform of SACU have been ongoing since 1994.

Another contentious issue is the planned Free Trade Area between the European Union and South Africa. The BLNS did not participate in this negotiation, and fear negative effects on their economy. The EU–South Africa FTA will reduce the size of the common revenue pool. It will expose the BLNS countries to increased competition, not only on the South African market where EU products will become cheaper, but also on the EU market where they would lose a preferential advantage over South Africa. However, some of the anticipated dynamic effects are positive for the BLNS and could more than compensate for the negative effects.

Despite divergent views among the BLNS and South Africa about some aspects of SACU, it is likely that all its member states derive significant benefits. The future success of SACU will be dominated by what happens with the South African economy. SACU could play an increasing role as the anchor economic zone for Southern Africa.

East African Cooperation (EAC)

Creation: East African Cooperation was revived in 1995 and builds on the legacy of the East African Community, which was created in 1965 and disbanded in 1977.

Membership: Kenya, Uganda and Tanzania.

Background and main objectives

The East African Community was preceded during the colonial era by a Customs Union between Kenya and Uganda to which Tanganyika was later added. Created in 1965, the Community was a clear example of the first-wave South–South regional integration. In addition to being a Customs Union, the East African Community constituted the umbrella for several joint companies of the member states such as East African Railways, the East African Shipping Company and the East African Development Bank.

Despite their common history and proximity, divergences in economic development strategy increased quickly during the post-independence period. This added to the tensions that were caused by the different levels of industrialization inherited by the newly independent states. Industrial capacity was concentrated in Kenya. There was some capacity in Uganda, but almost nothing in Tanzania. These unbalanced initial conditions strongly affected the trade patterns between the three countries. Tanzania considered that the result was an unfair distribution of the gains from the Community, with Kenya benefiting most. Tanzania believed that a more autonomous development strategy, involving import substitution and protection, would be more beneficial. At a more general level, Tanzania started its experiment of 'African socialism', which, in trade policy, implied high protection and extensive controls. The Tanzania experiment was widely supported by the donor community including the World Bank. Political problems added to the economic divergences, leading to the break-up of the East African Community in 1977.

During the second half of the 1980s and the 1990s, *de facto* convergence of the economic policies in the three countries increased. They all implemented structural adjustment programmes and subscribed to the integration objectives of the PTA and COMESA. The end of the civil war in Uganda in 1986 marked the beginning of an economic revival. Being a landlocked country, it needs regional cooperation in order to sustain its economic growth. Uganda strongly favoured a revival of East African Cooperation. Kenya and, to a lesser extent, Tanzania benefited from the economic growth in Uganda. Kenya again became one of the main suppliers for Uganda in addition to its vital transit role. In all three countries the revival of cooperation has been wholeheartedly promoted by the private sector.

In 1993, the three countries agreed on the establishment of the Permanent Tripartite Commission for East African Cooperation. The Secretariat of this Commission was installed in Arusha, Tanzania, in 1996. A draft Treaty was prepared during 1998. Its signature was planned by the end of 1999. It is interesting to observe that before putting this draft into the government decision-making mechanisms, it was widely discussed among academics, private operators and civil society in general. This contrasts with most other agreements and treaties in Africa which were decided without much public debate and scrutiny.

Main achievements and assessment

It is too early to discuss and assess the effects of the revival of East African Cooperation. Clearly, the new East African Cooperation differs from the old one in many respects. All three economies have significantly liberalized trade and payments. Unlike in the past, they all recognize the importance of the private sector. The new cooperation has led to progress in some concrete matters such as convertibility of national currencies, agreements to avoid double taxation and simplification of border formalities. The Commission for East African Cooperation is preparing actions in a large number of areas.

The draft Treaty envisages a deepening of East African integration. Such deepening is compatible with the more shallow integration at the level of COMESA of which all three countries are members. However, for Tanzania, there is a problem because it is also a member of SADC. Moreover, there is a fear in Tanzania of a repetition of the experience with the old East African Community, which was considered to be unfair to Tanzania.

The success of the revival of East African Cooperation will not only depend on its economic decisions, but also very much on political and security factors. The countries are affected by the problems in the neighbouring Great Lakes states and in Southern Sudan. Rwanda's application to join East African Cooperation, supported by Uganda, may change the nature of the cooperation arrangement. It is hard to predict whether this will strengthen or weaken East African Cooperation.

Latin America and the Caribbean

For a long time regional integration has been high on the agenda for the Latin American and Caribbean countries. Within the developing world, these countries were the most active in promoting the first wave of regional integration. This led, in 1960, to the creation of the Latin American Free Trade Association (LAFTA) comprising all the independent states in South America plus Mexico. The Central American Common Market (CACM) was founded in the same year. The intellectual basis for economic integration in the region was provided by the Economic Commission for Latin America. Under the leadership of Raoul Prebish, regional integration was advocated as the way towards successful industrialization via import substitution. The Andean Pact created in 1969 and the Caribbean Community (CARICOM) in 1973 completed the picture.

The regional integration initiatives of the first wave did not live up to the expectations held at the time of their creation. In 1980, LAFTA was transformed into the Latin American Integration Association (LAIA), better known by its Spanish abbreviation: ALADI. But ALADI did not represent a fundamental change. The debt crisis which confronted many countries was particulary severe during the first half of the 1980s. As in the African situation, economic difficulties interacted with political tensions, internal strife and sometimes conflict between different countries. Gradually, inward-looking economic policies were replaced by more outward orientation. In a parallel development, authoritarian rule was replaced by democratically elected governments. The 'lost decade' of the 1980s was followed by a return of economic growth during the 1990s.

The reorientation of economic policies and the political system was accompanied by a renewed regional integration drive. Two fundamental developments were the creation, in 1991, of the Southern Cone Common Market, better known as MERCOSUR and the participation of Mexico in NAFTA in 1994. Another striking event was the revitalization of the idea of hemispheric integration with the planned Free Trade Area of the Americas (FTAA).[4]

Central American Common Market (CACM)
Creation: The CACM Treaty was signed in 1960.

Membership: Costa Rica, El Salvador, Guatemala, Honduras, and Nicaragua.

Background and main objectives

CACM is a grouping of small economies. Regional integration is seen as a way to overcome the limitations of the small economic size. Following its creation, CACM made rapid progress in terms of tariff dismantling and movement towards a Common External Tariff (CET). Because of the import substitution objective, the CET rates were quite high, ranging from 11 per cent for capital goods to

106 per cent for consumer goods. Agriculture was largely excluded (as in many other integration agreements). This penalized Honduras. Still, intra-regional trade as a share of total trade went up rapidly and reached almost 27 per cent in 1970, which is a very high level, taking into account the limited overall size of the grouping: population of 31 million and GNP of US$ 41 billion (in 1996).

After the initial success, the integration process came to a halt and even reversed as a result of political and economic crises (including civil war and even armed conflict between some of the member states). Borders between some member states were closed, and there was a general increase in non-tariff barriers. The Clearing House and the Monetary Stabilization Fund that had been installed ceased to function. The share of intra-regional trade declined to around 15 per cent in 1989.

From the end of the 1980s onwards, following improved security and political stability, the Central American integration process was revitalized. Some of the member states implemented significant unilateral trade liberalization. Costa Rica went furthest in this direction. In 1991, Panama started collaborating with CACM. A new target structure for the CET was agreed in 1992 with rates between 5 and 20 per cent, much lower than the original rates. Costa Rica did not subscribe to these rates because its unilateral reductions had resulted in even lower values. In 1996, the target rates for the CET to be achieved by the year 2000 were lowered further to zero per cent for capital goods and 15 per cent for consumer goods.

Main achievements and assessment

The revitalization of the CACM can be considered as an example of the second wave of regional integration initiatives. It builds on the unilateral liberalization of most of the member states and is generally outward-oriented. The new approach has brought some success. From its low level in 1989, the share of intra-CACM trade in total trade has exceeded 20 per cent since 1994. Still, the transformation from inward-looking policies towards outward orientation is not yet completed. The weakest economies, Honduras and Nicaragua, have not yet seen much improvement.

Another aspect is that CACM is increasingly acting as a unit for the economic relations between the Central American states and the other countries and regional blocs in the Western Hemisphere. Relations with CARICOM were established in 1992, and an agreement was reached on free trade with the Dominican Republic in 1998. In the past, bilateral negotiations involving individual CACM member states were very common. There are clear advantages if CACM enters into deals as a bloc.

Andean Community

Creation: The Andean Pact Treaty was signed in 1969. In 1996 the name was changed to Andean Community.

Membership: Bolivia, Colombia, Ecuador, Peru and Venezuela.

Background and main objectives

The Andean Pact was set up in 1969 with the Cartagena Agreement as a subgroup of LAFTA to deepen integration. The creation of the Andean Pact was a reaction of the smaller countries to the larger ones that dominated LAFTA.

Venezuela joined the group in 1973 and Chile left in 1976. Among the integration groupings in the Americas, the Andean Pact has developed the most elaborate institutional structure.

The Andean Pact has made little progress towards its objective of a Customs Union. No agreement could be reached during the 1970s and most of the 1980s. Trade liberalization speeded up only at the time of the second wave of regional integration around the beginning of the 1990s. But even at that time, it was not possible to overcome divergent views about the tariff level. Bolivia and Peru preferred a lower level than Colombia and Venezuela. In 1992, Peru unilaterally decided to suspend preferential treatment to imports from within the zone.

The Cartagena agreement included the objective of harmonious regional development of industry. An attempt was made to install a joint industrial programming mechanism that provided for an allocation of specific industries to specific member states. These industries would be allowed to supply the protected regional market. This system of regional import substitution behind high tariffs did not work in practice. In 1989, the joint industrial programming approach was replaced by a more outward-oriented policy.

In 1996, the change of the name to Andean Community coincided with a second revitalization, including an institutional reform. Targets for achieving a Customs Union were again set. A Common External Tariff comprising four tariff levels: 5, 10, 15 and 20 per cent should be achieved by 2005. Trade in services will also be liberalized.

Main achievements and assessment

Despite a number of favourable factors, such as a common history and culture, and a shared dissatisfaction about the wider integration process advocated by ALADI, progress towards market integration has been very slow. Targets frequently had to be revised and it has generally been difficult to reconcile the divergent views of the member states. Political difficulties both within and between member states are a likely explanation. The reintegration of Peru into the preferential system is going slowly and the plan is for it to be completed fully only in 2005.

Nevertheless, the second revitalization has a good chance of being more successful than earlier efforts. The formation of MERCOSUR and NAFTA, and the hemispheric discussions on the FTAA have acted as a catalyst for Andean integration. On the other hand, the fact that Bolivia made an agreement for free trade with MERCOSUR illustrates that cohesion is still not yet very strong. However, a positive view of this agreement is that it could pave the way for an FTA between the Andean Community, MERCOSUR and Chile.

Caribbean Community

Creation: The Treaty of Chaguaramas establishing CARICOM was signed in 1973.

Membership: Bahamas, Barbados, Belize, Guyana, Haiti (1997), Jamaica, Trinidad & Tobago, Suriname (1995), and the OECS members (see below).

Background and main objectives

CARICOM was preceded by the Caribbean Free Trade Association (CARIFTA), established in 1966 and modelled largely on the European Free Trade Association.

CARIFTA's Secretariat was based in Guyana, which had pushed for its creation. During the early 1970s, it was decided to broaden the integration initiative beyond trade matters, and this led to the creation of CARICOM in 1973. From the beginning, a distinction was made between *more* developed member states and *less* developed member states. The more developed countries are the relatively larger ones: Barbados, Jamaica, Trinidad and Tobago and Guyana. The less developed countries are the OECS member states plus Belize. The latter receive special and differential treatment in the implementation of integration policies. All the member states of CARICOM are small economies. In 1994, the total population was only 6 million and overall GDP amounted to US$ 17 billion. With the recent accession of Suriname and, especially, Haiti, the population more than doubled to over 13 million, although the GNP went up by less than US$ 3 billion.

The main objectives of CARICOM are economic integration through the creation of a 'single market and economy', functional cooperation in specific sectors and coordination of foreign policies.

The Caribbean Development Bank (CDB) is an associate institution that was established in 1969. It is particularly geared to financing infrastructure in the less developed member states of CARICOM. Among comparable development finance institutions, the CDB has built up a good reputation.

Main achievements and assessment

Progress towards the CARICOM 'single market and economy' has been much slower than anticipated. The target dates for achieving internal trade liberalization and a Common External Tariff have been postponed several times. The target rates have been lowered in line with what has happened elsewhere. It has been difficult to reconcile the interests of the less and more developed member states. The former prefer a higher maximum tariff rate for revenue purposes and, at the same time, a lower minimum rate for import substitution (to provide cheap inputs). The goal, set in 1992, was to achieve minimum and maximum rates for industrial goods between 5 and 20 per cent by the end of 1998. The less developed members are allowed to apply a zero minimum rate. For agricultural products, the maximum rate is 40 per cent. However, there are several member states that apply other duties and charges and non-tariff barriers in addition to the CET.

Intra-CARICOM exports as a percentage of total exports went up from around 5 per cent in the early 1980s to about 13 per cent around the mid-1990s. Given the small size of the CARICOM economies, this is a very high share. However, intra-CARICOM trade is very much dominated by oil exports from Trinidad & Tobago. The Caribbean Common Market does not (yet) include the Bahamas and Haiti. In 1999 an agreement was reached about gradually including Haiti.

CARICOM has produced a number of positive results in the area of functional cooperation such as the University of the West Indies, the Caribbean Export Development Agency and the Meteorology Institute.

There has also been progress towards the coordination of foreign policy. Increasingly, the CARICOM member states have been speaking with one voice in international forums. Significant developments include the establishment of formal relations with the Central American Common Market in 1992. In addition CARICOM signed preferential trading agreements with Venezuela (in 1992) and Colombia (in 1994). In 1996, a *joint regional negotiation machinery* was created to increase capacity to participate in various trade arrangements. More recently, in 1998, agreement was reached in principle to liberalize trade between CARICOM and the Dominican Republic. However, the negotiations on practical implementation are moving slowly. The CARICOM was also instrumental in the launching of the Association of Caribbean States (ACS) in 1994. Trinidad & Tobago will host the Secretariat of the ACS (see note 4).

The CARICOM faces a number of major challenges. CARICOM's preferences in the markets of industrial countries have been eroded because of multilateral liberalization. The creation of NAFTA has aggravated this because of increased competition from Mexico in the United States and Canada. Future ACP–EU cooperation could entail the creation of a Free Trade Area between CARICOM and the EU. At the same time negotiations are under way towards the Free Trade Area of the Americas. It would be in the best long-term interest of CARICOM members to move in parallel towards free trade within the Western Hemisphere and with Europe. However, the adjustment cost at the level of specific industries and at the level of the government budget will be large. The challenge for the CARICOM region is to participate in the wider integration process, while at the same time strengthening its position in activities with a comparative advantage such as services. The OECS subgroup faces additional challenges (see separate section).

Despite the fact that many targets have not been met within the agreed deadlines, the achievements of CARICOM are sizeable. The organization also contributed towards raising the profile of its member states on the international scene.

Organization of Eastern Caribbean States (OECS)

Creation: The Treaty establishing OECS was signed in 1981.

Membership: Antigua & Barbuda, Dominica, Grenada, Montserrat, Saint Kitts & Nevis, Saint Lucia, and Saint Vincent & the Grenadines.

Background and main objectives

The OECS groups the very small English-speaking economies of the Eastern Caribbean. Its central secretariat is in Saint Lucia, while its economic affairs secretariat is based in Antigua. The combined land area and population are only 3000 square kilometres and half a million respectively. The OECS GNP is around US\$ 2 billion. All the OECS members are also members of CARICOM, so the OECS can be considered as an example of variable geometry. The OECS builds on cooperation arrangements that were already set up during the colonial era. Montserrat is an overseas territory of the United Kingdom.

The main OECS objectives are market liberalization and functional cooperation. An important aspect of cooperation has been the establishment of the Eastern Caribbean Central Bank in 1983, which maintains a common currency, the Eastern Caribbean dollar. Hence, the OECS constitutes a monetary union.

Main achievements and assessment

Despite the disadvantages resulting from their small economic scale, the OECS countries have been successful in maintaining a reasonable growth rate. With an average GNP per capita above US\$ 3000, the OECS is in the category of upper middle-income countries.

The OECS members have obtained good results in the area of functional co-operation. Examples include investment promotion, civil aviation and fisheries. They have also benefited much from relatively generous flows of concessional funds and preferential arrangements with industrial countries.

The dependence of the OECS countries on preferential arrangements such as the EU's banana regime illustrates their vulnerability. The banana industry has become established as a viable and regular source of revenue for small independent farmers that previously were plantation workers or subsistence peasants. In some OECS countries, the banana sector employs around a third of the labour force. The EU's preferential banana regime has been rejected under the WTO dispute settlement mechanism, following complaints from the United States (on behalf of large banana trading companies) and a number of Latin American banana producers. It is recognized that economic diversification is vital, but the extreme dependence on EU commodity preferences leads to a sizeable adjustment cost.

Southern Cone Common Market (MERCOSUR)

Creation: The MERCOSUR Treaty was signed in 1991.

Membership: Argentina, Brazil, Paraguay and Uruguay.

Background and main objectives

The origin of MERCOSUR can be traced to the gradual coming together, during the 1980s, of the two main economic powers in South America, Argentina and Brazil. This *rapprochement* took place against the background of political changes and economic policy reform leading to a more outward orientation in both countries. Two smaller economies in the region, Paraguay and Uruguay, asked to participate in this process and the four countries signed the Treaty of Asunción establishing MERCOSUR in 1991. Its secretariat is located in Montevideo, Uruguay. In 1996, the population of MERCOSUR was 205 million and its GNP reached US$ 1030 billion.

MERCOSUR is an ambitious integration initiative, partly inspired by the EU. Its main objectives include free movement of goods, services and production factors between the member states, and the adoption of a Common External Tariff towards third countries. Other objectives are the coordination of macroeconomic policies and functional cooperation in matters such as transport, communication and energy. In the area of trade liberalization MERCOSUR adopted a very different approach from that of ALADI. Rather than undertaking laborious product-by-product negotiations, MERCOSUR agreed on automatic across-the-board tariff reductions and elimination of non-tariff barriers.

Main achievements and assessment

Following its creation, MERCOSUR quickly captured the headlines as a new type of integration organization of developing countries. Even though the timetable for tariff dismantling was ambitious, progress was generally on schedule during the first five years of implementation. The share of intra-regional trade in total trade went up rapidly from 9 per cent in 1990 to 22 per cent in 1996.

By 1995, a Customs Union, albeit an imperfect one, was achieved. The Common External Tariff rates are between zero and 20 per cent, with an average of

12 per cent. However, temporary product exclusions are allowed. Paraguay has the largest number of exclusions, but the other countries also maintain sizeable exclusions. In addition, automotive products and sugar are subject to a special regime. At the end of 1997, Brazil and Argentina adopted an increase of 3 per cent in the maximum level of the CET. Paraguay and Uruguay reluctantly agreed, but were allowed to exempt certain products from the increase. In 1998, in the wake of the Asian financial crisis, intra-MERCOSUR trade fell for the first time in many years. At the beginning of 1999, Brazil devalued its currency. This led to trade tensions between Argentina and Brazil and some unilateral measures were taken. However, there has not been any serious backtracking. Rather, ideas for moving towards monetary and fiscal harmonization were put on the table.

In 1996, MERCOSUR signed agreements to gradually establish free trade with Chile and Bolivia. These agreements demonstrate the attraction of MERCOSUR as a trading bloc. Negotiations are taking place for a wider agreement between MERCOSUR and the Andean Pact. Discussions on trade liberalization between the EU and MERCOSUR have also started.

Asia and the Pacific

In contrast to Africa, Latin America and the Caribbean, regional integration has generally been a less prominent issue in Asia and the Pacific. The best-known regional organization is the Association of South East Asian Nations (ASEAN) that was founded as far back as 1967. ASEAN's original objectives were mostly political, regional integration only becoming an important agenda item at the beginning of the 1990s. It is fair to say that the first wave of *economic* integration initiatives hardly touched Asia and the Pacific. During the 1990s, interest in regional integration has been increasing in the Pacific.

Association of South East Asian Nations (ASEAN)

Creation: The Bangkok Declaration was signed in 1967.

Membership: Brunei (1984), Indonesia, Laos (1997), Malaysia, Myanmar (1997), Philippines, Singapore, Thailand and Vietnam (1996).

Background and main objectives

The origin of ASEAN, during the 1960s, was the desire to set up closer political and security cooperation in the South East Asian sub-region. The five original members that signed the Bangkok Declaration in 1967 were Indonesia, Malaysia, the Philippines, Thailand and Singapore. Brunei joined in 1984, Vietnam in 1995 and the most recent new members, Laos and Myanmar, were admitted in 1997. Cambodia's admission was foreseen for the same year, but was postponed because of renewed political problems and unrest. The founding member states are all large economies. Even though the population of Singapore is only 3 million, it is not a small economy because it has such a high per capita income. The size of its economy is US$ 90 billion. Brunei's population is very small, around 300 000. However, because of its high oil revenue, it cannot be considered to be in the category of small developing economies. On the other hand, Laos and Myanmar are small developing economies, although economic data for Myanmar are not reliable.

Following its creation, ASEAN served, in the first place, as a political discussion and collaboration forum. In addition to the promotion of peace and stability in the sub-region, ASEAN's objectives include functional and economic cooperation. Functional cooperation covers areas such as social development, culture, science and technology, the environment, drugs and narcotics. The most important elements of economic cooperation are trade liberalization, industrial development, finance and banking, and investment. The initial approach towards trade liberalization did not lead to much progress. Lengthy negotiations led to limited reciprocal opening of markets. Trade liberalization was intensified only in 1992, with the decision to establish the ASEAN Free Trade Area (AFTA) over a period of 15 years. The instrument to establish AFTA is the Agreement on the Common Effective Preferential Tariff (CEPT). During the 1990s, new themes have been added to the economic cooperation agenda, including tourism, services and intellectual property.

Various schemes of industrial cooperation have been set up during the 1970s and the first half of the 1980s. In 1976 ASEAN Industrial Projects (AIPs) began establishing large-scale industrial projects. Another scheme is the ASEAN Industrial Complementations (AICs), which was introduced to encourage specialization and trade in the automotive sector. The ASEAN Industrial Joint Venture (AIJV) scheme was designed to encourage greater investment into and within the region. Products of such joint ventures received tariff preferences in the ASEAN countries.

ASEAN has a light institutional structure: a small Secretariat was established only in 1976, in Jakarta, around the time of the first agreement on preferential trading arrangements. In 1992, following the agreement on AFTA and the broadening of functional and economic cooperation, the Secretariat was enlarged. A special unit has been set up to monitor the implementation of AFTA.

Main achievements and assessment

Until the early 1990s, ASEAN's main achievements have been in the domain of political and security dialogue and some aspects of functional and economic cooperation. Gradually, ASEAN has also become an instrument for expressing common positions of its member states in international economic forums. Even in the absence of progress towards economic integration, the fact that ASEAN acted as a bloc has increased the bargaining power of the member states. Most of ASEAN's member states experienced almost two decades of rapid economic growth, until the onset of the crisis in East and South-East Asia in 1997.

The share of intra-ASEAN exports in total exports decreased during the 1960s to around 15 per cent in 1970. The share gradually went up to around 19 per cent in 1990 and further to 22 per cent in 1995. A large part of ASEAN's intra-trade involves the hub economy, Singapore, and reflects networks among businesspeople of Chinese background.

In line with experience in Latin America, ASEAN's industrial cooperation schemes are not considered successful. It was not possible to strike a balance between diverse national public and private sector interests.

ASEAN's early trade liberalization initiatives did not lead to many results. This was due to a slow product-by-product approach, national safeguards and restrictive rules of origin (at least 50 per cent of the value-added must be from within the region). The approach initiated with the AFTA agreement in 1992 is much more general and automatic. The original target period was shortened from 15 to 10 years. The ASEAN Free Trade Area should be achieved by the year

2003. The origin rules have been somewhat relaxed in comparison to the earlier schemes.

AFTA will not lead to complete free trade within the sub-region. Each country must divide its tariff lines into four categories: inclusion list, temporary exclusion list, sensitive list and general exception list. For the products in the inclusion list, tariffs must be between zero and 5 per cent by the year 2003. All non-tariff barriers should also be eliminated. The general exceptions list contains products excluded for security reasons. Originally, all unprocessed agricultural products were also excluded. However, negotiations are underway gradually to include such products. At present, 82 per cent of the tariff lines are in the inclusion list, and 16 per cent are in the temporary exclusion list. This leaves only about 2 per cent of products in the sensitive or general exception lists. The newest member states (Laos and Myanmar) have much smaller inclusion lists to facilitate adjustment. Moreover, they receive technical assistance to help them with the implementation of AFTA.

There is no doubt that ASEAN has grown into an important regional integration grouping. In comparison to most groupings in Latin America and Africa, ASEAN has been modest in setting its trade liberalization targets. Following the adoption of the AFTA agreement in 1992, progress in this area has not been fast, but it has been steady. A Customs Union is not envisaged for the moment. Regional industrial policy at the ASEAN level was not a success. It seems that the initially more planned approach has given way to one aimed at harmonizing the regulatory framework for investment in the form of the ASEAN Investment Area (AIA). ASEAN has been successful in representing its member states in international negotiations.

South Asian Association for Regional Cooperation (SAARC)

Creation: The Charter was adopted in 1985.

Membership: Bangladesh, Bhutan, India, Maldives, Nepal, Pakistan and Sri Lanka.

Background and main objectives

The proposal for an association of the nations in South Asia was first made by Bangladesh in 1980. Preliminary contacts led to the adoption of a charter on the SAARC in 1985. SAARC groups some of the largest developing countries with some very small ones. The range of population size is from 950 million for India to only 260 000 for the Maldives. Four of the seven member states – Bangladesh, Bhutan, Maldives and Nepal – are least-developed countries.

The SAARC arrangement involves mostly functional cooperation in areas such as agriculture, poverty alleviation and people-to-people contact. Trade and economic cooperation was initiated through the South Asian Preferential Trading Arrangement (SAPTA) that was signed at ministerial level in 1993 and entered into force in 1995. SAPTA foresees the gradual reduction and eventual elimination of tariffs within SAARC. It is seen as a step towards the creation of a South Asian Free Trade Area (SAFTA).

Main achievements and assessment

SAARC's main merit is that it constitutes a forum for exchange of views among countries with a long common history and important common interests, but with often divergent views and in some cases territorial conflicts. History and geography dictate that there should be some measure of regional cooperation. Regular meetings of heads of state and government have been organized. India dominates the sub-region and has borders, often very long, with all the other member states except Sri Lanka and the Maldives, which are island states. Functional cooperation is vital in areas such as forestry and the struggle against erosion, management of inland water and coastal resources and transportation.

It is probably too early to make an assessment, but progress towards trade liberalization has been very timid. Genuine progress would call for an across-the-board approach rather than the proposal by each country of products to be liberalized. The share of intra-regional trade in total trade is small and declined from around 5 per cent during the 1970s to around 3.5 per cent by the early 1990s. In comparison to other developing regions, SAARC member states, with the exception of Sri Lanka, maintain relatively high levels of protection. Regional trade liberalization should move in parallel with liberalization towards the world economy.

Economic Cooperation Organization (ECO)

Creation: The Treaty of Izmir was signed in 1977 and amended in 1990 and 1992.

Membership: Afghanistan, Azerbaijan, Kazakhstan, Kyrgyzstan, Iran, Pakistan, Tajikistan, Turkey, Turkmenistan and Uzbekistan.

Background and main objectives

The present ECO is a successor to a cooperation agreement of 1964 between Iran, Pakistan and Turkey. In 1977, these three countries formalized their cooperation by signing the Treaty of Izmir. Two years later, with the change of regime in Iran, the organization became dormant until it was revived in 1985. In 1992, six newly established states in Central Asia, which emerged from the collapse of the Soviet Union, became members of ECO. Afghanistan also joined the organization at that time, bringing the membership to ten. The three founding members (Iran, Pakistan and Turkey) dominate ECO in terms of population and economic size. Three of the member states, Kyrgyzstan, Tajikistan and Turkmenistan, are small transition economies.

ECO's main objectives are functional cooperation in areas such as agriculture, education, industry, transport, energy and narcotics. Objectives in the trade and customs area are moving towards gradual reduction of trade barriers. A Protocol on an ECO Preferential Tariff Arrangement was signed by the three founding members in 1991.

Main achievements and assessment

ECO can be considered as a reactivation of long-standing historical and trade connections ranging from Central Asia to the Mediterranean. While progress is currently hampered because several member countries are confronted by conflicts, there is undoubtedly potential for increased cooperation and integration. The economic transformation of the Central Asian states towards market orientation will prepare the ground for deeper integration.

Even though ambitious cooperation plans already exist, practical progress has been limited so far. One such plan is for the development of new transport infrastructure more or less along the classic 'silk route'. Such a scheme would create a trade connection to compete with the infrastructure that was put in place in Russia by the former Soviet Union. Progress in the area of trade liberalization, even among the three founding members, is so far very limited.

Gulf Cooperation Council (GCC)

Creation: The Charter constituting the GCC was signed in 1981.

Membership: Bahrain, Kuwait, Oman, Qatar, Saudi Arabia and United Arab Emirates.

Background and main objectives

Regional cooperation between the Arab states in the Gulf region developed rapidly following the first oil price shock in 1974. This led to the creation of the GCC in 1981. The member states are all small in terms of population (except for Saudi Arabia). However, they are upper middle- and high-income economies, deriving the bulk of their revenue from petroleum exports. The objectives of the GCC comprise political, functional and economic cooperation. Functional cooperation covers a broad area including education, culture, health, social affairs, industry, water resources and scientific research. In the economic field, the aims are for deep integration in the form of a common market. The GCC headquarters is located in Saudi Arabia.

Main achievements and assessment

Important progress has been made in areas of functional cooperation. As regards economic integration, the GCC moved quickly to abolish tariffs and other restrictions on their mutual trade in 1983. Agreement has further been reached to move towards a relatively low Common External Tariff, but its implementation has not yet been possible. There has been some progress towards the free movement of workers.

An achievement of the GCC has been to act as a bloc in trade policy matters. An example is the negotiation with the European Union aimed at reaching a Free Trade Area. However, progress has been very slow and no agreement has yet been reached.

South Pacific Forum (SPF)

Creation: The SPF was established in 1971. There is no written charter.

Membership: Australia, Cook Islands, Federated States of Micronesia, Fiji, Kiribati, Marshall Islands, Nauru, New Zealand, Niue, Palau, Papua New Guinea, Samoa, Solomon Islands, Tonga, Tuvalu and Vanuatu.

Background and main objectives

The South Pacific Forum is an informal political grouping of 16 independent and self-governing states in the South Pacific region, constituted in 1971. Its Secretariat is located in Fiji. The 14 developing countries, that is, all member states except Australia and New Zealand, are collectively referred to as the Forum

Island Countries (FIC). They are spread over a vast geographical area. Individual countries constitute archipelagos with large distances between the small islands. The exception is Papua New Guinea, which covers the eastern half of the mini-continent of New Guinea and the adjacent islands. In terms of population and economic size all the FIC are small. The combined population is only a little over 6 million and the GNP is about US$ 8.5 billion. PNG represents approximately two-thirds of the population and GNP. The most important asset of the FICs is their large sea area, containing within its boundaries almost a third of the world's total fish stocks.

Of the 14 FICs, eight are Members of the ACP group. The six non-Members are: Cook Islands, Federated States of Micronesia, Marshall Islands, Nauru, Niue and Palau. All six have applied to become Members of the ACP group.

The South Pacific Forum is a well-structured organization that is active in a large number of cooperation themes. For some of these themes, separate regional bodies such as the Forum Fisheries Agency with headquarters in the Solomon Islands and the South Pacific Regional Environment Programme with headquarters in Samoa have been formed. Other cooperation themes are trade promotion, civil aviation, telecommunications and tourism.

Main achievements and assessment

The South Pacific Forum is considered to be a successful organization for functional cooperation in several key areas of common interest such as fisheries, environment and tourism. The Forum is also important for political dialogue and for raising the concerns of the small FICs at the international level (for example, their disagreement with the French nuclear testing programme).

The Forum has recently become more active in a number of subjects related to economic integration. In June 1999 the Forum Trade Ministers endorsed in principle a Free Trade Area between the members of the FIC. Furthermore, work is planned on collective trade facilitation covering subjects such as phytosanitary requirements and customs procedures. Additionally, the Forum Secretariat is preparing its member states for the next round of WTO trade liberalization and for negotiations of the future trade regime with the EU. The FICs are also considering steps towards investment liberalization.

Melanesian Spearhead Group (MSG)

Creation: MSG was created in 1991.

Membership: Fiji (1996), New Caledonia (1996), Papua New Guinea, Solomon Islands, and Vanuatu.

Background and main objectives

The Melanesian Spearhead Group was established in 1991 by PNG, Solomon Islands and Vanuatu as a relatively loose body for political and economic collaboration. In 1994 the three founding members agreed that MSG would become a Free Trade Area. In 1996 Fiji and the French overseas territory of New Caledonia joined the arrangement, without, however, taking part in the trade agreement. The MSG is a sub-group of the South Pacific Forum Island Countries (FIC). The MSG members are all small economies, but within the FIC they are by far the largest ones representing more than 85 per cent of the combined population and GNP.

Main achievements and assessment

It is premature to discuss the trade liberalization of MSG. In order to limit the costs, no permanent secretariat has been established. MSG matters are handled by units within the administration of the member states. Progress on trade liberalization is very slow. It is constrained by the product-by-product approach that was adopted. So far only 35 products, mainly primary ones, have been liberalized. Given the new interest of the Pacific Forum in trade liberalization, the Spearhead Group has the potential to become the fast track for such liberalization within the FIC group.

Appendix B: Characteristics of Small Developing and Transition Economies

Table B1 Characteristics of small developing economies: Africa

Economy	GNP[1] $ 1996	GNP p.c. 1996	Pop. (mln) 1996	Special status[2]	WTO[3]	Openness[4]	ACP[5]	LDC[6]
Angola	3.0	270	11.1	0	1	0	1	1
Benin	2.0	350	5.6	0	1	1	1	1
Botswana	4.4	3260	1.5	1	1	1	1	1
Burkina Faso	2.4	230	10.7	1	1	0	1	1
Burundi	1.1	170	6.4	1	1	0	1	1
Cameroon	8.4	610	13.7	0	1	1	1	0
Cape Verde	0.4	1010	0.4	2	0	–	1	1
Central Afr. R.	1.0	310	3.3	1	1	0	1	1
Chad	1.0	160	6.6	1	1	0	1	1
Comoros	0.2	450	0.5	2	0	–	1	1
Congo (Brazza.)	1.8	670	2.7	0	1	0	1	0
Congo (Kinsh.)	5.7	130	45.2	0	1	0	1	1
Côte d'Ivoire	9.4	660	14.3	0	1	0	1	0
Djibouti	0.5	780	0.6	0	1	–	1	1
Eq. Guinea	0.2	530	0.4	1	0	–	1	1
Eritrea	0.8	220	3.7	0	0	–	1	1
Ethiopia	6.0	100	58.2	1	0	0	1	1
Gabon	4.4	3950	1.1	0	1	0	1	0
Gambia	0.4	360	1.1	0	1	1	1	1
Ghana	6.2	360	17.5	0	1	1	1	0
Guinea	3.8	560	6.8	0	1	1	1	1
Guinea-Bissau	0.3	250	1.1	0	1	1	1	1
Kenya	8.7	320	27.3	0	1	1	1	0
Lesotho	1.3	660	2.0	1	1	–	1	1
Liberia	–	–	2.8	0	0	–	1	1
Madagascar	3.4	250	13.7	2	1	0	1	1
Malawi	1.8	180	10.0	1	1	0	1	1
Mali	2.4	240	10.0	1	1	1	1	1
Mauritania	1.1	470	2.3	0	1	0	1	1
Mauritius	4.2	3710	1.1	2	1	1	1	0
Mozambique	1.5	80	18.0	0	1	0	1	1
Namibia	3.6	2250	1.6	0	1	–	1	0
Niger	1.9	200	9.3	1	1	0	1	1
Rwanda	1.3	190	6.7	1	1	0	1	1
São Tomé	0.05	330	0.1	2	0	–	1	1
Senegal	4.9	570	8.5	0	1	0	1	0
Seychelles	0.5	6850	0.08	2	2	–	1	0
Sierra Leone	0.9	200	4.6	0	1	–	1	1
Somalia	–	–	9.8	0	0	0	1	1
Sudan	7.8	290	27.3	0	2	–	1	1
Swaziland	1.1	1210	0.9	1	1	–	1	0
Tanzania	5.2	170	30.5	0	1	0	1	1
Togo	1.3	300	4.2	0	1	0	1	1
Uganda	5.8	300	19.7	1	1	1	1	1
Zambia	3.4	360	9.2	1	1	1	1	1
Zimbabwe	6.8	610	11.2	1	1	0	1	0

Notes follow Table B4.

Table B2 Characteristics of small developing economies: Latin America and the Caribbean

Economy	GNP[1]	GNP p.c. $ 1996	Pop (mln) 1996	Special status[2]	WTO[3]	Openness[4]	ACP[5]	LDC[6]
Antigua and B.	0.5	7330	0.07	2	1	–	1	0
Barbados	1.7	6530	0.3	2	1	1	1	0
Belize	0.6	2700	0.2	0	1	–	1	0
Bolivia	6.3	830	7.6	1	1	1	0	0
Costa Rica	9.1	2640	3.4	0	1	1	0	0
Cuba	–	–	11.0	2	1	–	0	0
Dominica	0.2	3090	0.07	2	1	–	1	0
El Salvador	9.9	1700	5.8	0	1	1	0	0
Grenada	0.3	2880	0.1	2	1	–	1	0
Guyana	0.6	690	0.8	0	1	1	1	0
Haiti	2.3	310	7.3	2	1	0	1	1
Honduras	4.0	660	6.1	0	1	1	0	0
Jamaica	4.1	1600	2.5	2	1	1	1	0
Nicaragua	1.7	380	4.5	0	1	1	0	0
Panama	8.2	3080	2.7	0	1	–	0	0
Paraguay	9.2	1850	5.0	1	1	1	0	0
St Kitts and N	0.2	5870	0.04	2	1	–	1	0
St Lucia	0.6	3500	0.16	2	1	–	1	0
St Vincent	0.3	2370	0.11	2	1	–	1	0
Suriname	0.4	1000	0.4	0	1	–	1	0
Trinidad and T	5.0	3870	1.3	2	1	–	1	0

Notes follow Table B4.

Table B3 Characteristics of small developing economies: Asia and the Pacific

Economy	GNP[1]	GNP p.c. $ 1996	Pop (mln) 1996	Special status[2]	WTO[3]	Openness[4]	ACP[5]	LDC[6]
Afghanistan	–	–	24.2	1	0	–	0	1
Bhutan	0.3	390	0.7	1	0	–	0	1
Cambodia	3.1	300	10.3	0	2	–	0	1
Fiji	2.0	2470	0.8	2	1	–	1	0
Jordan	7.1	1650	4.3	0	2	–	0	0
Kiribati	0.07	920	0.08	2	0	–	1	1
Laos	1.9	400	4.7	1	2	–	0	1
Maldives	0.3	1080	0.3	2	1	–	0	1
Marshall Isl.	0.1	1890	0.06	2	0	–	0	0
Micronesia	0.2	2070	0.1	2	0	–	0	0
Myanmar	–	–	45.9	0	1	–	0	1
Nepal	4.7	210	22.0	1	2	1	0	1
Papua NG	5.0	1150	4.4	2	1	0	1	0
Samoa	0.2	1170	0.2	2	2	–	1	1
Solomon Isl.	0.3	900	0.4	2	1	–	1	1
Tonga	0.2	1790	0.1	2	2	–	1	0
Vanuatu	0.2	1290	0.2	2	2	–	1	1
Yemen	6.0	380	15.8	0	0	1	0	1

Notes follow Table B4.

Table B4   Characteristics of small transition economies

Economy	GNP[1]	GNP p.c. $1996	Pop (mln) 1996	Special status[2]	WTO[3]	Openness[4]	ACP[5]	LDC[6]
Albania	2.7	820	3.3	0	2	1	0	0
Armenia	2.4	630	3.8	1	2	0	0	0
Azerbaijan	3.6	480	7.6	0	2	0	0	0
Estonia	4.5	3080	1.5	0	2	1	0	0
Georgia	4.6	850	5.4	0	2	0	0	0
Kyrgyz	2.5	550	4.6	1	1	1	0	0
Latvia	5.7	2300	2.5	0	1	1	0	0
Lithuania	8.4	2280	3.7	0	2	1	0	0
Macedonia	2.0	990	2.0	1	2	1	0	0
Moldova	2.5	590	4.3	1	2	1	0	0
Mongolia	0.9	360	2.5	1	1	–	0	0
Tajikistan	2.0	340	5.9	1	0	0	0	0
Turkmenistan	4.3	940	4.6	1	0	0	0	0

Note
– = no information available.
1. US $ billion 1996.
2. 1 = landlocked; 2 = island; 0 = other.
3. 1 = member of the WTO; 2 = membership requested; 0 = not a member.
4. 0 = closed; 1 = open (as defined by Sachs and Warner, 1995).
5. 0 = not a member of the ACP group; 1 = member of the ACP group (the only ACP countries not in the tables are Dominican Republic, Nigeria and South Africa).
6. 0 = not a least-developed country; 1 = least-developed country (Bangladesh is the only least-developed country not in the tables).

Source: Population and GNP data World Bank, *1998 Development Report and Atlas*.

Notes

1 Introduction

1 During the Middle Ages, regular long-distance trade took place between China, India, the Middle East, North Africa and Europe.
2 There is also a microeconomic dimension of globalization, emphasized by Oman (1994 and 1995). In his view, competitiveness is more affected by the capacity to adopt innovations than by availability of raw materials.
3 The current list of applicants still includes several prominent trading nations such as China, Russia, Ukraine, Taiwan, Saudi Arabia and Vietnam.
4 The work to define and agree on standards in a particular industrial sector takes place through technical committees and working groups. These bring together the main economic players in the sector, including companies, consumer organizations and government authorities.
5 The Asian financial crisis, which started in mid-1997, did not fundamentally change the long-term picture. Still, it led to formidable economic problems and hardship for the countries affected and to unprecedented and controversial interventions by the international community. At the beginning of 1999, there were signs that economic growth would resume in some of the countries. The crisis led to a reassessment of the liberalization of capital flows and the importance of banking supervision.
6 There is also a debate on the complementarity and the sequencing between openness and other major areas of economic reform such as privatization and deregulation as well as reform in the area of political institutions, governance and the legal system.
7 This widely used formulation is attributable to Bhagwati (1992).
8 One might pose the question whether a hegemonic economy could *ever* be benevolent and resist the temptation of deploying its full power. Clearly, even such an economy will suffer in the long term if the consequence of its behaviour is to destabilize other nations. A hegemonic economy may therefore participate in a positive-sum game.
9 Critics point to the protectionist aspects of the Common Agricultural Policy (CAP) as well as protection in textiles. However, protection in those sectors has been a widespread phenomenon across most OECD countries. Sometimes, countries that are among the most liberal in industry can be the most protective for agriculture (for example, Norway and Switzerland). Agricultural protection has always been linked to the specific nature of agricultural markets and the social aspects of the rural economy. The gradual and orderly transition of rural societies is a long-standing objective of the CAP.
10 This should not be interpreted as providing an argument for *large* developing economies to pursue autarkic or closed policies. However, they have possibilities of integration into the world economy that are not available to *small* developing economies.
11 The characteristics of *Small Island Developing States (SIDS)* have been the subject of several international meetings. A programme of action was adopted

at the Barbados conference on sustainable development of SIDS in 1994.

12 For example, a report of the Commonwealth Secretariat (1985) defined a small state as one with a population of around one million or less. More recently, the Commonwealth Secretariat (1997) revised its cut-off point to one-and-a-half million to reflect the increase in world population. Another study of Armstrong and Kervenoael (1998) proposes an upper limit of three million persons to define small size. With the latter limit, Singapore just qualifies as a small state.

13 The arbitrariness of the criterion is demonstrated, for example, by the fact the Dominican Republic, usually considered to be a small developing country, is not included, because its GNP just exceeds the cut-off value.

14 A few countries below the cut-off point, but classified by the World Bank as high-income (with per capita GNP above US$ 9000 in 1996) are not included, because of their special situation.

15 The criteria used by the UN to define Least Developed Countries are: per capita GDP, physical quality of life index and an economic diversification index. The physical quality of life index comprises life-expectancy at birth, per capita calorie supplies, combined primary and secondary enrolment ratio, and adult literacy. The economic diversification index takes into account the share of manufacturing in GDP, the share of employment in industry, per capita electricity consumption and export concentration. The list is reviewed every three years.

16 There has been increased attention on the concept of *vulnerability* of small developing countries, whether or not they are least developed. It is argued, for example, by the Commonwealth Secretariat (1997) that the vulnerability of such countries justifies certain concessions of their industrial trade and cooperation partners that would not necessarily apply to large developing countries with a comparable per capita income. This reasoning is presently used by Vanuatu and the Maldives to underscore that their graduation from the list of Least Developed Countries should be postponed. Within the United Nations, work is ongoing to define a 'vulnerability index'. An example of such an index has already been worked out by Briguglio (1995). His index combines three groups of variables: exposure to foreign economic conditions (such as dependence on trade), remoteness and insularity, and disaster-proneness. Briguglio demonstrates that small island developing states have indeed a higher vulnerability index than other developing countries with similar per capita GNP.

17 Even though the emphasis is on trade aspects, it is understood that, in addition to WTO membership, the base-line strategy should also include membership of the IMF with subscription to current account convertibility.

2 WTO Membership: What's in it for Small Developing Countries?

1 The World Trade Organization was formally established on 1 January 1995. As an institution, the WTO has equal standing with the International Monetary Fund (IMF) and the World Bank. The WTO is responsible for administering the General Agreement on Tariffs and Trade (GATT) 1994, the General Agreement on Trade in Services (GATS), and the Agreement on Trade Related Intellectual Property Rights (TRIPs). 'GATT 1994' consists of (a) the

original 'GATT 1947', (b) the amendments to GATT 1947 and (c) the Under-standings reached under the Uruguay Round.

2 There is extensive literature on the topics covered in this chapter. This pre-sentation draws particularly on Hoekman and Kostecki (1995), IMF (1994), Krueger (1995), Martin and Winters (1995) and Page and Davenport (1994). It is not meant to provide a comprehensive treatment of the multilateral trading system, but a coverage that helps to demonstrate its importance and limitations for small developing economies.

3 It is remarkable that neither the GATT nor the WTO has a clear definition of developing countries. The practice is that developing-country status is based on self-selection. This is not the case for the sub-category of the least-developed countries (LDCs), where a UN definition based on objective criteria is employed (see also Chapter 1, note 15).

4 Tariff bindings are obligations not to raise tariff rates on specific products above a certain level without compensating reductions in other tariffs. The actual applied tariffs may be lower than the bound rates. The larger the difference between applied tariffs and bound rates, the easier a country can unilaterally raise its tariffs, while still fulfilling its WTO obligations.

5 The other basic principle is non-discrimination or Most-Favoured-Nation (MFN) as set out in Article I. MFN implies that any concession granted by a con-tracting party to a product or service of another country is automatically granted to like products or services of all the other contracting parties. The MFN obligation is complemented by the national treatment rule (Article III), requiring that foreign goods, once they have satisfied whatever border measures that are applied, such as customs duties, be treated no less favourably in terms of taxes and equivalent measures than identical goods of domestic origin.

6 Since 1973, the Multifibre Arrangement (MFA) has regulated trade in tex-tiles and clothing between importing industrial countries and exporting developing ones as well as Central and East European countries. Imports into industrialized countries are restricted through a complex system of country and commodity-specific quotas.

7 See, for example, Martin and Winters (1995). The predicted loss to sub-Saharan Africa reflects the anticipated rise in food prices resulting from the reduction of agricultural protection in industrialized countries.

8 The first ministerial meeting following the creation of the WTO, which took place in December 1996 in Singapore, demonstrated these tendencies. The WTO Secretariat proposed a draft plan of action in favour of the least-developed countries. With respect to market access, the plan called upon *developed and developing countries* to grant duty-free preferential access for the exports of least-developed countries. The plan also called for assistance in the area of capacity-building. What is remarkable about the plan is that, for the first time, it explicitly called on the more advanced developing countries to help the least-developed countries. The plan was broadly endorsed at the ministerial meeting and was further worked out during a meeting organized jointly by WTO, UNCTAD and the International Trade Centre (ITC) in October 1997.

9 Countries such as Mauritius and Jamaica that are members of the Lomé Convention have been exempted from the MFA for their textiles and cloth-ing exports to the EU. Hence, the phasing-out of the MFA implies a loss of their advantage (see Chapter 5).

10 Even though the EU and the US, which together account for about 40 per cent of agricultural trade, dominated the discussions on agriculture, the negotiations were also influenced by a new kind of coalition of traditional agricultural exporters called the Cairns Group. The coalition comprises industrial countries (Australia, Canada and New Zealand), developing countries (Argentina, Brazil, Chile, Colombia, Fiji, Indonesia, Malaysia, the Philippines, Thailand and Uruguay) and a transition economy (Hungary). Of the developing country members only one, Fiji, is a small developing economy.

11 For example during 1994–95 Mexico introduced 18 cases, Brazil 12 and India nine. This is to be compared with 37 cases for the EU, 30 for the United States and nine for Canada.

12 According to Sachs (1998), an estimated one-third of merchandise trade is composed of shipments among the affiliates of a single company, as opposed to trade among separate exporters and importers.

13 International investment regulations have long been discussed in the OECD. A Multilateral Agreement on Investment (MAI) has been under preparation. The MAI would be open to non-OECD members. It intends to establish non-discrimination, national treatment, protection and transparency. It also foresees a mechanism for dispute settlement complementing WTO provisions. However, developing countries and non-governmental organizations were not at all in favour of a system designed exclusively to serve OECD members, with little attention for social and environmental issues. During 1998, when it became clear as well that several OECD member states were not in favour, preparations were stopped. It has been suggested that the discussions on investment should move to the WTO in order that developing countries can also participate.

14 It is too early to guess the medium- and long-run effects of the economic crisis in East and South–East Asia that started in 1997 and deepened during 1998. There will certainly be a slower growth of their imports in the short run. By the beginning of 1999 there were signs of resumed growth in some of the affected countries.

15 The limitations for small countries in relation to dispute settlement were underlined in a presentation by the Ambassador of St Lucia at a hearing of the European Parliament in May 1997, in Brussels. In the banana regime dispute, St Lucia, together with its partners in the Organization of Eastern Caribbean States, used the services of a legal specialist. However, this lawyer could not attend the WTO panel because he was not an official delegation member. Larger countries can afford to have legal advisers as full-time members of their delegation.

16 Even though developing countries' contributions to the budget are not very high, at the beginning of 1997, 23 developing countries had not paid for more than three years. This excludes them from receiving technical assistance. Another seven developing countries were more than one or two years in arrears and therefore barred from chairing WTO bodies (see Michalopoulos, 1999).

3 Unilateral Economic Liberalization

1 See also the discussion on Trade Related Investment Measures (TRIMs) in Chapter 2.

2 A comprehensive overview of experience with trade liberalization in the context of structural adjustment programmes was made by Thomas, Nash and associates (1991).

3 Current-account convertibility means that local currency can be freely exchanged for foreign currency in order to import goods or to pay for factor services. However, capital transactions to invest or transfer funds abroad may still face various restrictions.

4 A weakness of the Sachs and Warner measure is that it does not reflect the intensity of openness or closedness. For example, a 20 per cent overvalued exchange rate is quite different from a 500 per cent overvaluation, but both lead to a classification as closed. A monopoly on major exports can still be compatible with an open economy, depending on how it is handled. Without a monopoly, small exporters of farm products may be at the mercy of monopsonist buyers.

5 Corden (1974) draws a distinction between divergences and distortions. A divergence can be any difference between private and social cost, or private and social benefits. A distortion is a divergence that is caused by government policy of some kind, such as a tariff or subsidy. Divergences that are not distortions are typically caused by market failures.

6 The welfare gain obtained through the optimal tariff occurs at the expense of the rest of the world. However, it is possible that other large economies or trading blocs retaliate by also imposing tariffs.

7 An exception is Lawrence and Litan (1986). They discuss how dislocation effects of trade liberalization in an affluent economy can be mitigated without restoring permanent protection. Possible measures include temporary relief to displaced workers while providing incentives for mobility. Such measures are difficult to set up in a small, poor economy.

4 South–South Regionalism

1 Integration initiatives of developing countries frequently take on board certain aspects of the European approach. This copying can be risky because the context is very different. It is therefore useful to explain some aspects of the European experience.

2 The terminology is somewhat problematic and even controversial. Bhagwati and Panagariya (1996) use the abbreviation PTA for 'Preferential Trading Area' which can be an FTA, a CU or even a Common Market. In their view, 'Free Trade Area' sounds too positive because imports from third countries are in fact not free. In other words, an FTA discriminates against third countries. In this text, we follow the more usual definition. Another term used by Frankel (1997) to refer to *one-way* concessions is *preferential trade arrangement*. These are the subject of Chapter 5.

3 The dividing line between free trade in services and free movement of production factors is not always clear. For example, provision of financial services across borders is closely related to capital movements and construction services require labour movement (see Frankel, 1997).

4 Deep integration is often associated in the literature with the 'new regionalism' (see, for example, Robson, 1993).

5 The principle of mutual recognition of standards was an important aspect of the completion of the European single market in 1993. The strategy was

to rely as much as possible on mutual recognition and limit harmonization to essential health and safety requirements. Furthermore, the task of developing harmonized standards was given to private sector standardization organizations (see Tsoukalis 1997).

6 For some of these discussions see Frankel (1997), McMillan (1993), Nagarajan (1998) and Snape (1993).

7 Even under Article XXIV, some exceptions are possible given the ambiguity of the concept of 'substantially all' trade. Sometimes, 90 per cent coverage of trade is used as a benchmark. Hence there may still be lobbying from pressure groups to exclude certain products. There may also be a case for temporary exclusion of infant industry products, with a potential of real productivity gains.

8 Nagarajan (1998) points out that the Understanding introduced a discrepancy between the rules for CUs and those for FTAs. The assessment for CUs shall be based on applied rates, but for FTAs it is not clear whether bound or applied rates shall be used. This ambiguity can have important practical implications. For example, there were negative consequences for EU exporters when Mexico, following its 1994 currency crisis, raised applied tariffs towards the EU and other third countries whereas it did not raise them towards its NAFTA partners.

9 An exception is Hufbauer and Schott (1994). In order to assess the prospects for Western Hemisphere economic integration, they developed the concept of 'readiness indicators'. These are price stability, budget discipline, external debt, currency stability, reliance on trade taxes, market-oriented policies and functioning democracy. Apart from the last one, they are all economic indicators. By assigning target values to the indicators they rank countries in terms of their chances of progress towards economic integration.

10 Casual observation and writing often simply point to the low level of recorded intra-regional trade as an explanation for the lack of success of regional economic integration of developing countries. The reasoning goes on to point out that many countries export identical primary commodities or labour-intensive manufactures and concludes that there is no potential for intensified trade. These views miss the point that in many cases, regional integration is simply not implemented because certain preconditions are not satisfied or because the design is not appropriate. Furthermore, it should not be forgotten that there is often a large amount of unrecorded trade, especially when the economies suffer from macroeconomic distortions. In the case of small or very small economies, it is natural that intra-regional trade is relatively small. In addition, cross-border infrastructure may be inadequate so that trade with more distant industrial countries is relatively cheap. Therefore a low *level* of intra-regional trade does not allow conclusions on the success or the potential of integration among developing countries.

11 This might change in the future. There are recent examples where developing country arrangements took into account political criteria. In April 1996, MERCOSUR partners made it clear that the anticipated military coup in Paraguay would have negative consequences for its participation. In August 1997, ASEAN countries decided to postpone Cambodia's accession, following a coup and renewed civil strife. However, around the same time, Myanmar did become a member of ASEAN even though many third countries criticized its human-rights situation. In Africa, the Democratic Republic of Congo

became a member of both COMESA and SADC despite political unrest and, later on, conflict involving several countries in the region.

12 This observation is consistent with the comment in Chapter 3 that adjustment programmes with a focus on unilateral liberalization can have negative spillover effects on countries in the same region. Hence the need to take into account the regional dimension in these programmes. Expressed differently, adjustment programmes that are regionally coordinated and compatible in terms of reform measures and pace will facilitate successful regional integration.

13 There are four convergence criteria to be met by a country for entry into the European Monetary Union: no more than 1.5 per cent inflation above the average of the three lowest-inflation member states; a government deficit no larger than 3 per cent of GDP; a public debt no higher than 60 per cent of GDP; long-term interest rates not more than 2 percentage points above the levels in the three lowest inflation countries. On the public debt it is added that a country qualifies if its debt/GDP ratio approaches the target level at a satisfactory pace. In addition, the national currency should not have been devalued within two years prior to the entry into the monetary union.

14 The European Commission 1997 Communication: 'Agenda 2000 for a stronger and wider Union' contains a detailed description of the accession criteria as well as an assessment of the extent to which these criteria are fulfilled by the present candidates for EU membership.

15 The Trade Policy Review Mechanism is briefly described in Chapter 2.

16 Differences in language and history did not, however, prevent Suriname becoming a member in 1996 and Haiti in 1997. The population of Haiti also exceeds the combined population of the other CARICOM members.

17 For more complete, but still concise overviews, see for example Bulmer (1994) or CEPR (1995).

18 It is also argued sometimes that rapid technological change and globalization erode the sovereignty of small countries, especially in economic decisions. By pooling resources and power, groupings of countries can recapture some of this loss and again become significant players – for example, in areas such as scientific research.

19 Referring to sub-Saharan Africa, it is striking that groupings with a large number of countries such as ECOWAS (16 members), COMESA (around 20 members) or SADC (14 members) are making slow progress on trade liberalization and other integration policies. While it is too early to draw firm conclusions, the progress of UEMOA (8 members) and EAC (3 members) seems to be faster.

20 Article 3b of the Maastricht Treaty states: 'In areas which do not fall within its exclusive competence, the Community shall take action, in accordance with the principle of subsidiarity, only if and in so far as the objectives of the proposed action cannot be sufficiently achieved by the Member States and can therefore, by reason of the scale or effects of the proposed action, be better achieved by the Community.'

21 Amendment ten of the US Constitution states: 'The powers not delegated to the United States by the Constitution, nor prohibited to it by the States, are reserved to the States respectively or to the people.'

22 As an illustration, one could refer to the overlap in the mandates of smaller and larger groupings in Africa. Under subsidiarity smaller groupings could

focus on matters such as cross-border infrastructure whereas larger groupings could deal with issues such as customs documentation and transport
regulations.

23   The line between variable geometry and multispeed integration cannot always be drawn accurately. Some member states may decide upon slower
implementation, but if implementation is further postponed, what seemed
only multispeed may turn into *de facto* variable geometry. This could be
applicable to the European Monetary Union. The Euro zone was launched
on 1 January 1999 by 11 countries. Two member states opted out (for the
moment) and for two others the entry conditions were not fulfilled. This
situation could be characterized as variable speed. However, if those who
opted out decide to stay out indefinitely it becomes variable geometry. Variable
speed or geometry is also applicable in the EU in the social field and in the
area of movement of persons where a subgroup of EU members created a
'passport union' (i.e. the Schengen agreement). This digression demonstrates
that some variable speed or geometry is likely whenever a grouping contains a relatively large number of member states.

24   In the European context, the main areas for the common base recommended
by the CEPR group are the single market, including trade and competition
policy, the structural and cohesion funds, the harmonization of indirect
taxation and a mechanism for coordinating monetary policy to avoid competitive devaluation. Moreover, in the non-economic sphere, the common
base should include an acceptance of basic principles such as democratic
government, respect for human rights, mutual non-aggression and the rule
of law. In the view of the CEPR group, a reformed version of the controversial Common Agricultural Policy (CAP) might be part of the common base,
but not monetary union and a common social policy.

25   By imposing a tariff, a large country, in contrast to a small one, can restrict
imports in order to obtain price concessions. In this way, a tariff can improve its terms of trade and hence welfare, at the expense of the welfare of
the trading partners. The *optimal tariff* is the one that maximizes the gains.
A large trading bloc has an incentive to use tariffs to its advantage. However, other trading blocs may retaliate and the end-result may be a trade
war in which all traders lose. One of the main objectives of the multilateral
system is to avoid a tariff war where welfare at world level would certainly
decline.

26   The supply curve of the partner country is horizontal over the import range
of the home country. This is compatible with the small-country assumption. At a larger supply level, the partner country's supply curve can be
rising.

27   Demand and supply of the home country can be subtracted for each price
so that only demand for imports remains.

28   These include: perfectly competitive markets, full capacity utilization, homogeneous goods and absence of other distortions. If other distortions are
present, because of market conditions or policy interventions, the theory of
second best applies. This means that it is not certain whether elimination
of one kind of distortion, for example tariffs, while others remain present,
will increase welfare.

29   Bhagwati and Panagariya's criticism is mainly addressed against regional
arrangements involving 'trade hegemons'. They consider arrangements of

developing countries such as MERCOSUR with some favour even though they do not find them the best strategy. More generally they consider regional arrangements justified when they deepen towards a common market with free movement of production factors or an economic union implying policy harmonization.

30 An example is De Rosa's (1995) estimate of the effects of the ASEAN-planned FTA, usually referred to as AFTA. Intra-ASEAN trade is estimated to expand by 19 per cent, largely in the form of trade creation. Welfare effects range from less than 0.5 per cent for the more protected economies of Indonesia, the Philippines and Thailand to 1.3 per cent in Malaysia and 3.9 per cent in Singapore.

31 The Kemp–Wan theorem is a direct application of the fundamental theorem of welfare economics, stating that any competitive equilibrium can be sustained by a suitable price vector. When a CU is formed, there exists an internal price vector that sustains the same level of trade and thus world prices. The difference between the internal equilibrium price vector and the unchanged world price vector defines the Common External Tariff.

32 See, for example, Perroni and Whalley (1994) and Whalley (1996). An illuminating overview is provided by Fernandez and Portes (1998).

33 The *domino theory of regionalism* proposed by Baldwin (1995) can be seen in the same light. If a large trading bloc is deepening its integration, the cost to private firms of being outside increases. This triggers lobbying to encourage outsiders to become members. With more countries joining, the pressure to apply for membership increases. The domino theory provides a nice explanation of why the East European countries wish to become part of the European Union.

34 These effects were mentioned in Chapter 3 in relation to unilateral liberalization, referring to Rodrik (1998).

35 Another possibility is that the CU comprises a dominant country which sets the CET unilaterally. In fact this is what has happened so far in the SACU where South Africa has decided on the tariff schedules. An example is the offer made during the Uruguay Round, without much involvement from the four smaller member states. One of the important aspects of the current negotiation on the reform of SACU is to set up a structure where all the member states are involved in decisions.

36 The concept of a Harmonized External Tariff (HET) has been encouraged in Eastern and Southern Africa by the African Development Bank, the European Commission, the IMF and the World Bank in the context of an initiative to facilitate cross-border economic activities (see European Commission 1998).

37 For example, the rules of origin of COMESA are as follows: 'Goods must be consigned directly from a member state to a consignee in another member state and:
 – be wholly produced or
 – contain an import content of not more than 60 per cent CIF value of the total cost of materials used in production or
 – contain not less than 45 per cent ex-factory value added or
 – contain not less than 25 per cent value added if the final product is considered to be of particular importance to the economic development of member states (a list of such approved goods is available at the Secretariat).
'All goods eligible for COMESA tariffs should be accompanied by a COMESA

Certificate of Origin, duly completed, stamped and authenticated by the authorized signatories in the country of origin.' (See COMESA website: www.comesa.int.)

38 Efforts are being made towards gradual harmonization of the different EU systems of origin verification.

39 An example to illustrate this possibility, worked out by Krueger (1993) is car assembly in Mexico. If an automobile carries a 50 per cent duty in the United States and the components carry comparable duties, a Mexican assembler will be obliged to import components from the US in order to fulfil the rule of origin (for example 80 per cent of the components' value must be from within NAFTA). It can be demonstrated that a higher origin requirement amounts to an extension of US protection of components to Mexico. In other words, Mexico is obliged to buy components within NAFTA rather than from the cheapest source, if it wishes to qualify for duty-free car exports to the US.

40 If the customs duties are pooled and flow to a common budget, it does not matter who collects the duties. This is the situation in the EU where all customs duties go the EU budget. However, in the European situation, customs duties are only 0.25 per cent of GDP and the EU budget represents around 1.2 per cent of GDP. For most developing countries, customs duties represent a sizeable part of government revenue and of GDP often exceeding 25 and 5 per cent respectively. Hence if customs duties are pooled, there must be a system that enables the funds to flow back to the national budgets. In fact, this is what happens in SACU. All duties are pooled and an agreed formula is applied to give a share to each member state. South Africa administers the system. An important discussion item in the SACU renegotiations is to agree on a formula that satisfies all member states (more background on this is provided in Appendix A). The alternative to pooling is that each member state collects duties on the goods that enter. For landlocked countries, a transit system must be set up involving a customs bond guarantee. An importer from a landlocked country must provide a financial guarantee to the transit country as long as the goods are in transit. Needless to say, such a system constitutes a trade barrier and an extra cost to the private sector. It is interesting to recall that Viner's (1950) original definition of a CU also includes a requirement of 'apportionment of customs revenue between the members in accordance with an agreed formula' (p. 5). This condition has been almost completely neglected in the literature, probably because it referred mainly to industrial countries for whom customs revenue was not significant.

41 This point is emphasized by the European Commission (1998). The theme is also developed by Mistry (1996) in relation to Southern Africa.

5 Non-Reciprocal Arrangements with Industrial Countries

1 Nevertheless, the US maintained a preferential trade relationship with the Philippines from 1900 to around 1940.

2 The Yaoundé Conventions stipulated that the associated states should not impose any customs duties or charges having equivalent effect on imports from the EC. However, they were allowed to retain or introduce customs duties necessary to meet development or budgetary needs. The Convention

did not stipulate free trade among the associated states, but only recommended the formation of customs unions or free trade areas. The associated states were required to give treatment to imports from the EC no less favourable than treatment of the most-favoured third country and to provide information on their trade policy. As it turned out, development and budgetary needs provided ample justification for import duties, so that there was, in reality, no free trade between the EC and the associated states.

3 The origin of UNCTAD is briefly described in Chapter 2.

4 The EU system was started by the six original member states. Following EU enlargement, the new member states integrated their own GSP into the EU scheme.

5 A comparable arrangement implemented by Canada in favour of the Caribbean Commonwealth states is CARIBCAN. Another non-reciprocal preferential arrangement set up by Australia and New Zealand, and benefiting the Pacific Island Countries, is the South Pacific Regional Trade and Economic Cooperation Agreement (SPARTECA).

6 See also the discussion on infant industry as an argument for protection at the country level in Chapter 3.

7 There is extensive literature on EU preferential trading arrangements. An interesting overview, including a description of the historical background, is provided by Grilli (1993). Another overview is Faber (1990). The Lomé trade system is described for example by Davenport, Hewitt and Koning (1995). The European Commission (1993 and 1997b) published two volumes on the role of EU as a world trade partner, including a description of preferential arrangements.

8 Some non-ACP countries have market access that is comparable to the Lomé regime. However, these are based on *reciprocal* arrangements such as the European Economic Area (EU, Norway, Iceland and Liechtenstein), the Customs Union with Turkey and the 'Europe agreements' with the Central and Eastern European countries. There remain only six countries with pure MFN treatment: Australia, Canada, Japan, New Zealand, Taiwan and the United States; and one country with less-than-MFN treatment: North Korea (Sapir, 1998).

9 The situation is evolving constantly. The Barcelona agreement in 1995 started a process that should lead to an EU–Mediterranean Free Trade Area. As a result, the non-reciprocal association agreements are gradually being replaced by FTAs between the EU and the Mediterranean states. The first agreements were concluded with Israel, Morocco and Tunisia. The move towards FTAs between the EU and developing countries falls under the subject of North–South integration dealt with in Chapter 6.

10 See Appendix Tables B1 to B3. Several Pacific states as well as Cuba are candidates to join the ACP group.

11 Respect for human rights, democratic principles and the rule of law were introduced as *essential elements* of the Lomé Convention. If the obligations in respect of essential elements are not fulfilled, the partial or full suspension of application the Convention is possible.

12 A brief general discussion of rules of origin can be found in Chapter 4.

13 The case of fish is rather complicated. Fish caught inside the territorial 12-mile zone is always considered originating. Outside the 12-mile zone, fish must be caught by ACP vessels. There are stringent provisions to determine

whether a vessel can be considered as an ACP vessel: registration, flag, ownership and crew composition.

14 The sugar protocol is a remarkable arrangement under which a number of developing countries can export cane sugar to the EU at the internally guaranteed EU price. Because the EU sugar market is protected, this price is generally well above the world market price. The system boils down to an income transfer. The protocol dates back to the first Lomé Convention signed in 1975. However, unlike the Convention, the sugar protocol was meant to be of unlimited duration. According to Hermann and Weiss (1995), it resulted from the political pressure of a coalition consisting of the UK government, the UK sugar-refining company Tate and Lyle and the sugar-exporting Commonwealth countries. Its adoption was facilitated by the unusual marketing conditions around 1975 with very high world market prices and extreme volatility. The main operation of the sugar protocol is the annual quota allocated to 19 beneficiary countries. All these countries, with the exception of India, are small ACP states. Of the total amount of around 1.3 million tons a few countries get a very high share: Mauritius (491 000 tons), Fiji (165 000 tons), Guyana (159 000 tons), Jamaica (119 000 tons) and Swaziland (118 000 tons). The other allocations are much smaller. The one for India is negligible. The income transfer in an absolute sense and in comparison to GDP is several cases quite high. For example, Mauritius received an average of €80.0 million per year between 1975 and 1991 which amounts to 4.6 per cent of GDP. The corresponding figures for Fiji are €26.5 million and 2.1 per cent and for Guyana €24.7 million and 9.1 per cent (see Hermann and Weiss, 1995). Even though the sugar protocol is of unlimited duration, its economic effect will gradually diminish as the EU implements the Uruguay Round agreement which will bring the internal EU price closer to the world market price.

15 For earlier Conventions, the EU justified the Lomé trade regime by invoking a combination of Article XXIV (on Free Trade Areas and Customs Unions) and Part IV (allowing special and differential treatment of developing countries).

16 A more complete description of the main characteristics and trade effects of the CBI can be found in Davenport (1995) and Gill, Pellarano and Hess (1996).

17 See Gill, Pellerano and Hess (1996).

18 Or the other comparable regimes such as CARIBCAN and SPARTECA (see note 5).

19 Detailed surveys were prepared by Brown (1988) and Langhammer and Sapir (1988). Another detailed overview, with empirical analysis for the ASEAN countries is by Davenport (1987). A brief description can be found in Faber (1990). Most of the research on GSP was carried out during the 1980s. In the 1990s research interest has shifted towards regional integration and the multilateral system.

20 The old system included tariff preference quotas for sensitive and very sensitive items that were divided into fixed shares for each of the EU member states. Imports that exceeded the quota automatically faced the MFN tariff rate. For the products covered by the Multifibre Arrangement (MFA), preferences were offered only when the exporting countries agreed to apply a 'Voluntary Export Restraint'.

21 Of the 71 ACP states, 39 are least-developed countries. The others are developing countries in the WTO system, except for South Africa, which is considered an industrial country. Thus, of the 48 least-developed countries, only nine do not belong to the ACP group. (See also Appendix B, Tables B1–B3.)
22 A wide variety of methods have been used as reported by Brown (1988) and by Langhammer and Sapir (1988).
23 The smaller and least-developed countries benefited more from the other arrangements specifically geared to them, such as the Lomé Convention and the CBI.
24 Though it should be recalled that a large part of the phasing out of the MFA will only take place shortly before the year 2005 and that liberalization of agriculture is only beginning. Further dismantling of barriers in the agricultural sector will be dealt with during the planned 'Millennium Round' of the WTO.

6 North–South Regionalism

1 It is sometimes forgotten that disparities within groupings of developing countries can also be very large. For example, Bahamas and Haiti, both CARICOM members, have very different per capita incomes (US$ 10 180 and US$ 310 respectively). The gap between Singapore and Vietnam, both members of ASEAN, is even greater (US$ 30 550 and US$ 290).
2 The other members are Brunei, Chile, Taiwan, Hong Kong, Korea, New Zealand and Singapore. Taken together, the APEC countries represent almost 40 per cent of the world population and around 55 per cent of world output. This makes APEC by far the largest economic grouping, even though it is a shallow one and there is no intention of deepening integration.
3 The planned widening of the EU towards Central and Eastern Europe can also be compared to North–South integration.
4 Since the beginning of the 1990s, new forms of conditionality for development assistance have been introduced. This is another way to address some of the problems of the new interdependence. Conditionality is now widely applied to areas such as human rights, the rule of law, democratization, good governance and correct financial management. The practical implementation of such conditionality is not easy. A particular problem arises in relation to applying the same standards across developing countries that may be very different in size and strategic importance (for example, China in comparison to Myanmar or Togo).
5 The collaborative research programme of the African Economic Research Consortium (AERC) on regional integration and trade liberalization analysed the situation in Kenya, Mauritius, Uganda, Nigeria, Ghana, Côte d'Ivoire, South Africa, Zambia and Zimbabwe. Only Mauritius and Uganda did not reverse their trade liberalization process. Most other countries partially reversed trade reforms, while Nigeria experienced a total reversal (see Oyejide 1996).
6 Some would argue that South Africa could play the role of regional anchor economy. South Africa already assumes such a role *vis-à-vis* the neighbouring countries that participate in the Rand zone and the SACU. These countries are very small and have been economically integrated with South Africa for

historical reasons. Whether South Africa can extend its role of regional anchor depends on three main conditions: strong political leadership, macroeconomic stability and a willingness to assist the least-developed countries in the region.

7 Diminishing time-inconsistency of policies is seen as an important explanation of the willingness of Central and Eastern European countries to agree on reciprocal arrangements with the EU. This led to the 'Europe agreements', that also prepare for future membership of the EU.

8 See the discussion in Chapter 4 on the static outcomes of regional arrangements.

9 This is not always the case. It was mentioned above that the Lomé Convention is not a unilateral, but a negotiated agreement. By negotiating as a group, the ACP countries can expect to get a better deal than would be the case if they negotiate separately.

10 The Enterprise for the Americas Initiative (EAI) started in 1990 by President Bush already included a vision of free trade in the Western Hemisphere. As an intermediate step, it foresaw the possibility of free trade areas between the US and groups of countries or single countries. In order to start negotiations, countries were required to fulfil various criteria such as elimination of tariff and non-tariff barriers, liberalization in services and investment, protection of intellectual property, and ending of foreign exchange controls. The EAI also included investment grants and debt-forgiveness. A number of assistance programmes were implemented and framework agreements signed. However, no formal trade negotiations were started under the EAI.

11 This approach is also in line with the recommendations of an independent group of experts on 'smaller economies and Western Hemispheric integration', chaired by Sir Alister McIntyre.

12 Please refer to the discussion of these principles in Chapter 4.

13 Within the ACP group, using a GNP of less than US$ 10.0 billion as a cut-off point, only the Dominican Republic, Nigeria and South Africa are not small economies. South Africa became a member of the Lomé group in April 1997 with a special status implying among other things that it does not benefit from the Lomé trade preferences. The negotiations to establish an EU–South Africa Free Trade Area were concluded at the beginning of 1999. Implementation could start during 2000, with a transitional period of 12 years on the South African side and 10 years for the EU.

14 As seen in Chapter 5, the lack of success of the Lomé preferences must be qualified. In an aggregate sense it is true, but at the level of specific countries and products there are a number of success stories. Besides, it is difficult to tell what would have happened in the absence of Lomé.

15 The political dimension will become more important in the future. This will encompass a wide range of themes such as democracy, human rights, good governance, conflict prevention, arms expenditure, migration, drugs, organized crime and ethnic discrimination. These themes reflect a desire to get a better grip on the new interdependence problems, which is also an aspect of the FTAA process.

16 Fifty-eight of the 71 ACP states are presently members of the WTO.

17 For an overview of some of these discussions see McQueen (1998) and Solignac Lecompte (1998).

18 It is not clear whether the rule of thumb that is sometimes referred to, of

90 per cent coverage of total trade liberalization, refers to the average of trade in both directions. If 90 per cent is indeed an average, and taking into account the fact that EU liberalization already reaches more than 97 per cent, the ultimate ACP tariff dismantling could remain well below 90 per cent. This would leave considerable scope for continued ACP protection on infant industry, revenue or other grounds.

19 There is a qualification in the mandate to protect the interests of non-least-developed countries who are, for objective reasons, not in a position to join an FTA with the EU in 2004. Alternative possibilities will be examined to provide these countries with a new trade framework, which is equivalent to the current situation and in conformity with the WTO. This could be done by introducing more differentiation within the GSP (see the discussion on GSP in Chapter 5).

20 The ACP countries will anyhow lose their relative advantage in comparison to the Central and East European countries that have entered into Europe agreements and other developing countries that accept FTAs (for example, the Mediterranean countries).

21 This is illustrated, for example, in the debate on the recent United States initiative towards Africa. Improved access to the US market is offered to countries that consolidate trade liberalization. However, there remain important constraints on textiles, reducing the value of the offer for the African countries.

22 In small economies, many customs duties may not be protective, because the products on which duties must be paid cannot be produced efficiently locally. Such duties are, in fact, disguised consumption taxes and may be fully justified. Redefining them as consumption taxes, they should not be eliminated in an FTA. An example is cars, which cannot be produced efficiently in many small economies. But it can make a lot of sense to tax car imports.

7 Summary and Conclusions

1 There are cases of policies in small countries that could lead to reaction in other countries because they may have sizeable effects, for example in the area of intellectual property.

2 Mauritius is a member of several regional organizations, including COMESA, IOC and more recently SADC. Economic growth in Mauritius has been mainly export-led. Most export growth has been towards the North. However, Mauritius now has the capacity to export more to its integration partners in the region, when opportunities arise. But trade liberalization of its regional partners has been much slower than envisaged under the agreements.

3 From the beginning of European integration, customs revenue has been pooled and used for Community or Union level policies. The low and declining level of customs revenue probably explains why there was never much controversy on this subject. At present, customs duties cover a relatively small part of the EU budget (around 20 per cent), the largest part of the budget is being collected as a share of the Value Added Tax base. The EU budget itself is relatively small as a share of GDP, at around 1.2 per cent, or less than half of defence expenditures, for example. Another example of pooling of customs revenue is the Southern African Customs Union (SACU). In fact, South

Africa collects almost all the revenue and pays the other member states according to an agreed formula. The SACU reform is at present being negotiated and the revenue pooling and sharing is a key topic for the small member states.

4 There is an obvious concern to preserve sovereignty. Regional integration is often presented as giving up sovereignty. Two observations can be made in this regard. First, globalization implies an inevitable loss of sovereignty in relation to economic policies. Second, regional integration is not about giving up (what is left of) sovereignty, but rather about exercising and sharing sovereignty in a wider context. Regional integration may, in fact, help to recapture sovereignty in some areas where collective action is more effective than unilateral action.

5 If there is a substantial and measurable redistribution of customs revenue among member states a compensation mechanism can be set up. An example is the 'solidarity levy' set up by the UEMOA countries. A percentage of external tariff revenue is set aside for budgetary compensation.

6 Some of the EU's arrangements, such as those for sugar and bananas, are actually paid for by the European consumers through higher prices.

7 In the case of small developing economies entering into deep integration with the North, one cannot really speak of sharing of sovereignty, because the weight of the partners is so unequal. The situation is quite different for South–South integration, where it is correct to speak of sharing sovereignty.

Appendix A: Regional Integration Arrangements Involving Developing Countries

1 This review does not cover organizations that have not been active recently for a variety of reasons. These include: the Mano River Union (MRU) comprising Guinea, Liberia and Sierra Leone; the Economic Community of the Great Lake States or in French the 'Communauté Economique des Pays des Grands Lacs' (CEPGL) involving Burundi, Rwanda and the Democratic Republic of Congo; and the Arab Maghreb Union (AMU) to which Algeria, Morocco, Tunisia, Libya and Mauritania belong. Even though the tasks of the Intergovernmental Authority on Development (IGAD) grouping countries in the Horn of Africa (Djibouti, Ethiopia, Eritrea, Kenya, Somalia, Sudan and Uganda) have recently been broadened to cover trade integration as well, it is not reviewed because, so far, not much has happened on this subject. The Indian Ocean Commission (IOC), comprising Comoros, Mauritius, Madagascar, Seychelles and the French Department of Réunion is not included because its main activities are in functional cooperation. More detailed descriptions of regional integration in Africa on which this overview draws can be found in Bach (1999), Faroutan (1993), Holden (1998), Maasdorp (1996) and Oyejide *et al.* (1997). A broad analysis of regionalism in Africa was recently prepared by Asante (1997). Drawing on his experience as senior adviser to UNECA he specifically sets out the historical context and the present challenges for regional integration initiatives in Africa.

2 Membership in this list and those that follow reflects the situation around the end of 1998. For countries that recently joined the arrangement, the year of accession is indicated.

3 Besides its central role in SACU and its membership of SADC, South Africa

maintains a set of bilateral agreements in the Southern Africa region (for example, with Mozambique, Malawi and Zimbabwe). This set-up can lead to a 'hub-and-spoke' system, benefiting mainly South Africa. Some of these agreements imply tariff preferences, such as the one with Malawi. But in the case of Zimbabwe, preferences were in fact reversed to the discontent of Zimbabwean exporters.

4   The FTAA is examined in Chapter 6. ALADI is not included in the organizations reviewed because its economic integration role has been overtaken by the other groupings, even though it remains the broadest Latin American forum to discuss integration matters. The Group of Three (G3) agreement, signed in 1995 between Colombia, Mexico and Venezuela is not included because it contains no small economies and its future role is not fully clear. The Association of Caribbean States (ACS) was founded in 1994 following an initiative of the CARICOM Heads of State. It involves all the member states of CARICOM, CACM and the Group of Three plus the Dominican Republic and Cuba. The objectives of ACS include both economic integration and functional cooperation (Gill, 1995). Because it is not yet possible to say whether the ACS will become a significant player on regional integration matters, it also is not discussed separately. More details on regional integration in Latin America and the Caribbean can be found in Bouzas and Ros (1994), Bulmer–Thomas (1998), Lipsey and Meller (1997) and Nogues and Quintanilla (1993).

References

Abbott, Kenneth. 1996. 'Trade Remedies and Legal Remedies: Anti-Dumping, Safeguards and Dispute Settlement after the Uruguay Round', paper presented at the Conference on the World Trading System, World Bank Economic Development Institute (June).

Altinger, Laura and Alice Enders. 1996. 'The Scope and Depth of GATS Commitments', *The World Economy* (19) 307–32.

Anderson, Kym and Richard Blackhurst, eds. 1993. *Regional Integration and the Global Trading System*. St. Martin's Press, New York.

Andriamananjara, Saomiely and Maurice Schiff. 1998. *Regional Groupings among Microstates*. World Bank.

Armstrong, H. and R.J. De Kervenoael. 1998. 'A Comparison of the Economic Performance of Different Micro-states and Larger Countries', *World Development* (26), 639–56.

Artis, and Lee, eds. 1994. *The Economics of the European Union*. Oxford, Oxford University Press.

Asante, S.K.B. 1997. *Regionalism and Africa's Development: Expectation, Realities and Challenges*. Macmillan, London.

Axline, Andrew W. 1994. *The Political Economy of Regional Cooperation: Comparative Case Studies*. Pinter Publishers, London.

Bach, Daniel, ed. 1999. *Regionalisation in Africa: Integration & Disintegration*. James Currey, Oxford.

Baldwin, Richard E. 1995. 'A Domino Theory of Regionalism' in *Expanding Membership of the EU*, eds Pertti Haaparanta and Jaakko Kiander. CEPR and Cambridge University Press, Cambridge.

Baldwin, Richard E. and Anthony J. Venables. 1995. 'Regional Economic Integration' in *Handbook of International Economics* Volume III, eds Gene M. Grossman and Kenneth Rogoff. Amsterdam, Elsevier.

Bernal, Richard L. 1994a. 'CARICOM: Externally Vulnerable Regional Economic Integration' in *Economic Integration in the Western Hemisphere*, eds Roberto Bouzas and Jaime Ros. Notre Dame University Press, Notre Dame.

Bernal, Richard L. 1994b. 'From NAFTA to Hemispheric Free Trade', *Columbia Journal of World Business* (24), 3, 23–31.

Bernal, Richard L. 1995. 'Regional Trade Arrangements and the Establishment of a Free Trade Area of the Americas', *Law and Policy in International Business*, December.

Bernal, Richard L. 1996. *Strategic Global Repositioning and Future Economic Development of Jamaica*. North–South Agenda Papers, no. 18, May.

Bhagwati, Jagdish. 1992. 'Regionalism versus Multilateralism', *The World Economy* (15), pp. 535–55.

Bhagwati, Jagdish. 1993. 'Regionalism and Multilateralism: an Overview', in De Melo and Panagariya, 1993, pp. 22–51.

Bhagwati, Jadish. 1997. 'The Global Age: from a Sceptical South to a Fearful North'. *The World Economy* (20) 259–83.

Bhagwati, Jagdish and Arvind Panagariya. 1996. 'Preferential Trading Areas and Multilateralism: Strangers, Friends or Foes' in Bhagwati, J. and A. Panagariya, eds, *The Economics of Preferential Trade Agreements*, American Enterprise Institute Press, Washington, DC.

Blackhurst, Richard. 1997a. 'Regionalism in a Rules-Based World Trading System', paper presented at European Commission and World Bank Seminar on Regionalism and Development, June, Brussels.

Blackhurst, Richard. 1997b. 'The WTO and the Global Economy', *The World Economy* (20) 527–44.

Bouzas, Roberto and Jaime Ros, eds. 1994. *Economic Integration in the Western Hemisphere*. Notre Dame University Press, Notre Dame.

Briguglio, Lino. 1995. 'Small Island Developing States and Their Economic Vulnerabilities', *World Development* (23), 1615–32.

Brown, Drusilla K. 1988. 'Trade Preferences for Developing Countries: a Survey of Results', *Journal of Development Studies*, pp. 335–63.

Bulmer, Simon. 1994. 'History and Institutions of the European Union', in Artis and Lee, 4–31.

Bulmer-Thomas, Victor. 1998. 'The Central American Common Market: from Closed to Open Regionalism', in *World Development* (26), 313–22.

Centre for Economic Policy Research. 1995. *Flexible Integration: Towards a More Effective and Democratic Europe*. London.

Collier, Paul. 1995. 'The Marginalization of Africa', *International Labour Review* (134), 541–57.

Collier, Paul and Jan Willem Gunning. 1995. 'Trade Policy and Regional Integration: Implications for the Relation between Europe and Africa', *The World Economy* (18), 387–410.

Collier, Paul, Patrick Guillaumont, Sylviane Guillaumont and Jan Willem Gunning 1997. 'The Future of Lomé: Europe's Role in African Growth', *The World Economy* (20), 285–305.

Commonwealth Secretariat. 1985. *Vulnerability: Small States in the Global Society*. Commonwealth Secretariat, London.

Commonwealth Secretariat. 1997. *A Future for Small States: Overcoming Vulnerability*. Commonwealth Secretariat, London.

Cooper, C.A. and B.G. Massel. 1965. 'A New Look at Customs Union Theory', *Economic Journal* (75), pp. 742–7.

Cooper, C.A. and B.G. Massel. 1965. 'Towards a General Theory of Customs Unions for Developing Countries', *Journal of Political Economy* (73), pp. 471–6.

Corden, W.M. 1974. *Trade Policy and Economic Welfare*. Clarendon Press, Oxford.

Davenport, Michael. 1986. *Trade Policy, Protectionism and the Third World*. Croom Helm, London.

Davenport, Michael. 1992. 'Africa and the Unimportance of Being Preferred', *Journal of Common Market Studies*, June, pp. 233–51.

Davenport, Michael. 1995. *Impact of the Uruguay Round and NAFTA on Commonwealth Caribbean Countries*. Commonwealth Secretariat, London.

Davenport, Michael, Adrian Hewitt and Antonique Koning. 1995. *Europe's Preferred Partners? The Lomé Countries in World Trade*. Overseas Development Institute, London.

De La Torre, Augusto and Margaret R. Kelly. 1992. *Regional Trade Arrangements*. Occasional Paper 93, IMF, Washington, DC.

De Long, Bradford J. and Barry Eichengreen. 1992. *The Marshall Plan: History's Most Successful Structural Adjustment Program*. CEPR Discussion Paper 634.

De Long, Bradford J., Christopher De Long and Sherman Robinson. 1996. 'The

Case for Mexico's Rescue', *Foreign Affairs* (73), no. 3, pp. 8–14.

De Melo, Jaime and Arvind Panagariya. 1992. 'The New Regionalism', *Finance and Development*, December, pp. 37–40.

De Melo, Jaime and Arvind Panagariya, eds. 1993, *New Dimensions in Regional Integration*. Cambridge University Press.

De Rosa, Dean A. 1995. *Regional Trading Arrangements among Developing Countries: the ASEAN Example*. IFPRI Research Report 103, Washington, DC.

Edwards, Sebastian. 1993. 'Openness, Trade Liberalization, and Growth in Developing Countries', *Journal of Economic Literature* (31), 1358–93.

European Commission. 1993. 'The European Community as a World Trade Partner', *European Economy*, no. 52, Brussels.

European Commission. 1996. *Green Paper on Relations between the European Union and the ACP Countries on the Eve of the 21st Century*. Brussels.

European Commission. 1997a. *Agenda 2000 for a Stronger and Wider Union*, COM (97) 2000.

European Commission. 1997b. *Improving Market Access for the Least Developed Countries*, COM(97) 156.

European Commission. 1997c. *The European Union as a World Trade Partner.* European Economy, Reports and Studies, no. 3.

European Commission. 1998. *Cross-Border Initiative to Facilitate Regional Trade, Investment and Payments in Eastern and Southern Africa and the Indian Ocean*, Vol. 3. Brussels.

Faber, Gerrit. 1990. 'Trade Preferences of the European Community as Instruments of Development Cooperation', in *Trade Policy and Development*, ed. Gerrit Faber. Universitaire Pers Rotterdam, Rotterdam.

Faroutan, Faezeh. 1993. 'Regional Integration in Sub-Saharan Africa: Past Experience and Future Prospects', in *New Dimensions in Regional Integration*, eds Jaime De Melo and Arvind Panagariya. Cambridge University Press, Cambridge.

Fernandez, Raquel and Jonathan Portes 1998. 'Returns to Regionalism: an Analysis of Nontraditional Gains from Regional Trade Agreements', *The World Bank Economic Review* (12) 197–220.

Francois, Joseph F. 1997. 'External Bindings and the Credibility of Reform', in *Regional Partners in Global Markets*, eds A. Galal and B. Hoekman. CEPR, London.

Frankel, Jeffrey A. 1997. *Regional Trading Blocs in the World Economic System*. Institute for International Economics, Washington, DC.

Frankel, Jeffrey, Ernesto Stein and Shang-jin Wei. 1996. 'Regional Trading Arrangements: Natural or Supernatural?' *American Economic Review*, May, pp. 52–6.

Gibb, Richard. 1994. 'Regionalism in the World Economy', in Richard Gibb and Wieslaw Michalak, eds, *Continental Trading Blocs: the Growth of Regionalism in the World Economy*. John Wiley, New York.

Gill, Henry S. 1995. *The Association of Caribbean States: Prospects for a 'Quantum Leap'*, North-South Agenda Papers, no. 11, North–South Centre, University of Miami.

Gill, Henry S., Fernando Pellerano and Richard Hess. 1996. 'A New Strategy to Promote Regional Integration in the Caribbean Region'. Report prepared for the European Commission, Brussels.

Grilli, Enzo R. 1993. *The European Community and the Developing Countries*. Cambridge University Press, Cambridge.

Gunning, Jan Willem. 1994. 'Trade Reform in Africa: the Role of Donors', in

Trade, Aid and Development: Essays in Honour of Hans Linnemann, eds J.W. Gunning *et al.* St. Martin's Press, New York.

Haggard, Stephan. 1995. *Developing Nations and the Politics of Global Integration*. The Brookings Institution, Washington, DC.

Hallet, Andrew H. and Carlos A. Primo Braga. 1994. *The New Regionalism and the Threat of Protectionism*. Policy Research Working Paper 1349, the World Bank.

Helleiner, G.K. 1996. 'Why Small Countries Worry: Neglected Issues in Current Analysis of the Benefits and Costs for Small Countries of Integrating with Large Ones', *The World Economy* (19) 759–63.

Herrmann, Roland and Dietmar Weiss. 1995. 'A Welfare Analysis of the EC–ACP Sugar Protocol', *Journal of Development Studies* (31), August, 918–41.

Hoekman, Bernard and Michel Kostecki. 1995. *The Political Economy of the World Trading System*. Oxford University Press, Oxford.

Holden, Merle. 1998. 'Southern African Economic Integration', *The World Economy* (21) 457–69.

Holmes, Peter and Alisdair Smith. 1997. *Dynamic Effects of Regional Integration*. Paper presented at European Commission and World Bank Seminar on Regionalism and Development, June, Brussels.

Hudec, R.E. 1987. *Developing Countries in the GATT Legal System*. Gower, London.

Hufbauer, Gary Clyde and Jeffrey Schott. 1993. *NAFTA: an Assessment*. Revised Edition, Institute for International Economics, Washington, DC.

Hufbauer, Gary Clyde and Jeffrey Schott. 1994. *Western Hemisphere Economic Integration*. Institute for International Economics, Washington, DC.

Imani Development. 1995. *Evaluation of the Trade Provisions of the Lomé Convention*. Report prepared for the European Commission, Brussels.

International Monetary Fund. 1994. *International Trade Policies: the Uruguay Round and Beyond*, 2 vols. World Economic and Financial Surveys. Washington, DC.

Kahler, Miles. 1995. *International Institutions and the Political Economy of Integration*. The Brookings Institution, Washington, DC.

Kemp, Murray C. and Henry Y. Wan. 1976. 'An Elementary Proposition Concerning the Formation of Customs Unions', *Journal of International Economics* (6) 95–7.

Krauss, Melvyn B. 1972. 'Recent Developments in Customs Union Theory: an Interpretative Survey', *Journal of Economic Literature* (10) 413–36.

Krueger, Anne. 1993. *Free Trade Agreements as Protectionist Devices: Rules of Origin*. NBER Working Paper 4352.

Krueger, Anne. 1995. *Trade Policies and Developing Nations*. The Brookings Institution, Washington, DC.

Krueger, Anne. 1997. 'Free Trade Agreements versus Customs Unions', *Journal of Development Economics* (54) 169–87.

Krugman, Paul. 1991. 'The Move towards Free Trade Zones', Policy Implications of Trade and Currency Zones, Federal Reserve Bank of Kansas City Symposium, pp. 7–41.

Krugman, Paul. 1992. 'Does the New Trade Theory Require a New Trade Policy?' *The World Economy*, July, 423–41.

Kuruvila, Pretty. 1997. 'Developing Countries and the GATT/WTO Dispute Settlement Mechanism', *Journal of World Trade*, 171–205.

Landau, Alice. 1996. *L'Uruguay Round Conflit et Coopération dans les Relations Economiques Internationales*. Bruylant, Brussels.

Langhammer, Rolf. 1992. 'The Developing Countries and Regionalism', *Journal of Common Market Studies*, June (30) 2, pp. 211–31.

Langhammer, Rolf J. and André Sapir. 1988. *Economic Impact of Generalized Tariff Preferences*. Gower, London.

Lawrence, Robert. 1996. *Regionalism, Multilateralism and Deeper Integration*. The Brookings Institution, Washington, DC.

Lawrence, Robert Z. and Robert E. Litan. 1986. *Saving Free Trade*. The Brookings Institution, Washington, DC.

Lipsey, Richard G. and Patricio Meller, eds. 1997. *Western Hemisphere Trade Integration*. Macmillan, London.

Maasdorp, Gavin. 1996. 'Can Regional Integration Help Southern Africa?', in *Can South and Southern Africa Become Globally Competitive Economies?* ed. Gavin Maasdorp. Macmillan, London.

McMillan, John. 1993. 'Does Regionalism Foster Open Trade? Economic Theory and GATT's Article XXIV', in Anderson and Blackhurst, pp. 292–310.

McQueen, Matthew. 1998. 'Lomé versus Free Trade Agreements: the Dilemma Facing the ACP Countries', *The World Economy* (21), 421–43.

McQueen, Matthew. 1999. *The Impact Studies on the Effects of REPAs between the ACP and the EU*. ECDPM Discussion Paper no. 3, Maastricht.

Martin, Will and L. Alan Winters. 1995. *The Uruguay Round: Widening and Deepening the World Trading System*. World Bank.

Michalopoulos, Constantine. 1999. 'The Developing Countries in the WTO'. *The World Economy* (22) 117–43.

Mistry, Percy. 1996a. 'Regional Dimensions of Structural Adjustment in Southern Africa'. Paper prepared for the Conference on Regional Integration in Africa, Johannesburg, February.

Mistry, Percy. 1996b. *Regional Integration Arrangements in Economic Development: Panacea or Pitfall?* Forum on Debt and Development, The Hague.

Morrissey, Oliver and Yogesh Rai. 1995. 'The GATT Agreement on Trade Related Investment Measures: Implications for Developing Countries and their Relationship with Transnational Corporations', *Journal of Development Studies* (31) 5, pp. 702–24.

Nagarajan, Nigel. 1998. 'Regionalism and the WTO: New Rules for the Game?' forthcoming in Economic Papers, European Commission, Brussels.

Nogues, Julio and Rosalinda Quintanilla. 1993. 'Latin America's Integration and the Multilateral Trading System', in *New Dimensions in Regional Integration*, eds Jaime De Melo and Arvind Panagariya. Cambridge University Press, Cambridge.

Oman, Charles. 1994. *Globalization and Regionalization: the Challenge for Developing Countries*, OECD, Development Centre Studies, Paris.

Oman, Charles. 1995. *The Policy Challenges of Globalization and Regionalization*, Policy Brief No. 11, OECD, Development Centre, Paris.

Organization for Economic Cooperation and Development. 1995. *Regional Integration and the Multilateral Trading System: Synergy and Divergence*. Paris.

Organization of American States. 1996a. *Mechanisms and Measures to Facilitate the Participation of Smaller Economies in the Free Trade Area of the Americas*. Washington, DC.

Organization of American States. 1996b. *Small and Relatively Less Developed Economies and Western Hemisphere Integration*. Washington, DC.

Oyejide, Ademola. 1996. *Regional Integration and Trade Liberalization in Sub-Saharan*

Africa (Summary Report). African Economic Research Consortium, Nairobi.

Oyejide, Ademola, Ibrahim Elbadawi and Paul Collier (eds). 1997. *Regional Integration and Trade Liberalization in Sub-Saharan Africa*. Volume 1: *Framework, Issues and Methodological Perspectives*, Macmillan, London.

Paemen, Hugo and Alexandra Bensch. 1995. *From the GATT to the WTO – the European Community in the Uruguay Round*, Leuven University Press, Leuven.

Page, Sheila and Michael Davenport. 1994. *World Trade Reform*, Overseas Development Institute, London.

Palmeter, David. 1993. 'Rules of Origin in Customs Unions and Free Trade Areas', in Anderson and Blackhurst, pp. 326–43.

Pelkmans, Jacques. 1997. *European Integration: Methods and Economic Analysis*, Addison Wesley Longman, Harlow, England.

Perroni, Carlo and John Whalley. 1994. *The New Regionalism: Trade, Liberalisation or Insurance?* NBER Working Paper 4626.

Robson, Peter. 1993. 'The New Regionalism and Developing Countries', *Journal of Common Market Studies*, September (31) 3, pp. 329–48.

Robson, Peter. 1998. *The Economics of International Integration* (4th edition). Allen and Unwin, London.

Rodrik, Dani. 1995. 'Comments on Anne Krueger'. *Trade Policies and Developing Nations*. The Brookings Institution, pp. 101–11.

Rodrik, Dani. 1997. *Has Globalisation Gone Too Far?* Institute for International Economics, Washington, DC.

Rodrik, Dani. 1998. 'Why Is Trade Reform So Difficult in Africa?' *Trade Reform and Regional Integration in Africa*, eds Zubair Iqbal and Moshin S. Khan. International Monetary Fund, Washington, DC.

Ruggiero, Renato. 1996. *The Road Ahead: International Trade Policy in the Era of the WTO*, Fourth Annual Sylvia Ostry Lecture, Ottawa, 28 May.

Sachs, Jeffrey. 1998. 'International Economics: Unlocking the Mysteries of Globalisation', *Foreign Policy*, Spring, 97–111.

Sachs, Jeffrey and Andrew Warner. 1995. 'Economic Reform and the Process of Global Integration', Brookings Papers on Economic Activity (1).

Samson, Gary. 1996. 'Compatibility of Regional and Multilateral Agreements: Reforming the WTO Process', *American Economic Review*, May (86) 2, 88–92.

Sapir, André. 1998. 'The Political Economy of EC Regionalism', *European Economic Review*, April.

Sawyer, W. Charles and Richard L. Sprinkle. 1989. 'Alternative Empirical Estimates of Trade Creation and Trade Diversion: a Comparison of the Baldwin–Murray and Verdoorn Models', *Weltwirtschaftliches Archiv* (125) 61–73.

Schiff, Maurice. 1997. 'Small is Beautiful: Preferential Trade Agreements and the Impact of Country Size, Market Share and Smuggling', *Journal of Economic Integration* (12) 359–87.

Schiff, Maurice and Alan Winters. 1998. 'Regional Integration as Diplomacy', *The World Bank Economic Review* (12) 271–95.

Snape, Richard H. 1993. 'History and Economics of GATT's Article XXIV', in Anderson and Blackhurst, pp. 273–91.

Solignac Lecompte, Henri-Bernard. 1998. *Options for Future ACP–EU Trade Relations*. ECDPM Working Paper No. 60, August, Maastricht.

Sorsa, Piritta. 1996. 'Sub-Saharan African Own Commitments in the Uruguay Round – Myth or Reality?' *The World Economy* (19) 287–305.

Srinivasan, T.N. 1996. *Developing Countries and the Multilateral Trading System:*

from GATT (1947) to the Uruguay Round and the Future Beyond, Paper presented at the Conference on the World Trading System, World Bank Economic Development Institute, June.

Stevens, Christopher, Jane Kennan and Richard Ketley. 1993. 'EC Trade Preferences and a Post-Apartheid South Africa', *International Affairs* (69) 89–108.

Summers, Lawrence H. 1991. 'Regionalism and the World Trading System', *Policy Implications of Trade and Currency Zones*, Federal Reserve Bank of Kansas City Symposium, pp. 295–301.

Thomas, Rosalind H. 1996. 'Regional Arrangements and the World Trade Organisation: the Case of the Southern African Development Community'. Paper presented at the 8th Annual Conference of the African Society of International and Comparative Law, Cairo.

Thomas, Rosalind H. 1997. *Regional Arrangements and the World Trade Organisation: the Case of Southern Africa*. Paper presented at EC Seminar, February, Brussels.

Thomas, Vinod, John Nash and associates. 1991. *Best Practices in Trade Policy Reform*. Oxford University Press, Oxford.

Thurow, Lester. 1992. *Head to Head: the Coming Economic Battle among Japan, Europe and America*, William Morrow, New York.

Tsoukalis, Loukas. 1997. *The New European Economy Revisited*. Oxford University Press, Oxford.

UNCTAD. 1996. Handbook of Economic Integration and Cooperation Groupings of Developing Countries, Vol. I, New York and Geneva.

Vamvakidis, Athanasios. 1996. *Trade Openness and Economic Growth Reconsidered*. Department of Economics, Harvard University, Cambridge, MA.

Viner, Jacob. 1950. *The Customs Union Issue*. Carnegie Endowment for International Peace, New York.

Wade, Robert. 1990. *Governing the Market – Economic Theory and the Role of the Government in East Asian Industrialization*. Princeton University Press, Princeton.

Wallace, William. 1994. *Regional Integration: the West European Experience*. The Brookings Institution, Washington, DC.

Weintraub, Sidney. 1993. 'The NAFTA and Developing Countries', in *NAFTA as a Model of Development*, eds Richard Belous and Jonathan Lemco. National Planning Association, Washington, DC.

Weintraub, Sidney. 1996. 'Caribbean Integration into Today's World', in Keith Worrell and Anthony Gonzales, eds, *Whither the Caribbean Region: Whither CDB in its Support*, Caribbean Development Bank, St Michael, Barbados.

Whalley, John. 1996. *Why Do Countries Seek Regional Trade Agreements?* National Bureau of Economic Research Working Paper 5552. Cambridge, MA.

Wonnacott, Ronald J. 1996. 'Trade and Investment in a Hub-and-Spoke System versus a Free Trade Area', *The World Economy* (19) 237–52.

World Bank, 1996. *Global Economic Prospects and the Developing Countries*, April.

World Trade Organization. 1994. *The Results of the Uruguay Round of Multilateral Trade Negotiations*. Geneva.

World Trade Organization. 1995. *Regionalism and the World Trading System*, Geneva, April.

Yin, Pierre. 1993. 'Economic Success: Why Mauritius?', *The Courrier*, May–June.

Index